BODY SHOW/S:

Australian viewings

of

live performance

edited by

Peta Tait

Monograph No. 8 in the series

AUSTRALIAN PLAYWRIGHTS

SERIES EDITOR: VERONICA KELLY

Amsterdam - Atlanta, GA 2000

Cover

Kathryn Niesche, *Going Down*, Winterdaze 1998.
Photographer Angela Bailey.

The paper on which this book is printed meets the requirements of "ISO 9706:1994, Information and documentation - Paper for documents - Requirements for permanence".

ISBN: 90-420-1483-0 (bound)

Printed in The Netherlands

Contents

Foreword by the Series Editor

This volume of Australian views of contemporary physical theatre and performance is the eighth in the series 'Australian Playwrights' commenced by Ortrun-Zuber Skerritt of Griffith University, Brisbane. Since 1985 seven monographs or edited collections and eight video interviews have been produced. The book studies are *Louis Nowra* edited by Veronica Kelly; *Patrick White* by May-Brit Akerholt; *Jack Hibberd* by Paul McGillick; *David Williamson* by Ortrun Zuber-Skerritt; *John Romeril* by Gareth Griffiths, *Alma De Groen* by Elizabeth Perkins and *Our Australian Theatre in the 1990s* by Veronica Kelly.

The recent publications in the series are focussed less on author studies and more upon industrial developments, contemporary theorisations and the works of specific artists and theatre companies, thus mapping the cultural and industrial contexts in which Australian theatre-making occurs. It provides information about the general theatrical field and documents and analyses the work of specific groups. This covers a broad range of drama, performance, dance and physical theatre being currently devised both inside and outside the now problematic fields of text-based or authored writing. The illustrations are a major feature of the series, allowing readers to glimpse Australian theatre and its performers in front of their varied audiences.

Future plans for the 'Australian Playwrights' series include more author studies and further historical, thematic and theoretical studies.

The following video programmes are available from the Australian Film Institute, 49 Eastern Road, South Melbourne, Victoria 3205, Australia, where playwrights speak about their work.

Louis Nowra (1985)	36 min
Dorothy Hewett (1986)	52 min
Jack Hibberd (1986)	42 min
David Williamson (1986)	50 min
Stephen Sewell (1986)	59 min
Alma De Groen (1990)	44 min
Michael Gow (1991)	49 min
John Romeril (1992	54 min

My thanks are due to the founding editor for initiating and tenaciously sustaining this series, and to the playwrights, editors and contributors for their scholarly work, patient collegiality and enthusiasm for Australian theatre-making in all its aspects.

Veronica Kelly
Australian Drama Studies Centre,
University of Queensland
July 2000

Acknowledgments

I sincerely thank Veronica Kelly for initiating this book, a sequel to her own *Our Australian Theatre in the 1990s*, and for asking me to edit what has become this collection of fascinating essays. My grateful thanks to Mary Bartlett for her assistance during the editing process, to Dr Diane Carlyle, and to Marlowe Russell for making me so welcome and giving me her home office. My thanks to all the contributors for their hard work and enthusiasm; it's been worth it.

Peta Tait

Sincere appreciation is due to all the companies and artistes who have generously contributed photographic documentation. The work of individual photographers is acknowledged in the 'List of Photographs' and in individual captions.

Without the unfailing professionalism and warm supportiveness of Jeanette Champ, who encoded the typescript, the production of *Body Show/s* would have been a far more arduous project. Thank you Jeanette, Harley, Joseph and Melanie.

Veronica Kelly

Contributors

JANE GOODALL is an Associate Professor in the Faculty of Social Inquiry at the University of Western Sydney. She has published widely on performance and cultural studies and is the author of *Artaud and the Gnostic Drama* (Oxford UP, 1994). Her current work is on the relationship between the performing arts and the development of nineteenth-century evolutionary theory.

BILL DUNSTONE is an academic, actor and director. He is a research fellow at Curtin University of Technology, Perth, Western Australia. He taught at the University of Western Australia, and continues to teach and perform in Thailand, Singapore and India. He is currently writing a cultural study of theatre performance in Western Australia from colonial times.

DAVID WILLIAMS, currently Professor of Theatre at Dartington College of Arts, England, has taught and made theatre and performance in Australia, France and England. He is compiler of the sourcebooks on Peter Brook's CICT and the Théâtre du Soleil, and co-author of *Director's Theatre*. He is a contributing editor to *Performance Research*.

PETA TAIT is a Senior Lecturer at La Trobe University. Her books include *Converging Realities: Feminism in Australian Theatre* (Currency Press, 1994) and she is co-editor of *Australian Women's Drama: Texts and Feminisms* (Currency Press, 1997). She publishes on bodies in physical theatre and circus, and queer performance, and works with The Party Line performance group.

KERRIE SCHAEFER is a lecturer in the Drama Department at the University of Newcastle, NSW. She has written for *Real Time* and completed her Ph D, 'Poaching and Parody in Postmodern Performance: A Rehearsal Case Study of the Sydney Front's *Don Juan*' at Sydney University's Centre for Performance Studies.

ANGHARAD WYNNE-JONES is dance-trained and worked as a theatre practitioner in the UK and producer at London's Institute of Contemporary Arts. She did large scale site specific events in Sydney from 1989 onwards, and was Artistic Director of The Performance Space 1994-97. She was Executive Producer of the contemporary dance company, Chunky Move, and is Associate Director of the Adelaide Festival.

EDWARD SCHEER is a lecturer in theatre and performance theory at the School of Theatre, Film and Dance at University of New South Wales. He is secretary of the board of Sydney's The Performance Space and is editor of *100 Years of Cruelty* (Power Publications/Artspace, in press) on Antonin Artaud. He contributes regularly to the *Sydney Morning Herald*'s Good Weekend Magazine and *Real Time*.

SHARON MAZER is Head of the Department of Theatre and Film Studies at the University of Canterbury, New Zealand. Her articles have appeared in *The Drama Review* and *Theatre Annual*, and she is author of *Professional Wrestling: Sport and Spectacle* (UP of Mississippi, 1998).

ADRIAN KIERNANDER is Professor of Theatre Studies at the University of New England in Australia. He has written on the work of Ariane Mnouchkine, and is currently working on books on Australian theatre practitioners John Bell and Meryl Tankard. These are part of a larger research project into physical theatre and dance theatre in Australia since 1985.

PETER ECKERSALL is a theatre studies Lecturer in the School of Studies in Creative Arts, University of Melbourne and works with the Not Yet It's Difficult performance group. He completed his Ph D on Japanese avant-garde theatre at Monash University in 1999. He is co-editor of *Disorientations: Cultural Praxis in Theatre, Asia, Pacific, Australia* (Monash Theatre Papers, 1999).

JULIAN MEYRICK is a professional theatre director and a lecturer at the University of Newcastle, NSW. He completed his Ph D on the Australian Nimrod Theatre 1970-85 (Currency Press, in press), and publishes on arts policy. He was Artistic Director of the experimental kickhouse theatre and won numerous awards for his productions.

ANNE MARSH is a Senior Lecturer and Head of the Department of Visual Culture at Monash University. She was a practising artist till 1984, and continues to curate, lecture and publish internationally, in the areas of performance art, photography and contemporary media. Her book *Body and Self: Performance Art in Australia 1969-1993* (Oxford UP, 1993) is now available on CD-Rom.

JONATHAN BOLLEN's research has been published in *The Drama Review* and *Australasian Drama Studies*. He is a graduate of the University of Sydney's Centre for Performance Studies and completed his Ph D, 'Queer Kinaesthesia: On the Dance Floor at Gay and Lesbian Dance Parties, Sydney 1994-1998' at the University of Western Sydney, Nepean in 1999.

CYNTHIA BARNES has a M.Ed. and a research M.Ph. in drama from Goldsmith's College, University of London. Since 1995, after a long career in further education lecturing in English, she has travelled the world following her interest in theatre, including two extended trips to Australia. She teaches now in a variety of educational contexts in the UK.

KAREN PEARLMAN has a BFA in Dance from Tisch, NYU, and is doing postgraduate work. She was a dancer with Bill T. Jones/Arnie Zane Dance Company and other NY choreographers. With Richard Allen, she has been co-artistic director of That Was Fast, Tasdance, and The Physical TV Company and co-editor of a number of texts including *Performing the Unnameable* (Currency /Real Time, 1999).

RACHEL FENSHAM is a Senior Lecturer at the Centre for Drama and Theatre Studies at Monash University. Her intersecting research interests are in feminist theory, the philosophy of the body and performance genres such as dance, circus and theatre, and cultural history and politics. She co-edited *Disorientations: Cultural Praxis in Theatre, Asia, Pacific, Australia* (Monash Theatre Papers, 1999).

MARY MOORE is an established theatre designer whose career spans thirty years and three continents. In 1997, with the assistance of an Australia Council Fellowship, she created *Masterkey*, an intercultural work commissioned by the 1998 Adelaide Telstra and Perth festivals. *The Exile*, her most recent work, will tour Australia in 2001.

JULIE HOLLEDGE is Professor of Drama and Director of the Drama Centre at the Flinders University of South Australia. She is author of *Innocent Flowers: Women in Edwardian Theatre* and has worked in the theatre as a director, actor, and dramaturg. She is co-author of *Women's Intercultural Performance* with Joanne Tompkins.

Photographs

Cover

Kathryn Niesche, *Going Down,* Winterdaze 1996.
Photographer Angela Bailey.

Photographic essay: *Under Southern Eyes.*

Photographer Mary Moore. Text Julie Holledge

Under Southern Eyes, a series of performance installations based on the history of Port Adelaide was commissioned for the 1988 Adelaide Festival of Arts and performed in a wharf shed. It was directed by Julie Holledge, designed by Mary Moore and devised with student actors from the Flinders University Drama Centre, with choreography by Michael Fuller and music by Robert Lloyd.

Entering the 'Ghost Ship' the audience encountered tableau images evoking migration, and symbolically linking the ship to the maternal body inspired by Melanie Klein's theories of inner worlds, desire and childhood fantasies. The audience moved next to 'The Fairground' and performances of fire-eating, stilt-walking, waxworks, contortionists, magicians and freak show acts based on local oral histories, including that of Port Adelaide's pioneering actor-manager, George Coppin.

Part One: The Ghost Ship. A series of twelve performance installations based on maritime migration.

Photo 1

Travelling through the Roaring Forties.

Photo 2

Drowned bodies.

Part Two: The Fairground of Memory. The history of Port Adelaide told through fairground performance.

Photo 3

1924: fire at Number 2 Wharf on the cargo ship *City of Singapore.*

Photo 4

1928: The Workers' Waxworks perform the strike on the wharf.

Photo 5

1930s: the Depression.

Photo 6

1950s: The ventriloquists discuss social banditry at the Police Academy Floral Show.

Photo 7

1980s: Port Adelaide industrial alchemy. Mustard gas and industrial pollution.

Photo 8

1980s: Port Adelaide – a refuge for freaks and social outcasts.

Photo 9

Club Swing's Simone O'Brien holding Kareena Oates at the Victorian Arts Centre, Melbourne, January 1998. Photographer Angela Bailey.

Photo 10

Airated's Isabel da Silva, Deborah Batton and Anna Shelper 1997. Photographer Lyn Pool.

Photo 11

Sydney Front's *Don Juan,* 11 April 1991: 'Thump Rump' scene. Christopher Ryan, Annette Tesoriero and Nigel Kellaway. Photographer Heidrun Lohr.

Photo 12

Sydney Front's *Don Juan*: 'Java Dance'. Christopher Ryan, Andrea Aloise, John Baylis, seated seduction victim, Nigel Kellaway and Elise Ahamnos. Photographer Heidrun Lohr.

Photo 13

Sydney Front's *Don Juan*: 'Pavan/Fuck Me' scene. Andrea Aloise, Nigel Kellaway, John Baylis, Elise Ahamnos, Annette Tesoriero, Clare Grant. Photographer Heidrun Lohr.

Photo 14

Azaria Universe. Photographer Heidrun Lohr.

Photo 15

Barbara Karpinski. Photographer Heidrun Lohr.

Photo 16

Moira Finucaine as Romeo. Photographer Heidrun Lohr.

Photo 17

'Masculine Force and Intimate Exchanges in the Wrestlers' Gym'. Gleason's Gym, Brooklyn, New York. Larry Brisco (De Garis) offers Chris Moniz some tips. Photographer Sharon Mazer.

Photo 18

Tess De Quincey. Photographer Simon Hunter.

Photo 19

How Could You Even Begin to Understand. Umi Umiumare and Tony Yap. Photographer Sonia Tan.

Photo 20

Fleeting Moments. Yumi Umiumare. Photographer Brad Hick

Photo 21

Yoni Prior, Michael Kantor, Elisa Gray in *The Dybbuk.* Gilgul Theatre, Everleigh Railyards, Redfern (Sydney), 1991. Photographer Tracey Moffatt.

Photo 22

Milijana Cancar in Lyndal Jones' *Spitfire 123,* Section 3. Lonsdale Power Station, Melbourne, 1996. Photographer Petray Cancar.

Photo 23

David Wicks in Going Through Stages' *Dazzle of Shadows,* Melbourne 1993. Photographer Ian de Gruchy.

Photo 24

Stelarc, 'Sitting/Swaying: Event for Rock Suspension'. Tamura Gallery, Tokyo, 1980. Photographer K. Nozawa.

Photo 25

Stelarc, 'Amplified Body, Laser Eyes and Third Hand'. Maki Gallery, Tokyo, 1986. Photographer T. Shinoda.

Photo 26

Possessed by the Meryl Tankard Australian Dance Theatre. Photographer Regis Lansac.

Photo 27

Sara-Jayne Howard in *Furioso* by the Meryl Tankard Australian Dance Theatre. Photographer Regis Lansac.

Photo 28

Louise Fox, Matthew Whittet and John Bell. *King Lear* (1998) by the Bell Shakespeare Company directed by Barrie Kosky. Photographer Jeff Busby.

Photo 29

Hellen Sky and Louise Taube in Company in Space's *Escape Velocity*. Photographer Jeff Busby.

Photo 30

Helen Sky and Louise Taube in Company in Space's *Escape Velocity*. Photographer Jeff Busby.

Introduction: A/live performance

Peta Tait

Body Show/s: Australian Viewings of Live Performance asks in what ways do physical bodies in live performance present vital and compelling expressions of ideas? Over the past two decades a substantial number of performance groups in Australia and internationally have presented performing bodies in experimental works informed by cultural theory. These performances, as expansions of theatre, contain an implicit premise that expressions of thinking need not be spoken and written. Instead, they can be interpreted in reception directly through bodies in/at performance; that is, intellectual ideas can be embodied. Where bodies perform ideas, the words that prefigure theories including those about bodies become an unspoken presence in the text. Moreover, such embodiments of thinking are considered communicable – perhaps it is also assumed that some spectators will be familiar with alternative written expressions.

The quality common to these hugely variable bodies in performance is liveness. It is like the self of postmodern texts, imminent, irrational, dispersed. Therefore, it is important that commentaries on this performance are responses to the live body and its action as it makes cultural significances, rather than merely extracting authorial thinking – rewriting the intended text – since a body in performance often produces unintended significances. What is the contribution of liveness to the embodiment of ideas and in what ways can it also be (re)viewed?

Body Show/s investigates performances by live bodies as texts, past and present.[1] It discusses and describes bodies in contemporary performance, theatre, visual art and dance; in circus, ethnographic and animal shows; in performance training, butoh and wrestling; at gay and lesbian dance parties, and in relation to digital images. It investigates the meanings of physical bodies as cultural spectacles. Chapters in the book are grouped in three sections. **Citings** explores how performing bodies sign social identities inclusive of animals and concepts of otherness. Reviewings arise from historicised bodies and postcolonial understandings – these body shows exist as the antithesis of, but forerunners to, contemporary shows. **Sightings** are viewings of contemporary performances that bodily represent and interrogate masculinity, femininity, maleness, femaleness, sexualities and interculturalism. **Sitings** locates performing bodies in architectural, social and virtual spaces, in intersecting cultural geographies. These explorations of how the staging of bodies codes racial, gender and queer identity link contemporary performance to historical shows such as circus.

The contributors to *Body Show/s* are theorists and critics who work in Australasia, a number of whom are performance-makers. While explorations of how bodily knowledges and thinking are embodied underscores both the form and content of many of the performances discussed in this book, elsewhere words about and in direct response to live performing bodies continue to be more the terrain of the journalist than the cultural theorist. *Body Show/s* attempts to redress this imbalance with theoretical viewings of live bodies – thinking that ghosts their action. While approaches reflect prevailing theories of subjectivity, desire, and absence in the reception of representation, contributors find phenomenological and kinaesthetic concepts more pertinent to body shows. Both by coincidence and design, *Body Show/s* presents phenomenological discussions of sensory body to body liveness.

Theatre based on spoken words generates written critiques with more frequency because it can be captured after the event. The difficulty of matching the viewing of live performing bodies in the present to thinking and writing after the event means that they exist as remembered e/motion. (The widespread strategy of speculating about bodies and inferring an (universalising) actor's presence from the drama (written page) actually disappears the complex artistry of specific theatre and performance texts, and of bodies, although it avoids the huge difficulties of responding to the instabilities of live body-texts). Thinking about the porous meanings of live performing bodies in action is related to perceiving the specificities of physical bodies, but this process must be distinguished from the alternative interpretative possibilities of fixing them in photographs and film for reviewing. Even video records of live performance reflect an imperfect version of a whole text by banishing its liveness. Despite the increasing importance of visual texts in cultural discourse, theoretical analysis of live performance remains underdeveloped.[2]

As Peggy Phelan, who does write philosophically in response to live performance explains, it is difficult to write about what is not there; live is like her Real-real, unverifiable, disabled, a visible blind spot, unmarked (3). If live bodies are like 'truth-effects' (Phelan 3), they do not align with words nor do they stabilise for the viewing. They continue their motion even in memory and therefore, as she has pointed out, they are always in translation. It is important to attempt to engage with this elusive quality of the liveness of performing bodies, because complex ideas about cultural identity implicate live sensory exchanges in visual codings. While the struggle to retain the residue of corporeality in thinking and writing has become a preoccupation of much recent discourse and, interestingly, the metaphors of theatre and performance are widely used in critical theory and philosophy,[3] explicit examples of theatrical bodies and their discourses are less in evidence (Carlson 7). Liveness is crucial to the meanings of contemporary performance and contains significances for critical theory. For example, feminist theoretical approaches to the commodified sexual body and the structuring of desire, the female body as a sign of masculine desire, emphasise its seen inscription (Schneider 5).[4] Given that liveness is a sensory condition, what are the bodily implications of engaging with notions of live for cultural knowledges? Analysis of the desired body as artifact or sign obscures the relentlessly dynamic motion but seeming randomness of bodily sensations and responses; their capacity to pass through even the spatiality of language, to revoke it. A live body might, therefore, present flows and exchanges that resist the Symbolic order, its totalising effects, eschewing its logic in poetics of liveness.

Philip Auslander ('Liveness') explains that because a pure originating condition is associated with liveness that has come to signify (and simulate) authenticity, live exposes cultural anxieties as well as theoretical unease. He points out that the televisual image has become integral to much live performance and even reverses relations so that some live events might be considered to arise out of technological production (197). Auslander claims that staged together the televisual overpowers the live (*Liveness*). In disputing a binary opposition between liveness and its mediatisation, Auslander extrapolates that liveness was meaningless before the technology for its reproduction (the flattening of bodies into a unified surface) was invented. Nonetheless theatre and its bodies have been cited (flattened) with the written word at least since the ancient Greek theatre Auslander ('Liveness') mentions. Jane Goodall argues that cultural anxiety about mechanical reproduction substitution is centuries old, yet theatre's live copying of mechanical movement offers long established resistant discourses to anxiety about the loss of agency and the failure of liveness (death).

I contend that the ongoing fascination with performing bodies in action is also because kinaesthetic awareness is unstoppable within the yearnings of fleshed phenomenologies (see Chapter 4 'Fleshed, Muscular Phenomenologies'). These invite and resist their reconfiguration through technological stimuli, for example, with film. Looking for meaning in a live performing body is not simply in Derridan terms finding 'what it is not' but more about culturally forgetting what is there. Profuse, erratic sensory reactions defy language's taming strictures. While the condition of liveness is recognised as arising with the spatialities established between and within physical bodies, in performance reception the liveness of spectatorial bodies is ongoing and inclusive of thought responses. Future opportunities for staging nonreflective liveness seem compromised by technology because of economies of scale, but they evoke possibilities for new viewings of alive as interactive. How the growing trend in performance to stage technological with live – there is evidence of this in performances discussed here – impacts on visceral responses requires further consideration.

Live performing bodies are ephemeral. They are experienced as moving and in exertion, elastic and vibratory in their visual appearance and through their voices, aurally; as physical entities they are always active even when appearing still. The boundaries of live do not finish with visible surfaces; live can be heard and sensed. These are differentiated bodies despite their congruent potential to belong to categories of bodies. Live performance offers an insubstantial materiality, a visually tactile condition of unpredictable dynamic potentialities. It manifests as the qualities of a specific body framed within social identity and named to imply its specific distinctiveness.[5] Live is the starting point for all bodily knowledges and imagery; it counter/acts the captured static image: an immobility that mimics deadness.

Live performance is, as Marvin Carlson explains, praxis (195) and it is as unstable and variable as the countless, endless trajectories for moving bodies. Yet the speech of a speaking live body might serve to mask the paradoxical materiality of an ongoing separation between speaking and moving to show physical presence. A performer who is moving to capacity in athletic exertion cannot use his or her own voice easily. These separations are replicated in cultural responses to performance; spoken words make the reception of meaning less ambiguous. The literal potentialities in what Derrida terms a '"language" of action', an 'athletic writing', seem to require speechless embodiment (9). An assumption that bodies are like words makes them conduits of social meanings that accommodate how bodies are categorised, but avoids the complexity of observing and receiving via particular body shapes, actions and differences in their specificities. Perhaps bodies constantly collide and oscillate along singular and multiple layered moving lines.[6]

As Maurice Merleau-Ponty argues, thinking has a history of excluding self-awareness of embodiment and although this provides substance in thinking, it also requires forgetfulness (*Phenomenology* 58). (In psychoanalytic approaches this might coincide with the condition of loss (Phelan 15). Contributors to *Body Show/s* are not simply asking how spectators think consciously or unconsciously about performing bodies; they consider the ways in which such body works contribute bodily to the social performance of ideas as bodies.

As Phelan argues, live performance evokes a sense of an ontology as like performance (196). To what extent are experiences of live performance, as like ontology, engagements across visceral, sensory bodies experienced in spatially dispersed physiologies, some of which express cognitive languages? Carlson defines performance as 'a self consciousness about doing and re-doing' and a 'physicality of theatrical performance' (199). Forgetfulness and/or loss are always latent within the practice of bodily doing. This is not to argue for the evaporation of language or to deny its constitutive power for identity, but to suggest that performance reception may not be manifestly thought, but rather embodied, felt and known. Without doubt, interpretative meanings about bodies need to be made visible, to be written. The written body, however, only echoes live and its perceptions.

Nonetheless, bodies are outlined within shared meanings which inadvertently or otherwise linger across performed body-texts. Phenomenologies of performance reception argue that spectatorship also involves responses to body-specific actions that expand cerebral perception. Involuntary responses: a postural shift, a smile, a sudden intake of breath, a sensory tingle, a slight itch, a yawn, are not mimicking the actions of a performer but are almost imperceptible and inexplicable responses to the other's physicality. The audience functions like a visceral meta-body, as if its articulated, distinctive reactions happen unpredictably within the whole. In the instance of writing about live, liveness surfaces in the embodied perceptions of the writer; the separations between knowings and bodies bridged here in words, conjoined to imagined and re-imaged spatialities of movement. While written responses clearly disappear the initial qualities of a performance, there is a residue of liveness in the thinking responses of the writer/reader (embodied), in awakened embodied knowledges of live. The accumulative effects resound with cultural yearnings for liveness with bodies.

Chapter summaries

I am delighted that the chapters in this book, all drawn from research in progress, convey such a wide diversity of body shows and interpretative frameworks. As representative examples, they point to where future research can address the gaps in the record while offering young performance-makers a sense of the achievement and intellectual significance of contemporary Australian performance. The advent and legacies in circus of English and French equestrian shows in the late eighteenth century coincided with the end to overt public spectacles in the social disciplining of bodies (Foucault). In retrospect, the strength of the hundred and fifty-year-old tradition of circus in colonial Australia, the most popular entertainment until the 1920s (St Leon), was its capacity to reflect the imperatives of a conquering, unfettered physicality indicative of colonising Australia. The emergence of internationally influential Australian new circus and physical theatre aligned with radical politics by the late 1970s reveals an ongoing artistic and cultural adaptation of body shows in hugely different contexts.

Section one, **Citings**, spans nineteenth-century ethnology and daring human and horse acts, emphasising their historical confluence in circus. In 'Acting Savage' Jane Goodall thoughtfully and provocatively questions whether recent views indicative of our shame, that exhibited native bodies in the nineteenth century were completely victimised, also deny agency to the Aboriginal people involuntarily kidnapped in this abhorrent practice. Goodall considers how the prescriptive expectation of performing the savage produced an identity other than the exhibited person's own and argues, therefore, that identity relations are far more complex when the watched body was also skilfully performing. Bill Dunstone's very entertaining and comprehensive argument in 'Performing Colonial Bodies and (as) Work', reveals how a boy, cross-dressed as Britannia, walking a slack-wire and stripping to his underwear in 1870s Perth, Australia, was discursively transgressing colonialism and its corollary of masculine dominance through risk-taking and displays of physical strength. Although nineteenth-century popular theatre and circus performance – the distinctions remain arguable – were leisure activities, they were nonetheless work, paid or otherwise, and produced the colonial subject while mocking imperialist culture.

David Williams' performatively written 'Performing Animal, Becoming Animal' cleverly exposes culture's longstanding objectification of horses. Their utilitarian and aesthetic value speaks more of the controlling and patrolling boundaries of human identity and subjectivity than animality. The homogenising and privileging of species perpetuates a barbaric ignorance of bodily properties and differences, and this persists in the visual arts. Théâtre Zingaro, however, work with specific horse bodies in unpremeditated work-play. In my chapter on 'Fleshed, Muscular Phenomenologies: Across Sexed and Queer Circus Bodies' I investigate the reception of muscular performing bodies of two all-female aerial groups doing fast action as muscular drag, to envisage identity politics within phenomenological theory. Aerial action is the performance of liveness. This is a rereading of some of Merleau-Ponty's ideas to ask how, if dispersed physicality and habitual patterns of motion in the phenomenal field contribute to the reception of bodily acts, this might then impact on, or even overpower, thinking about socially symbolic bodies. Radical ideas of bodies pre-empt fleshed, muscular interventions.

In section two, **Sightings**, contemporary performances that were viewed live are remembered, described and critiqued. In her insightful and revealing discussion of *Don Juan*, 'Staging Seduction: The Sydney Front and The Postmodern Geopolitics of Theatre's Bodies and Spaces', Kerrie Schaefer explores two major concepts evident in much contemporary performance over the past two decades: realignments in performer-spectator relations and the dynamics of seduction. The implications for both *Don Juan*'s form and content provide a superb example of performance, its preoccupations and its symmetry. Importantly, Angharad Wynne-Jones was the only person to see every show at Sydney's The Performance Space (TPS) from 1991 to 1997. In 'Catalogue Notes: Independent Female Artists at the Performance Space 1991-97', she (re)members body shows that delighted her and attributes the emergence of these female artists to artistic and pragmatic circumstances. In Edward Scheer's politically relevant 'Of Fears and Violent Fantasies: Performance and Responsibility in Open City's *All That Flows*', this influential ensemble group's approach to spoken language is explored through its seminal performance text about the male body – its interiority, masculinity and voyeuristic potential – and discourse about fascism and racism. If the confessional conversational delivery of Open City's Keith Gallasch and Virginia Baxter make their shows seem personal, their performance personae repeatedly revoke assumptions of a subjective body-self and authenticity in form and content.

In her exhilarating discussion of American male wrestlers in 'Real Men Don't Wear Shirts: Presenting Masculinity in Professional Wrestling', Sharon Mazer points out that what is being contested in male wrestling is definitions and expressions of masculinity in an unstable field of signifiers. She argues that professional wrestling is carnivalesque in its display of male bodies and that their masculine expression as real men is outrageous, even feminine. The relationship between styles of acting and cultural theories of the body is a hugely neglected field of research, so Adrian Kiernander's far-reaching, incisive 'The Unclassic Body' is extremely welcome. He explores how the acting and directing of Shakespeare in Australia by the acclaimed John Bell depicts a different actor's body. Bell rejects classical acting styles and delivers a Bakhtinian comic grotesqueness that undercuts more conventional stagings of canonical plays.

In two effective companion articles on butoh performance in Australia, Edward Scheer discusses 'Liminality and Corporeality: Tess De Quincey's Butoh', her performance style and approach to training, and Peter Eckersall writes on the work of Melbourne-based Yumi Umiumare and Tony Yap in 'What Can't Be Seen Can Be Seen: Butoh Politics and (Body) Play'. In the mid-1980s Japanese physical methods such as butoh seemed to become the preferred international disciplines for physical theatre training in performance, replacing the French mime training dominant since the 1960s. (Circus skills offered a separate although often overlapping physical discipline during these decades for physical theatre performers.) While De Quincey began to reframe the form away from Japanese butoh, Umiumare and Yap continue to engage with cultures of origin, although in varying interpretative modes that challenge Australian resistance to body difference. While butoh spans dance and theatre, the form is most specifically that of body show.

Section three, **Sitings**, locates performing bodies in cultural geographies of space; in expanded public and controlled private spaces, in self-selecting communities, in the promise of limitless virtual worlds. In his compelling account of 'Filthy Spaces: The Investment of Non-Theatre Venues in Melbourne 1990-95', Julian

Meyrick discusses the work of three important Melbourne performance-makers, Barry Kosky, Lyndal Jones and Peter King, chosen in part because of their use of venues away from theatres.[7] Meyrick describes how the use of industrial spaces for artistic and practical reasons began to impact on design aesthetics in conventional theatres. Kosky and Gilgul Theatre used a disused machine engine shop to convey nightmarish decay, Jones sought bigness and brutality in a power station to overpower intimate moments, and King continued to echo previous architectural spatialities in his subsequent use of other spaces. The cultural resonances of found spaces added greatly to the significances of performances.

In 'Obsolescent Bodies and Prosthetic Gods', Anne Marsh's profound questioning of Stelarc's proclamation that he is replacing obsolescent biology with a cyborg and cyberspace body highlights the contradictory crucible produced by theories of disappearance in postmodern performance. Specific physical bodies such as Stelarc's bleeding and pulsating body remain ever-present; and he subjectively experiences pain. Marsh asks whether Stelarc's work reiterates mind-body, nature-culture, masculine-feminine separations at a time when they are disavowed by identity politics. In 'Animated Suspension: Dance Parties and the Choreography of Community', a lucid and original account of the Sydney Gay and Lesbian Mardi Gras private dance parties, Jonathan Bollen elaborates on the difference between spectators viewing a designated performance on a dance party stage and party-goers in participatory showings through costuming and action that make the party event. Bollen asks: where do party-goers belong in discourses about performance? Participants are surrounded by the party, but (like actors in theatre texts) experience it as fragmentary and fractured; they cannot encompass the event.

Cynthia Barnes' extensive research into 'Death Defying Theatre and Community: Organisational Body Transformed' reveals how it redefined its communities and body politics from outdoor physical theatre displays of the 1980s to staging racially and ethnically representative bodies indoors in the 1990s. Their notion of community travelled from small-town Queensland to Sydney's outer western suburbs. In the first of three complementary articles on dance, Adrian Kiernander's 'The Impossibilities of the Dance Body' describes how the internationally acclaimed dance choreographer Meryl Tankard works with unconventional body shapes and sizes, and moves dancers into spaces above the stage on harnesses and behind screens as distorted shadows. In 'Learning to Read the Physical Mind'

Karen Pearlman demonstrates what she seeks, that dancers conceive of expanded intelligences in their training and in reading performance. She considers the kinaesthetic dancer's body in conjunction with theorists who argue that the mind is dispersed in the body. In the timely and forward-looking practices and ideas outlined in 'Mediating the Body: Dance and Technology', Rachel Fensham discusses filmed dance works by West Australian Chrissie Parrott and Melbourne's Company in Space that combine live and virtual spaces in which bodies are mediated by theory and technology, and are artistically adventurous as well as expanding audiences. This final chapter, where live and technological bodies converge, points to an important emerging direction in performance at the end of the twentieth century and to future exploratory spaces for interactive, live bodies.

References.

Allen, Richard & Karen Pearlman, ed. *Performing the Unnameable: An Anthology of Australian Performance Texts*. Sydney: Currency/Real Time, 1999.

Auslander, Philip. 'Liveness: Performance and the Anxiety of Simulation.' In Diamond, 196-213.

— *Liveness: Performance in a Mediatized Culture*. New York: Routledge, 1999.

Broome, Richard & Jackomos, Alick. *Sideshow Alley*. Sydney: Allen & Unwin, 1998.

Carlson, Marvin. *Performance: A Critical Introduction*. London: Routledge, 1996.

Derrida, Jacques. *Writing and Difference*. Trans. Alan Bass. Chicago: U of Chicago P, 1978.

Diamond, Elin, ed. *Performance and Cultural Politics*. London: Routledge, 1996.

Fischer-Lichte, Erika. *The Semiotics of Theater*. Trans. Jeremy Gaines & Doris L. Jones. Bloomington: Indiana UP, 1992.

Foucault, Michel. *Discipline and Punish*. Trans. Alan Sheridan. New York: Vintage Books, 1979.

Fuchs, Elinor. *The Death of Character: Perspectives on Theater after Modernism*. Bloomington: Indiana UP, 1996.

Goodall, Jane. 'Transferred Agencies: Performance and the Fear of Automatism.' *Theatre Journal* 49. 4 (1997): 441-453.

Merleau-Ponty, Maurice. *The Phenomenology of Perception*. Trans. Colin Smith. London: Routledge, 1996.

— *The Visible and the Invisible*. Trans. Alphonso Lingis. Evanston: Northwestern U P, 1995.

Murray, Timothy. *Mimesis, Masochism and Mime: The Politics of Theatricality in Contemporary French Thought*. Ann Arbor: U of Michigan P, 1997.

Phelan, Peggy. *Unmarked*. London: Routledge, 1993.

Schneider, Rebecca. *The Explicit Body in Performance*. London: Routledge, 1997.

St Leon, Mark, ed. *Circus in Australia*. Spec. issue of *Australasian Drama Studies* 35 (1999).

Notes

1 For discussion of body-texts see Fischer-Lichte. For a discussion of the Australian adaptation of the word 'show' into 'showies' for show people, see Broom & Jackomos, 28.

2 However, for a stimulating theoretical book developed from viewing performances see Fuchs.

3 See e.g. Murray. While several essays in this fascinating collection refer to specific theatre productions, most use theatre as a generic term, which seems at odds with its history of experimentation.

4 Rebecca Schneider describes body performances that she believes reveal how the gaps of the sign and signified collapse across the female body and its visceral spatiality.

5 Maurice Merleau-Ponty (*Visible*) denotes a 'lived body' with consciousnesses of knowing and physicality dispersed throughout the body and inseparably perceiving surroundings and other bodies.

6 These possibilities are evident in the word-filled Deleuzean philosophy of a nomadic self, but philosophies of ontology do need to be reinterpreted for the temporalities and artificial circumstances of performance.

7 It should be noted that the work of Jenny Kemp, and other important Melbourne-based performance-makers, is discussed elsewhere: See Allen & Pearlman.

Part I

Citings

1. Acting savage

Jane Goodall

The photograph shows nine figures, four standing and five (including a child) seated in front of them. As in any other formal group photograph from the Victorian era, all are posed neatly with their hands folded, and look directly at the camera. These, though, are 'savages', recently acquired for P.T. Barnum's Great Ethnological Congress, a massed entertainment in which they will appear as the Australian Cannibal Boomerang Throwers, alongside the Wild Moslem Nubians, Ferocious Zulus and Wild Men of Borneo. The nine figures in the photograph are indigenous Australians from Palm Island and nearby areas in North Queensland, who left their homelands in 1883 at the persuasion of R.A. Cunningham, who worked as a recruiting agent for Barnum. After appearing in the Great Ethnological Congress they were exhibited at a Dime Museum in Cleveland, then at the Crystal Palace in London before touring Europe. At each stage of their journey, the party dwindled as its members succumbed to diseases for which they had no immunity, brought on by an unfamiliar climate.

Their story is told in a touring exhibition entitled *Captive Lives* curated by Roslyn Poignant for the National Library of Australia in 1997. The photograph is a visual keynote for the exhibition, which portrays the group unequivocally as victims and presents the image as a record of capture. Cunningham is described as 'a cunning recruiter who proved merciless in his exploitation of human beings'. Caption boards reinforce the polemical message:

> The unwilling travellers were exposed to Western curiosity both scientific and popular, captive actors in a performance they did not choose.[1]

The same polemical message comes to the fore in an address for the Canberra launch of the exhibition by Sir William Deane, the Governor General of Australia:

> To the people who stared at them, caught up in the spectacle of performance and display, they were not fellow human beings. Rather, they were commodities.[2]

The address concludes by linking the exhibition with the current issue of reconciliation which, it is emphasised, depends upon present understanding and acknowledgement of past injustices. The reconciliation issue, so urgent during the three years of the exhibition's tour in Australia, is linked especially with one member of the group of 'captives'. This is Tambo, a Palm Islander who died in Cleveland and whose body Poignant was instrumental in returning to his homeland after it was rediscovered in 1993. Tambo's return to Palm Island over a century after his death was a healing symbolic reversal of the scene of abduction in which the 'odyssey of sorrow' began.[3] Members of the Palm Island family and other senior members of their community were present at both the Canberra and Sydney launches of the exhibition, and gave their endorsement to its presentation.

Looking at these images of bodies on show, caricatured in poster drawings or photographed in awkwardly staged groups, is a confronting experience. White spectators in the twentieth century may shy away, embarrassed to see too closely the damage done through the pathological tendencies that belong to their own cultural heritage, or angry at the continuing failure of non-Aboriginal Australia to make wholehearted efforts towards reconciliation. The images themselves were created for a very different kind of spectatorship, for a gaze that eagerly lingered on them, demanding to see more, to be ever more amazed and intrigued, to take possession of all the details and process them with a sense of complacency.

Captive Lives offers us a particular kind of insight into the dynamics between spectacle and spectator in ethnological shows. The exhibition's perspectives have much to do with the state of race relations in Australia in the late 1990s, when the country is going through what might be called a crisis of shame, torn between denial and the need for redress. The figures of the 'captives' in these images seem to express what the American psychologist Sylvan Tomkins calls shame-humiliation.

> It does not matter whether the humiliated one has been shamed by derisive laughter or whether he mocks himself. In either event he feels himself naked, defeated, alienated, lacking in dignity or worth. (Sedgwick & Adam 134)

Tomkins describes shame, though, in terms that cut both ways, between the spectator and the faces staring back from within the photographs. He sees shame-humiliation as intimately linked with contempt-disgust; they are two sides of a human inter-action in which each produces the other. If shame-humiliation is what is shown in the photographs, then contempt-disgust is what produced them.

> Whenever an individual, a class or a nation wishes to maintain a hierarchical relationship, or to maintain aloofness, it will have resort to contempt of the other.

Social change can give the spectator a very different positioning, however:

> In a democratic society, contempt will often be replaced by empathic shame ... or by distress in which the critic expresses his suffering at what the other has done, or by anger in which the critic seeks to redress the wrongs committed by the other. (Sedgwick & Adam 139)

Comments in the visitors' book for *Captive Lives* bear this out. A historical narrative of shame produces a contemporary experience of empathic shame.

What we see now, though, are only the images from what was originally an elaborately structured performance situation. It is hard, if not impossible, to get any sense of the figures in them as live bodies whose actions and behaviour could send complex messages. As exhibited bodies, they had no control over their situation, but as bodies engaged in performance they had opportunities to exercise very significant forms of control in their relationship with spectators. Without wanting to contest the 'shame narrative' presented in *Captive Lives,* I propose to explore some of the disjunctions in this and a number of other narratives about the showing of racial groups in the nineteenth century. At one level these exhibitions were indeed just bodies on show, there to be measured, described and analysed by self-styled men of science: evidence to be factored into theories of race. From an audience point of view, they were there to be scrutinised for their physiological characteristics and gawped at for their exotic behaviour. On another level, though, the tradition of ethnological shows as public entertainments had a destabilising relationship with prevailing scientific and political views about racial hierarchy. The destabilising factor was performance itself. As performing bodies, those on show were engaged in sequences of action that could be calculated for particular kinds of effects. If the scenarios were devised in the first instance by managers seeking to cater to preconceived images in the minds of their audiences, the performance was ultimately in the control of those who enacted it, and whose success as entertainers would feed back into management strategies for the promotion and design of the show. There were opportunities for parody, for the creation of ironic or contradictory impressions, and for the development of generic roles whose distance from any 'natural' human model grew to a point where serious scientific interpretation was turned back on itself in mockery.

A discussion of some earlier examples of ethnological shows may help to illustrate this point. Such shows belonged to a binary tradition, in which the entertainment industry and the so-called science of ethnology were braided together, their interdependence fraught with tensions. The tradition went back to the early decades of the nineteenth century, but became a prominent cultural practice in the 1840s after the foundation of the Ethnological Society in London in 1843. The Society was established with the express purpose of contributing to 'the Natural History of Man' by studying 'the causes of the varieties of the physical and mental development of nations' (Dieffenbach 2). Racial difference between humans presented a special kind of taxonomic problem: there were disagreements as to whether or not it was equivalent to species difference. How should races be classified? In order to decide this question and to determine where particular races belonged in the hierarchy of nature, racial difference needed to be thoroughly assessed, preferably through close physical examination of live subjects.[4] Members met to hear lectures about races from remote parts of the globe and, where possible, to consider live 'specimens' who had been brought to London, usually by show business entrepreneurs.

One such opportunity occurred in 1845 when two children from a family of African Bushmen were present at a Society meeting, to stand by as 'living illustrations' whilst the lecturer described their physiognomy, their native environment and their way of life, endeavouring as he did so to offer a considered assessment of their place in the hierarchy of racial varieties. In this situation there was no sense of a performance being given: the two children were simply under scrutiny. The lecturer made comments on their stature, the growth of their hair, the angle of their foreheads, the formation of their hands and feet and the set of their eyes (*Athenaeum*, 6 December 1845: 117). As objects of the ethnological gaze, they were accorded no agency or dignity: they were, in Tomkins' terms, shamed, however benevolently the Society believed itself to be regarding them. Tomkins explicitly associates shame-humiliation with transgressions against 'the universal taboo on looking.' (Sedgwick & Adam 144). Mutual looking creates intimacy between equals, and so is subject to social constraint. Members of the Ethnological Society presumably felt themselves exempt from such constraints because there was no such assumption of mutuality in the looking.

The Bushmen children subsequently appeared at the Egyptian Hall (a popular show place in Piccadilly), where they were exhibited together with 'the Great Ursine Baboon' and 'some exceedingly rare varieties of the monkey tribe'. The implication was clearly that the Bushmen represented the variety of the human species immediately adjacent to the monkey, but their status as specimens was confused by the introduction of a performance structure, in which both children (a boy aged sixteen and a girl of eight) played a series of adult roles. The bills advertising their appearance also include details of what amounted to a simple performance:

> 1st— Bushmen Children in the Dress of their Tribe.
> The Bushman will throw his Assigi (or Spear)
> Dance, &c.
>
> 2nd—The Bushman representing a Corporal of the
> Army, will go through the Manual and Platoon
> Exercise, with wonderful precision.
> The Bush Girl appearing as a Soldier's Wife.
>
> 3rd— The Bushman as a Gentleman's servant (Tiger)
> The Bush Girl as a Lady's Maid.[5]

Here there is evidence of the ethnological gaze, which lingers on people as exhibited bodies, being converted to the theatrical gaze which follows a sequence of action and registers bodies as vehicles of communication rather than sights in themselves. The latter moves away from a dynamic of shame towards one in which personal dignity can be shielded from humiliation through the mask of role play. The dynamics of control in ethnological shows changed as those on show became more skilled and confident, and could take the measure of their audiences, if perhaps not so literally as they themselves were sometimes measured.

Ethnology and show business engaged in different forms of exploitation, with potential for different kinds of effects on those who were exhibited. Ethnologists did not seek to exploit their 'specimens' financially, but they were certainly looking for gains in a knowledge economy. In return, they wanted to offer education and civilisation to those they regarded as most in need of it. Ethnological accounts tended to infantilise their subjects (since the lower races were equated with a condition of infancy in the evolution of humankind) and to represent their condition as terminal (since inferior races were considered necessarily at risk of extinction in the face of the great march of progress). Show business entrepreneurs may have stereotyped particular races as natives and/or savages, but at the same time they de-naturalised these types by turning them into roles for performance. The commercial exploitation associated with theatrical display allowed some scope for developing agency through performance, and for acquiring market value which could lead to financial independence. There are numerous cases of successful 'exhibits' changing or even abandoning their managers and setting up on their own terms.[6]

The Bushmen show was sufficiently successful to prompt a return season at the Egyptian Hall two years later with a different cast, this time of two adult couples and an infant. The *Times* (19 May 1847: 7) referred to the group as 'a stunted family of African dwarfs' and commented:

> In appearance they are little above the monkey tribe and scarcely better than mere brutes of the field ... They are sullen, silent and savage, mere animals in propensity, and worse than animals in appearance. The exhibition is however one that will and ought to attract. The admirers of 'pure nature' can confirm their speculations on unsophisticated man, and woman also, or repudiate them, by a visit to these specimens.

Concluding that 'in short, a more miserable set of human beings ... was never seen', the writer finally noted that they were 'about to perform some curious feats of activity' (*Times*, 19 May 1847: 7). This last statement seems to divorce itself from the rest of the account: the promise of 'curious feats of activity' carries implications of skill, ingenuity and planning that do not correlate well with images of brutes in the field. A more obvious mismatch of ethnological and theatrical points of view is evident in the account published in the *Illustrated London News* (12 June 1847). The Bushmen were 'a fine subject for scientific investigation' and afforded an opportunity to reflect on the contrast between 'the lowest and the highest of the race', which the visitor could take in at a single glance by looking through the window at the gentry in the street outside before returning his attention to 'the benighted beings before him' (381). The same review, though, described the setting in which the Bushmen were placed as 'a vigorous piece of scenic effect' and expressed admiration for the performance of one of the men, who addressed the audience with vigour and mimed the process of stalking and catching a lizard with appropriate dramatic cries. 'This fellow would make a capital melodramatic actor' was the verdict, and the show was progressively developed accordingly into a scenic pantomime with episodes such as 'Killing the Puff Adder', 'War Dance', 'Tracing the Footsteps of the Enemy', 'The Surprise' and 'Quarrels of the Bushmen'.[7] The Bushmen act continued to flourish as an item of popular theatre. An 1853 program for a variety show in Portobello Gardens features the Bushmen Savages alongside Negro Melodists, a Military Band, Signor Silvani's Wonderful Feats and Mademoiselle Volante's tightrope ascent across the lake.[8] The savage act, spiced up so that the performers tracked the lion, leopard and buffalo, rather than the mere lizard, was becoming a vaudeville performance in its own right.

If the ethnological gaze worked to fix racial typologies in a sharply graded racial hierarchy, the theatrical gaze was attuned to taxonomies of performance, or genres, and the savage show was becoming a genre. An ethnological aspect was part of the composition and was presented through lectures or in information leaflets that accompanied the shows. Show business entrepreneurs were well aware that the pseudo-scientific information they offered merely provided a pretext for audiences who preferred to think of themselves as motivated by educated curiosity than by prurient interest in strange human bodies. The information itself was formulaic. The generic savage narrative, for example, described a wild place of origin where the living conditions were harsh and precarious. The people themselves would be characterised as brutish in their features and stunted through poor nutrition. Most were cannibals. They were supposed to be ungoverned by reason, childlike in their over-excitability but at the same time dangerous in their violent impulses. Their favourite custom was the war dance. Since they had yet to reach the stage of civilisation at which language was properly developed, they were semi-articulate and, being closer to the animal than the human estate, they lacked basic forms of knowledge and skill. Groups described according to this formula included the Bushmen, Fiji Cannibals, Pigmy Earthmen, Wild Men of Borneo, Pigmy Cannibals and Botocudos.

Thus, whilst ethnologists minutely documented the specific similarities and differences between races, show business entrepreneurs collapsed a wide range of exotic races into one prototype, making a mockery of the ethnological project even as they seemed to be emulating it. To ethnologists 'savage' was a designation of shame invading the personhood and indelibly marked upon the bodies of those they scrutinised, whereas to showmen it was a role to be enacted. They soon realised that the exotic savages residing in the European imagination could be obtained far more easily from the wilder zones of the city than from the inaccessible areas of distant continents. George Sanger tells how his father discovered 'Tamee Ahmee and Orio Rio, the savage cannibal pigmies of the Dark Continent' in a Bristol slum. These 'two rather intelligent mulatto children' (aged nine and ten) were dressed up with feathers, beads and face paint to be introduced as near-animal species with the required whiff of horror and danger.

> Ladies and Gentlemen: These wonderful people are fully grown, being, in fact, each over thirty years of age. They were captured by Portuguese traders in the African wilds, and are incapable of ordinary human speech. Their food consists of raw meat, and if they can capture a small animal they tear it to pieces alive with their teeth, eagerly devouring its flesh and drinking its blood. (Sanger 45)

When the showman's bluff was called, the two children were returned to a Bristol workhouse, but Sanger assures us they 'did very well in later life' and often returned to his show as audience members (46).

The characterisation of Tambo and his group as the 'Australian Cannibal Boomerang Throwers' in Barnum's *Advance Courier* keeps firmly to the savage prototype. They are, it is claimed, 'the only members of their monstrous, self-disfigured and hopelessly embruited race ever to be lured from the remote, unexplored and dreadful interior wilds ... Undersized and disturbed in form, with bestiality stamped on their faces; their cruel eyes reflecting but a glimmering of reason; having no gift of speech beyond an ape-like gibberish, utterly unintelligible to anyone else' ('Australian Cannibals').[9] Offensive as this sounds, it was probably not even an attempt at a specific description of the group being put on show. There is a fundamental contradiction in the text between the generic portrayal of the Australians as cannibal-savages, and the claim – in the same broadside – that they are the creators of a radically original technology whose use is a highly refined accomplishment. The boomerang is 'made to reverse the accepted laws of projection and gravitation. It is not thrown at but from the object it is destined to strike, with unerring skill and crushing force. No other people have ever been able to master this extraordinary weapon'.

The contradiction in the account of the Australians also follows precedent. Showmen tended to use the savage narrative to lure audiences to see an exhibition in the first instance, but then if those exhibited demonstrated performance skills and showed signs of flourishing in the show business, their description would be changed so as to portray them as uniquely talented individuals with strongly appealing personal qualities. Thus in the case of the Earthmen their race in general is described as brutish and bereft of language, but the two children being shown as exemplars are introduced as having learned to speak English with elegance. They have also acquired a range of performative charms suitable to the English drawing room: they play the piano and sing 'in a pretty, childish style', their countenances are pleasing and their movements 'remarkably graceful' ('Erdermanne'). The Earthmen, together with two other children designated 'Aztec Lilliputians' were being marketed to the upper echelons of British society for private visits to prestigious households or for receptions in well appointed apartments specially rented for them. Promotional strategies for them were based on those for the prodigiously successful Tom Thumb, that 'pocket sized edition of humanity' who charmed the crowned heads of Europe. Here we see how the savage genre began to divide into subgenres. The Earthmen and Aztecs were examples of the drawing room savage: tamed, diminutive and cute, and generally epitomising the most appealing aspects of the state of childhood.

The Australian Cannibal Boomerang Throwers were closer to the subgenre of the outdoor or spectacular savage, which reached the peak of its success in Bill Cody's Wild West Shows. The best exponents of this version were promoted from brutishness not to be assimilated into European society but to become virtuosos of spectacular action, often on their own terms. The spectacular savage performance – with its whoops and yells, and its moments of lurking cunning leading to sudden outbursts of wild movement often with dangerous-looking weapons in hand – had obvious appeal for audiences with a taste for melodrama.

Amongst the most successful ethnological exhibitions of the mid-nineteenth century were a group of Iowa Indians who were featured in George Catlin's Indian Exhibition in London. This group had the capacity to offer performances that constituted a polished dramatic entertainment, whilst also offering the required level of wildness and *frisson* of threatened violence. The Iowa presented a series of nine scenes, individually detailed and collectively amounting to a varied program of action, narrative and characterisation. The synopsis for the opening scene, 'The Encampment', was included in the advertising literature:

> The Doctor, or Mystery Man, on Monday at 3.00, will select the ground for the encampment, according to the mode of the country; and having done this, will invoke the countenance and protection of the Great Spirit, by making the usual sacrifices of Tobacco by sprinkling it on the ground, and will then direct the Squaws where to pitch their tents, or Wig Wams, which they put up in a sudden and masterly manner, whilst the men are seated, lighting and smoking the pipe.[10]

A special outdoor performance in the Vauxhall Gardens followed this scene with an all-action presentation that included the Wild Horse Dance, the Eagle Dance, an archery competition, and a demonstration of combat techniques on horseback. Catlin has been referred to frequently as the inventor of the Wild West Show, but the Vauxhall Gardens performance was much closer to the Wild West genre than the indoor performances that Catlin devised and supervised for his Indian Gallery. The fully fledged action show with feats of archery and an equestrian spectacle was more likely to have been of the Iowa's own devising.

There is evidence that it was Cunningham's practice to graduate performers from the basic savage act to the spectacle performance. In 1889 he wrote to a friend about a second group of Queensland Australians he had acquired, complaining that they 'walked the block like dudes' and were not suitable for showing as wild men. The comment in *Captive Lives* remains relentlessly negative:

> However, with the assistance of his manager, Frank Frost, he found a way to exploit them. He hired race courses and baseball pitches where the Aborigines 'hurled the boomerang'.[11]

It is surely worth speculating a little further on this part of the story. Those who experience shame-humiliation do not 'walk the block like dudes'. Such an image suggests that the group in question were conscious of their dignity and confident of communicating it to others. Clearly Cunningham got the message and changed his management strategy accordingly. Barnum's publicity for the first group of Australians hints that he was keeping his options open: he was starting with the basic savage act, but signalling the potential for an action-based show featuring exceptional skills. To dismiss this simply as 'another form of exploitation' is to fail to do justice to the performers.

In an important new study of American Indians in Wild West Shows, L. G. Moses sets out the need for a revision of prevailing assumptions that the show Indians were 'artless victims'. The result of such a view, he claims, is that they 'have remained merely caricatures, as wooden and artificial as supposedly were the images they created'(7). Throughout the study, Moses provides evidence of the resourcefulness and self-determination of the Indians as performers, and he emphasises that it was precisely their skills as performers that entrepreneurs sought to market. 'Enterprising men quickly learned that Indians could work "Old World" crowds with as much facility as they could work "New World" mines' (11). The predicament of Australian Aboriginal performers taken to the other side of the world was obviously very different from that of American Indians working in the Wild West Shows, but there are similar questions to be raised. It is all too easy to present an image of these groups as artless victims, and to do so is to preclude any consideration of the skills and strategies they may have employed. In the case of Tambo and his companions we know too little to be able to tell how they dealt with the performance situation itself, and whether they had any sense of themselves as entertainers, but we need to be alert to the ways in which a performance situation that begins in exploitation may be turned into a situation of opportunity. There are many Aboriginal performers who made this transition and whose contribution to popular entertainment has yet to be properly acknowledged.[12]

Performance skills involve sophisticated communication strategies and for performers in ethnological shows, opportunities were created by the very fact that their audiences assumed savages to be incapable of such strategies. Savages could not but act naturally. As the *Athenaeum* (10 February 1844) reported of an appearance by a group of Ojibbeway Indians:

> These dusky savages are here more to instruct than to amuse us. They are not actors, representing dead or distant heroes, but the originals themselves. They are what they seem, and we have no standard to try them by, but what they wish to set up.

Exactly. But whilst the audience was taking instruction, what is to say that the savages may not have been getting considerable amusement by playing across the performance codes applied to them? In their study of a pigmy group exhibited at the Louisiana World's Fair in

1904, Phillips Verner Bradford and Harvey Blume observe that there are grounds for believing that the pigmies 'were involved in a subtle, ongoing parody of the exposition. But the authorities were not ready to give the forest dwellers credit for so much craft' (6). Bradford and Blume suggest that mimicry served as 'a form of disguise', allowing the pygmies to pose as the semi-retarded natives their audiences were expecting to see, whilst 'peering out from behind their masks, giving no indication of what they really thought, and keeping their own belief systems safe from inspection' (24). In assuming that ethnological performers were artless victims, we may ourselves fall victim to a very nineteenth-century illusion about inter-racial communication in which the indigenous 'other' is assumed to be naked as a communicator, incapable of artifice, strategy and parody.[13] Perhaps the empathic shame of late twentieth-century sympathisers may cause them to see nothing but shame in the plight of those about whom they are concerned, and so fail to see the devices of masking that live performance may have made available.

In arguing this, I have no wish to deny the injurious nature of the relationship entrepreneurs often had with ethnological performers, but rather to plead for more attention to the complexities of the performance situation itself. Show business does not thrive on the grossest forms of exploitation, because the power of the live performer is its main form of appeal and the humiliated do not make good entertainers. Inevitably, too, the live performance situation gives power to those in the show: what they do will determine whether there is boredom, laughter, irritation, amazement or sentimental empathy in those who are watching. The live performance is a volatile medium, constantly demanding new perspectives and sensations. Its destabilising influence is always potent, and often the more so in highly controlled social environments. Ideas and values may be treated with reverence or didactically reinforced in the theatre, but sooner or later performers will start to experiment with such stolid material, to seek out intrinsic absurdities, create playful inversions, over-sell the message to the point of buffoonery. This, I would suggest, is what happened with ethnological shows in the nineteenth century. They began as earnest lectures and frigid exhibitions, then diversified into a wide range of entertainments with all kinds of contradictory messages.

Barnum's Great Ethnological Congress was a development in his long-term strategy of playing off the worlds of science and show business to get the best profit out of both. As he was himself a showman rather than a scientist by profession, show business inevitably got the upper hand, often making a mockery of the scientific ideas it pretended to illustrate. Thus, Barnum's ever-expanding freak show became a parodic inversion of the earnest exercises in taxonomy taking place in the natural history museums; Darwinian theory became an excuse for diverse and often vaudevillian impersonations of the missing link; the idea of the savage took hold on the theatrical imagination to a point where it was the show itself that had to go wild, becoming ever faster, noisier, more unpredictable, more daring. Peta Tait's work has drawn attention to the ways in which circus performance destabilises categories and evokes 'a social fantasy of liberation from regulatory systems of order' (27). A circus, then, is of all nineteenth-century institutions perhaps the least reliable collaborator with a form of scientific enquiry whose core commitment was to taxonomy and hierarchy. Barnum liked to play both sides of the fence, keeping systematically arranged and comprehensive natural history collections alongside his freak shows and anarchic experiments with action and representation.

This is the context in which Tambo and his companions were introduced as performers. It is surely right that late twentieth-century non-aboriginal Australians should join with the Palm Island community to witness the telling of their lost history, a feat that was enabled after a decade of courageous scholarship on Roslyn Poignant's part. As one of the audience at the crowded Sydney opening of the exhibition recently, though, I felt that it was easy for us to slip into a way of seeing these images as some primary source of our own shame, and so fetishising them. It was also too easy to demonise 'those responsible' in ways that might salve our sense of shame, without contributing to any very worthwhile understanding of the dynamics of the story we were trying to follow. In the context of the huge Barnum entertainment machine, ethnological shows took on a highly ambiguous status, and to the extent that they enabled diversifying forms of live performance they could make a mockery of the typologies of race that were taking hold in science. The circus itself was no mere vehicle for peddling what is now called 'racism', a word that would have had no meaning in a social and cultural context where there was no perspective from which to see it as such. An evaluative view of racial difference prevailed everywhere. However, where science sought to create fixed evaluations of particular races, the performance of race made such fixture into a nonsense exercise by tampering with the behavioural signals that were being noted down and taken in evidence. Instead of seeing ethnological shows as an old and disgraceful cultural practice, long 'thank goodness' abandoned, perhaps we should instead face up to some of the still continuing elements in the overarching political and economic structures of the last century and the ideologies they enshrined. By performing liveness in the way they did, show people created a feral element inside the cultures of colonialism.

References

Broome, Richard & Alick Jackomos. *Sideshow Alley*. Sydney: Allen & Unwin , 1998.

Dieffenbach, Ernest. *On the Study of Ethnology*. Lecture delivered at a meeting on the Formation of the Ethnological Society, 31 January, 1843. London: Richard Watts, 1843.

'The Erdermanne, or Earthmen of South Africa'. *Illustrated Magazine of Art*, n.d. John Johnson Archive, Bodleian Library.

Goodall, Jane. 'Objects of Curiosity, Subjects of Discovery'. *Australasian Drama Studies* 34 (April 1999): 123-41.

Holland, Wendy. 'Reimaging Aboriginality in the Circus Space.' *Journal of Popular Culture* (June 1999): 14-26.

Moses, L. G. *Wild West Shows and the Images of American Indians, 1883-1933*. Albuquerque: University of New Mexico P, 1996.

Ramsland, John & Mark St Leon. *Children of the Circus: The Australian Experience* Springwood, NSW: Butterfly, 1993.

Sanger, 'Lord' George. *Seventy Years a Showman*. London: Dent, 1926.

Sedgwick, Eve Kosofsky, & Adam, Frank , eds. *Shame and Its Sisters: The Work of Sylvan Tomkins*. Durham: Duke UP, 1995.

St. Leon, Mark. *Spangles and Sawdust: The Circus in Australia*. Melbourne: Greenhouse 1983.

Stocking, George W. Jr. *Victorian Anthropology*. New York: Free Press, 1987.

Tait, Peta. 'Feminine Free Fall: A Fantasy of Freedom.' *Theatre Journal* 48 (1996): 27-34.

Verner Bradford, Phillips & Blume, Harvey. *Ota Benga: The Pygmy in the Zoo*. Melbourne: Bookman Press, 1992.

Notes

1 Caption board for *Captive Lives: Looking for Tambo and his Companions*. Exhibition curated by Roslyn Poignant for the National Library of Australia, Canberra, 1997.

2 Address by Sir William Deane, the Governor General on the Occasion of the Opening of *Captive Lives*, National Library of Australia, Canberra, 3 November, 1997.

3 'Odyssey of sorrow' is a phrase from Sir William Deane's Address.

4 There were two major branches of study in the Ethnological Society: the physical history of mankind, and comparative philology. I have not discussed the latter here as it is not directly relevant to my line of enquiry. A fuller

account of the Society's purposes and their context can be found in Stocking, chapters 2 and 3.

5 Handbill for 'Bushmen Children' at the Egyptian Hall, August 1845. Westminister Archives, Egyptian Hall folder.

6 One of the earliest documented cases is that of the Botocudos, a family of South American Indians who acquired their independence in London in 1822, and issued handbills declaring: 'The Indian Family of Botocudos ... have relieved themselves of the persons who enticed them to this country from their native home, and have exhibited them, and turned the whole of the profit to their own advantage'. As free agents, the Botocudos 'have deemed it expedient to exhibit themselves, and presume to hope that the liberality of the public will continue unabated towards them'. Handbill for The Botocudos at 23 New Bond Street, 1822. John Johnson Archive, Bodleian Library, Oxford.

7 Poster for the Bushmen at the Egyptian Hall. John Johnson Archive, Bodleian Library, Oxford.

8 Handbill for 'A Grand Day Performance' at Portobello Gardens, 1853. John Johnson Archive, Bodleian Library, Oxford.

9 'Australian Cannibals.' Caption Board for *Captive Lives*. From Barnum's *Advance Courier* (1883).

10 Program for the Iowa Indians at the Vauxhall Gardens, Sept 16, 1844 in John Johnson, Human Freaks series, Box 4.

11 Caption board for *Captive Lives*.

12 The work of St. Leon, Holland, Broome and Ramsland has begun this work of acknowledgement and celebration.

13 I have written at greater length on this topic in Goodall, 'Objects of Curiosity.'

2.
Performing colonial bodies and (as) work[1]

Bill Dunstone

In 1878 in the Town Hall, Perth, Western Australia, an eleven-year-old Melbourne-born boy hailed as 'Young Blondin, the Australian wonder', ventured out dressed as Britannia to the centre of a slack rope high above the floor, and divested himself of his costume down to his 'underdress' (*West Australian Times*, 10 September 1878). The politics of this balancing act seem to embody divergent aspects of theatre as imperial spectacle and as post colonial moment. The Young Blondin's parody of a Britannia stripped to a boy's underwear, 'her' body cross-gendered, but still out to seduce 'her' subjects, locates imperialism and colonialism in interlocking, transgressive discourses of desire, embodiment, masculinity and performance. The balancing boy Blondin seems to have offered his fellow colonials a carnivalesque laugh at pretentious spectacles of empire, and a reflexive laugh at their own role as spectators of empire. His simultaneous 'strip' and balancing act appears to have embodied the imperilled gender status of an apparently stable icon of empire, and to have offered a commentary, from the position of 'low other' (Stallybrass & White 175), on the ambiguous status of himself and his spectators as colonial subjects in a heirarchy of empire which his performance had, for the moment, turned topsy-turvy.

This chapter attempts to examine retrospectively some of the ways in which social and cultural meanings were produced in theatre and in circus performances such as Young Blondin's in colonial Western Australia. It specifically asks how the bodies and minds of colonial performers and spectators can be understood to have been at work during performances, especially, but not exclusively, during spectacles such as trick-riding, high wire and trapeze acts, in which performers demonstrated their physical skills in more or less dangerous circumstances.

A good way to tackle this issue is to re-examine the classificatory spatial and temporal differentiations which are conventionally employed to distinguish spectators from performers, and amateur performers from theatre professionals. Performance is conventionally classified, on the one hand, as paid work-time activity for professional performers, and on the other as a leisure-time activity for spectators and amateur performers. In colonial Western Australia these conventional boundaries were frequently invoked and policed for ideological reasons, both from within the theatre and from outside it. The lines between work time and non-work time in the colony were formed under a masculinist economic discourse which disregarded or undervalued the cultural work implicated in theatre performance. Vexed social and industrial issues about the right of employers to control the actions of employees outside working hours were sometimes projected onto theatre as a form of leisure which allegedly encroached on working time. In 1869 'Censor' grumbled, in a letter to the editor of the *Inquirer and Commercial News*, that the current influx of touring professional performers had encouraged local amateur performers to [mis]spend time away from their designated work:

> A Fremantle friend writes – 'Every second well-dressed official and government clerk you meet is 'studying his part' in some forthcoming Amateur Dramatic performance ... to the great surprise of old-fashioned folk, brought up with the idea that tradesmen and clerks are 'but engaged in their shops and at their desks". How heads of families can quietly look on, and allow their sons and clerks to idle away their time, is a matter of surprise to all who are not infected with the mania. (1 September 1869)

Representations of amateur theatre production and theatre-going as theft of work time were intimately bound up with patriarchal valorisations of the home as a source of respectability and, by extension, of social order. As Keith McClelland observes, in British society in the latter half of the nineteenth century 'the actual construction and sustenance of respectability was ... often heavily dependent on the work of women [in the home]' (208). For such ideological reasons, colonial women and men participated differently in amateur theatre. Colonial women did not perform on the amateur stage for almost four decades following a controversy surrounding the appearance of several respectable women in the colony's first amateur theatricals in July 1839. In the interim, female roles were customarily played by males.

However economic distinctions between professional theatre as paid employment and amateur theatre as unpaid recreational time broke down time and again in the multiple transformative processes of colonial theatre performance. Theatre performance imbricates multiple forms of work, and colonial Western Australian theatre can best be understood *as* work if historically-produced economic notions of leisure as non-work time are abandoned, and leisure itself is acknowledged as one of the many forms which work takes. Theatre performers and spectators in colonial Western Australia were engaged in forms of cultural work which more or less directly promoted imperial cultural unity and the hegemony of British culture within the empire, even while at times mocking these things. The Young Blondin's colonial parody of Britannia seems to have retained elements of respect and affection for the Empire and its iconography, even while taking 'a rise out of it'.

The particular performances with which this chapter is concerned took place in Western Australia between 1860 and 1880. During these decades amateur theatre, which had continued sporadically in Perth from its beginnings in 1839, underwent a significant revival. From 1865 professional companies began regularly to tour the major centres of Perth and Fremantle, as well as the remoter regions, on their way to and from the Eastern Australian colonies. But on 20 February 1861 the *Inquirer and Commercial News* had reflected: 'As regards amusements, we have but few and are contented with little'. This perception is hardly surprising, given that the colony was in severe economic depression in 1860, and given the demographics of settlement since 1829 when the colony was founded. According to the colonial government's Blue Book of 1860, a non-Aboriginal population of just 15,543 people inhabited the colony's two and a half million square kilometres – nearly one third of the Australian land mass. The total non-Aboriginal population of the colony had almost doubled to 29,561 by 31 December 1880, but the great majority of colonists lived within a few hundred kilometres of Perth in the south-west corner of the colony. The population of Perth, which had been proclaimed a city only in 1856, was about 5,000 in 1860, and it had grown marginally, and mostly by natural increase, to just under 6,000 by 1870. The colony was not socially or economically vigorous enough in these years to sustain a resident theatre company, nor to possess a dedicated theatre building. But the performances which took place in the colony during these two decades were deeply implicated in constructions of the colonial subject, and they drew on and re-constituted certain conventions of representing the Empire which were, as James Ryan says, 'deeply set in the British imagination' (11). Any theatre representation must, as representation, displace and transform the dominant to some degree, rather than simply replicate it. The spectators, performers, managements and other agencies and institutions which participated in these colonial performances were each engaged in the cultural work of constructing parallel and sometimes contestatory representations, or imaginaries, of both the Empire and the Swan River colony's place in it.

H. F. Moorhouse includes leisure among the many forms which work can take, and he argues that the meanings ascribed to these many forms of work are culture-specific. According to Moorhouse, the meanings and values ascribed to work differ from each other across cultures and within cultures, and these meanings resist incorporation into a single work ethic. If that is the case, then theatre work itself cannot be narrowly equated with a single dominant craft ethic or professional ethic. The concept of professional theatre has tended increasingly to converge with economic notions of work as paid employment, since the latter began to emerge in the West in the eighteenth century. Definitions of professional theatre as paid work valorise the performer's capacity to earn, through her or his mastery of materials and techniques, control over technologies, and adherence to broadly accepted work practices and values which affirm the performer's membership of a vocational élite (241). This economic approach to work has major shortcomings when it is applied to professional and amateur theatre. By defining theatre work entirely in terms of performer practices, the vocational model devalues the integral part which spectators play in the transformative work which goes on in theatre. The tendency to quantify professional theatre as paid employment is also at odds with qualitative attempts to distinguish professional from amateur theatre. Most importantly, definitions of work as paid employment devalue the significance and value of amateur theatre as cultural work in communities such as the settler colony of Western Australia in the decades from 1860 to 1880, when amateurs worked *pro bono,* and when neither the colony's economy nor its society could support a local professional theatre.

Patrick Joyce argues that in order to understand what work means in specific contexts, we need to look beyond our understanding of work as material production, and beyond our assumption that work is always and only located in paid employment (249). This must especially be the case with theatre, in which spectators and performers are engaged in transformative acts of embodiment, reception and signification. To understand performance as work, we need to acknowledge the various forms which actual work takes, and we need to approach work and its concomitant, leisure, as cultural constructions which both produce and are produced by the political and social agencies and institutions in which they are embedded. According to Joyce, work as material production is 'incomprehensible without an understanding of work as reproduction, both in its limited sense as the reproduction of the labour force and its larger sense as the reproduction of society itself (1-2). 'Reconstitution' is a more appropriate term than 'reproduction' for the transformative processes of theatre and circus performance. If we transpose these terms, then Joyce's statement begins to make better sense: theatre performance can be said to reconstitute its body of workers in the narrow sense through the transmission of practices and values; and in the larger sense, theatre can be said to reconstitute the social by re-positioning it and displacing it through representation.

As Moorhouse says of work in general, the meanings of performance as work are not likely to be simple and neat. Nor is theatrical work reducible to a univocal professional ethic. Rather, the meanings of theatre work are always and already implicated, and contested, in the politics of representing class, gender and race. Performance in colonial Western Australia from 1860 to 1880 can be understood as cultural production which was linked, on the one hand to stresses within colonial power relations, and on the other to promotions of the British Empire as an imaginary cultural and geographic unity. This chapter is concerned with the power relations that invest performance, and the agents and institutions that produce theatre and circus and give them meaning, but it does not maintain that performance is always and only legible as the product of discursive power. As the Young Blondin spectacularly embodied in his Britannia 'strip', the convention-bound bodies of performers could be potent sites for such contentious representations of power.

The Young Blondin, like several other child performers on the colonial Western Australian stage, was for a time technically a professional, contributing by his performance, even at that early age, to his family's living. Professional theatre performance undoubtedly had an important economic role as an historically and ideologically produced form of paid employment in colonial Western Australia. Professional theatre could, and did, have powerful impacts, for better and worse, on the small colonial economy based on scarcity. In 1880, the critic 'Odites' argued in the *Victorian Express* for a resident amateur theatre in the central regional town of Geraldton, some four hundred kilometres north of Perth. Odites argued, questionably, that while professional touring companies took money out of the local community, a local amateur theatre would re-circulate money within it (23 June 1880). The press was on firmer ground when, from time to time, it promoted the value of amateur performance as socially, culturally and ideologically productive work in the colony. The colonial press frequently invoked received hierarchical distinctions between professional and amateur theatre when it reflected on standards of amateur performance. But the same press strongly supported amateur theatre as socially productive leisure.[2] It frequently acknowledged the importance of both amateur and professional theatre as means of representing the Empire to colonial-born spectators, Aboriginal and non-Aboriginal alike. The optimism shown on 7 July 1839 by the *Perth Gazette and West Australian Times*, which dwelt on the virtues of amateur theatricals as a means of socialising colonial-born whites and Aborigines into the mystique of Empire, was undoubtedly misplaced. But there is no doubt that theatre performance came to articulate for colonial Western Australians many of those 'cultural formations, attitudes, beliefs and practices' which, Ryan reminds us, were involved in British imperialism (12-3). Ryan comments that 'Britain's Empire, like much in the Victorian age, had the atmosphere and aesthetic charge of a grand spectacle' (15). Without wishing to exaggerate the uniformity of the cultural forms which the Empire took, I would like to propose that local amateur groups and the professional theatre companies which toured Western Australia between 1860 and 1880 collectively promoted parallel spectacles of empire within a range of discourses to do with the power relations between leisure and work, and the gendering of spaces and bodies. The body which presented itself as spectacle, at risk – its energies focussed, its movements and gestures dilated – was always linked in this context with issues of imperial and colonial power, authority and desire. Mappings of bodies in performance were implicated, with geographical cartographies, in the construction of an imaginary of empire.

Colonial performance was well-placed, in its pivotal role between the élite world of imperial and colonial governments and the wider public sphere, to promote and play upon imperial imaginaries. In their journeys along intercolonial sea routes and across the colony's inland touring circuits, visiting theatre companies mapped out a geography of colonial settlement and linked it into an imaginary unified geography of the Empire. Professional and amateur companies functioned in their different ways as cultural texts which generally promoted, but sometimes questioned, imperial cultural unity and British cultural hegemony. Visiting performers positioned themselves as spectacle before the colonial gaze, and it was not uncommon for aspiring colonial youngsters to imitate in turn what they saw. In 1873 the Masters Lapsley of Perth, assisted by some of their schoolmates, a pony and a performing goat, raised seven pounds with a performance of 'some very clever acrobatic, athletic and equestrian feats' in imitation of Weiland's and Lyons's Circus, which was touring the colony at the time (*Perth Gazette and West Australian Times*, 25 April 1873). In their turn, visiting performers directed an imperial 'land-scanning eye' on the colony (Ryan 144). Frank Towers vividly recorded the rigours of a journey his family company made by stage coach in 1876 along hundreds of kilometres of flea-infested sand track from the southern seaport of Albany, which he described as 'truly the town of the dead', to Perth (*West Australian Times*, 13 February 1877). When May Vivienne and four other actors travelled the same track in 1882 the journey lasted sixteen days and two of the party's four horses died on the way. As Vivienne remarked: 'the pleasure of that expedition can be imagined' (2-3). If the tourists directed an imperial gaze upon the colony, then colonial spectators reciprocated from their position as 'other'. The bodily presence of the performers themselves was a potent cultural text, which served to reinforce the paradoxical status of the British performer as an object of colonial cultural desire and as a signifier of colonial cultural subjectification.

It would be mistaken to assume that theatre performance and colonial Western Australian society converged upon a single model of imperial beliefs, attitudes and practices, or that theatre performance simply replicated imperial and colonial dominants. Nevertheless, local commentators themselves drew parallels between the physical skills and mental ingenuity displayed in professional performance, and the skills which settlers, and sometimes the performers themselves, needed in order to survive in the colony. To the extent that such parallels were drawn, the bodies of performers represented points of entry into a colonial imaginary.

On 1 June 1869, Harry Bartine, an American acrobat who had recently come to Western Australia from Adelaide, South Australia, with Stebbing's Intercolonial Circus, gave two performances at Fremantle in honour of the fortieth anniversary of the founding of the colony. In the afternoon Bartine performed on the tight wire in the open air at the Old Convict Establishment, Fremantle. That evening in the Odd Fellows' Hall, Fremantle, Bartine repeated his act on the tight wire, and then performed his 'Antipodean act', which the *Herald* described as 'a dangerous and trying' feat requiring great muscular strength:

> It is performed thus: – An iron bar about 30 feet long with large rings attached is fixed to the ceiling. The performer mounting to the end of the bar by means of a rope, swings himself up, puts the fore part of one of his feet through the first ring – and suspending himself by the instep of his foot, puts the other foot in the next ring; hanging by his foot, he moves the foot that was in the first ring into the third ring and so on from ring to ring till he has traversed the whole length of the bar. The progress is backwards. (12 June 1869).

Newspaper reviewers bestowed similar approval on other displays of male muscularity and athleticism by performers who visited Western Australia that year. Reporting on 9 April 1869, about the first Perth performances by Lyons's Rocky Mountain Troupe of acrobats and comedians, the *Perth Gazette and West Australian Times* singled out Messrs Laurie and Nelson for 'their wonderful feats, of which we consider those on the horizontal bar as the most extraordinary exhibition of muscular power, and those with the pole as perhaps the more extraordinary still for the skill required in maintaining a perfect balance with the execution of difficult movements'. Such displays of athleticism and physical control by visiting male performers appear to have appealed all the more to the local inhabitants for their novelty value. The press wrote that Lyons's Rocky Mountain Troupe was 'astonishing the natives', by which it meant colonial-born non-Aborigines, during the troupe's tour of the colony's Eastern Districts. '[N]one of our colonial bred population', according to the *Perth Gazette and West Australian Times* 'had ever seen anything of the kind before' (23 April 1869). The same newspaper welcomed the subsequent arrival of Stebbing's equestrian and acrobatic troupe by sea from Adelaide in April 1869, with a similar emphasis on the prospective novelty value of its performances:

> As equestrianism is somewhat of a passion with [the] colonial-born, and this is the first opportunity they have had of seeing anything of the kind in the colony, we have little doubt that Mr Stebbing's troupe will have no reason to complain of the reception they will receive. (30 April 1869) [3]

The popularity of equestrian performances in a colony whose social and economic well-being depended crucially on the work of horses is attested to by the eloquent praise bestowed in the press on performances by a Geraldton-bred mare, acquired in 1880 to tour internationally with the Great London Circus as the equine lead in *Dick Turpin's Ride to York; or, the Death of Black Bess*.[4] The popular reception given to Lyons's and Stebbing's troupes reflected a desire on the part of local males to emulate the bodily skills and strength displayed by visiting male performers. According to the *Perth Gazette and West Australian Times*, several boys, 'ambitious of performing the acrobatic feats they have lately seen performed on the trapeze, etc.', sustained serious injuries (11 June 1869). The *Inquirer and Commercial News* reported that a juvenile had broken his collar-bone while trying to imitate Harry Bartine's acrobatic performance at Bunbury in the south-west of the colony (7 July 1869). In Perth, a 'venturesome youth' escaped unhurt when his improvised 'fixture' gave way while he was entertaining an audience of some twenty others with imitations of some of Young Blondin's feats, on vacant ground near the intersection of Hay and Milligan Streets (*West Australian Times*, 13 September 1878). The opening performance of Stebbing's Intercolonial Circus at the Fremantle Cricket Ground on 26 April 1869 was the first performance by a circus in Western Australia. The prospect aroused some of the male residents to such a riot of enthusiasm that the police responded with brutal whippings and arrests of spectators at the entrance to the Ground (*Herald*, 1 May 1869). The highlight of the show was a trapeze act featuring Mr Stebbing, his eight-year-old son, and the boy's still younger brother. Only one equestrienne, Madame Henriques, was listed on Stebbing's programme at Fremantle (*Herald*, 24 April 1869). The status accorded the male performer as an object of colonial desire glaringly reproduced the glamorous and the darker aspects of imperialist masculinist supremacism.

As Moorhouse reminds us, 'work as an area for the experience and display of sheer strength, endurance and courage [has not] been much discussed, yet, for males at least, such values are of some importance' (242). Equestrian, acrobatic, tight wire and trapeze performances attracted colonial spectators and acquired meaning precisely because they allowed spectators to witness performers in exhibitions of skill in non-routine confrontations with physical danger. Of course, those Swan River colonists who engaged in physical work, and especially those colonists who managed animals for work or leisure, routinely faced their share of dangers. Teamsters were sometimes crushed to death under dray wheels, women and men were fatally kicked or thrown to the ground by horses, and many colonists died of injury or privation in the bush. Performing groups themselves experienced the physical dangers of colonial and intercolonial travel. The Great London Circus lost its most valued horse in transit by sea from Adelaide, and its remaining animals were in poor condition when they arrived to perform at Fremantle (*Herald*, 1 May 1869). Sloman and Smith's Bijou Troupe, which appeared at the Odd Fellows' Hall,

Fremantle, prior to their departure for Java in July 1874, was forced to cut large parts of the programme because three company members had been injured when the horse drawing their vehicle bolted on the road from Perth to Fremantle (*Herald*, 4 July 1874). In July 1878, the ship *James Service*, on its way from Calcutta to Melbourne, was lost with no survivors during a violent storm at night on the Murray Reefs, about one hundred kilometres south of Fremantle. The only two bodies washed ashore were unrecognisable. One body was identified 'by the marking of the linen' as the remains of Mrs Frank Towers, 'the popular actress, who with members of her family performed [in the colony] with considerable success some short time ago' (*West Australian Times*, 2 August 1878). A luggage label indicated that the other body was probably the remains of Miss Bessie Edwards, of the Theatre Royal, Calcutta.

There would appear to have been cultural links between the staging of calculated risks in performance and the very real confrontations with death which performers experienced in transit, and which colonists faced in their lives. Performances such as Harry Bartine's on the ceiling of the Odd Fellows' Hall, Fremantle, relied for their appeal on deliberately calculated, explicitly staged risks, which the performer sought to overcome with muscular strength and control of the body. Physically-based performances in which performers faced the risk of injury or death could have spoken to colonists as liminal embodiments of the experience of physical danger, and perhaps even as stagings of transformative rites of passage towards death. Announcing the Young Blondin's intention to cross Perth's Swan River on a tight rope, the *West Australian Times* reflected, tongue in cheek, that '[a]s it is not often one gets a chance of seeing an individual pretend to commit suicide, or perhaps actually do it, by falling from a rope, the young gentleman will doubtless be well patronised' (*West Australian Times*, 9 August 1878). Repeat performances of Young Blondin's rope-walking, or of Bartine's 'Antipodean act', could be read as efforts to renew a consolatory illusion that death could be kept 'outside the circle of life" (Foucault 102). The survivor status implicitly accorded these two performers, and others like them, was the ideologically produced opposite of their historical function as markers of the fear of injury or death.

Physically-oriented performances seem to have held social appeal as affirmations of the links between bodies and colonial subjectification. Gymnastics and acrobatics enjoyed high status among local-born male performers and their acts were included in a wide range of social events. The local Australian Brothers, Messrs

Stokes and Bryan, performed on the horizontal bar as part of the first musical entertainment offered by the Perth Philharmonic Society in the Perth Town Hall in September 1877 (*West Australian Times*, 18 September 1877). Visiting artists commented on the high standards attained by local acrobats, and came increasingly to include local gymnasts in their programmes. The Brothers Bryan, members of a family long associated with brass bands, amateur theatre and minstrelsy in Perth, performed 'their Graceful Bending and Somersault Act' in support of Young Blondin's appearance as Britannia at the Perth Town Hall in 1878 (*West Australian Times*, 10 September 1878). The frequency and popularity of juvenile performances on the colonial stage suggests that child performers pointed up, more or less unconsciously, ambiguities in the gender and power relations of the adult world. This would seem to have been the appeal of visiting colonial juveniles such as the 'lilliputian' singer Katie Towers, the juvenile acrobat John Crosby, or the Young Blondin, who were able to sustain performances and engage spectators on their own terms, rather than simply be reactive. The appeal of such commanding colonial child performers seems to have resided, in large part, in their bodily and social ambiguity and liminality. It is possible that physical theatre by children and adults was also implicated in a discourse of aesthetics which had as its rationale the imperial conquest of space (Ryan 21). The colonial cultural referent of such an aesthetics would have been the settler/invaders' masculinist desire to acquire more land by expropriation from its Aboriginal owners.

It seems that physical risk and the mastery of skills in performance were both implicated in a masculinist discourse of colonial identity. The *Western Australian Catholic Record* (26 September 1878) appropriated the Young Blondin into a masculinist colonial myth of identity when it puffed him, on his departure from the colony, as 'a credit in his line to colonial pluck and enterprise'. In a review of the Great London Circus at Geraldton in June 1880, the critic 'Odites' affirmed local masculine identity when he wrote:

> ... it's too bad to be charged four shillings to look at a horse being lunged round a [circus] ring [by a visiting performer]. You could see more fun and far more skilful riding in Mr Brown's stockyard at Newmarracarra. (*Victorian Express*, 9 June 1880).

Crucial elements of risk and skill seem to have been lacking from the equestrian acts of the Great London Circus. On the other hand, when Harry Bartine overbalanced, fell almost five metres to the ground and badly bruised his body while tight-rope walking in the yard next to the Harbour Master's Barracks, Fremantle, in April 1873, his failure seems to have won him further public acceptance (*Herald*, 26 April 1873). The Young Blondin, too, was loudly applauded when he returned aloft and successfully crossed the tight rope, after having fallen from it in the Perth Town Hall, in September 1878 (*West Australian Times*, 13 September 1878). The public seems to have accepted these falls as more or less expected outcomes to calculated, even ritualised, confrontations with physical danger. It is possible that Bartine and the Young Blondin won acclaim precisely for having yielded themselves to potential self-sacrifice for the entertainment of the public – and, of course, for having the physical skill and fortitude to survive for another show.

In a colonial society in which most people valued respectability, the social visibility of performers' bodies exposed performers to allegations of impropriety. Masculinist fears of sexuality, and especially women's sexuality, as socially disruptive and morally debilitating were sometimes projected onto performers' bodies. But paradoxically, the containment policy of allocating female roles to male actors in amateur theatricals after 1839 did much to equivocate patriarchal constructions of the feminine. Fremantle's Master Mackey was one of a number of lads who made names for themselves as androgynous amateur actors of female roles. In 1869 Master Mackey won praise from the critic 'Jaques' for his surprisingly mature dramatic performance as Rose Briarly in the Fremantle Amateur Dramatic Company's production of Isaac Pocock's *The Robber's Wife* at the Odd Fellows' Hall, Fremantle. A few months later when young Mackey played an ambiguous gender role as Ernestine in the Fremantle Amateur Dramatic Company's 'laughable Vaudeville' *The Loan of a Lover*, 'Jaques' wrote: 'This lad displays capabilities for the stage that could scarcely be expected of a lad born in the colony' (*Herald*, 17 April & 10 July 1869). Few accounts survive of plays performed by working people and the poor in public houses, but extant material suggests that casts in these plays were also all-male. In 1875 the critic 'Yorick' favourably reviewed a cast of working-class men who performed D.W. Jerrold's melodrama *Black-Eyed Susan* in the bar room of the Federal Hotel, Fremantle. The title role was played by an unnamed fourteen-year-old boy (*Herald*, 20 November 1875).

The advent of professional touring provoked attacks on the impropriety of displaying male and female bodies, however costumed, as objects of desire to the public gaze in performance. The letter from

'Censor' to the editor of the *Inquirer and Commercial News* (1 September 1869) condemned performers on moral grounds and accused the press of indirectly encouraging public debauchery through reviews and advertisements of performances. In the course of his attack on the alleged social evils engendered by 'the present inundation of dramatic and acrobatic companies', 'Censor' warned of the moral danger of allowing working-class women to view 'these penny-gaff exhibitions', and condemned 'the humbug of deputations [of young men]' to present an 'amiable but by no means "first rate"' visiting actress with jewellery. Michael Samson and Samuel Solomon junior, members of the Fremantle Amateur Dramatic Club, responded in the following issue with the standard defence that amateur theatre was a rational and productive leisure time pursuit (8 September 1869). Colonial apologists for amateur theatre asserted its compatibility with domestic virtue and respectability; the critic 'Jaques' maintaining in 1869 that 'objections [of immorality] ... urged against professional performers cannot be made against amateur representations' (*Herald*, 23 January 1869). In the event, the presence of respectable professional female performers such as Louise Arnot, who visited the colony with the Theatre Comique in 1868, Mrs Lyons, who performed and resided in the colony between 1869 and 1873, and Miss Adelaide Stoneham, who toured twice with her family between 1871 and 1873, gradually eased the way for local women to re-appear with respectability on the colonial amateur stage. As early as 1865 the *Inquirer and Commercial News*, announcing the arrival of Edith Mitchell and Annie Hill, the first professional female actors to tour Western Australia, observed that the unwonted appearance of professional actors from London could be expected to 'draw crowded houses ... but where the performers were known to be women, everyone [would feel] himself bound to view a sight never before ... witnessed in Swan River' (27 September 1865).

Further decisive support for women amateur actors came from Lady Robinson, wife of Governor Sir William Robinson. Lady Robinson supported programmes of amateur theatricals at Government House, Perth, and set up the côterie Dorcas Society for women of the social élite in 1876 during her husband's first tour of duty. Governor Robinson himself strongly supported the construction of St George's Hall, which opened in Howick [now Hay] Street, Perth, in 1879, initially as a venue for dramatic and musical performances by the vice-regal côterie. As the result of these and other social interventions, socially eminent women such as Lady Louise Leake, wife of the Speaker of the Legislative Council, and Mrs

John Forrest, wife of the future premier Sir John Forrest, regularly appeared in amateur theatricals in Perth from 1878. Changes in the gendering of performers were more gradual in Geraldton. Respectable local women appeared with propriety on stage there from at least 1878, but several young men, known by their respective stage-names as Mlle Mordaunt, Miss Francesca Vere de Vere and Miss Claire de Lune, continued to play female roles for the Geraldton Amateur Theatrical Company into the 1880s.

Joyce notes that work retained its significance as a major source of values in Victorian England. But he also notes that, with the increasing tendency to demarcate separate spheres of work and non-work time in nineteenth century Britain, 'social values and identities were increasingly explored and defined in terms of leisure' (Joyce 24). Successful defences against charges of impropriety in the theatre, increasing participation by clerks and 'mechanicals' in amateur theatre, regular professional tours, and the gradual return of women to the colonial stage, implicate theatre in shifts of power concerning work, leisure, identity, class and gender in the ordering of colonial Western Australian society from 1860 to 1880.

Ryan describes imperialism as 'a pervasive and persistent set of cultural attitudes towards the rest of the world, informed to various degrees by militarism, patriotism, a belief in racial superiority, and loyalty to a "civilizing mission"' (12-13). While not wishing to overplay 'the consistency and uniformity of cultural forms of imperial power' (26), it is true that theatre performance in colonial Western Australia was implicated in these attitudes. Amateur theatre in Western Australia was linked with imperial militarism through its associations with the bands of various colonial Rifle Volunteer units, and through collaborations such as that between the Fremantle acting fraternity and the Royal Engineers Dramatic Corps while the regiment was based at Fremantle in the early to mid 1850s. The increasing numbers of colonial-born young people who participated in, or helped found, amateur theatre companies in Perth, Fremantle and Geraldton, represented small but decisive moves towards the emergence of new, self-confident re-formations of colonial identity and the status of the colony within the Empire. In these respects, amateur and professional theatre were directly implicated in formations of the colonial subject. The peculiar contribution of theatre performance in these years was to situate the corporeal presence of performers within the spectacle of empire, and to implicate performers' bodies in the social ordering of the colony.

References

Foucault, Michel. 'What Is an Author?' In Paul Rabinow, ed. *The Foucault Reader*. London: Penguin, 1984: 101-120.

Joyce, Patrick, ed. *The Historical Meanings of Work*. Cambridge: Cambridge UP, 1987.

McClelland, Keith. 'Time to Work, Time to Live: Some Aspects of Work and the Reformation of Class in Britain, 1850-1880.' In Joyce, 180-209.

Moorhouse, H.F. 'The "Work Ethic" and "Leisure" Activity: The Hot Rod in Post-war America.' In Joyce, 237-257.

Nicolay, Rev Charles G. *The Handbook of Western Australia*. Perth: B. Stern, 1891, repr. and rev. 1896.

Ryan, James R. *Picturing Empire: Photography and the Visualization of the British Empire*. London: Reaktion, 1997.

Stallybrass, Peter & White, Allon. *The Politics and Poetics of Transgression*. London: Methuen, 1986.

Vivienne, May. *Travels in Western Australia, Being a Description of the Various Cities and Towns, Goldfields, and Agricultural Districts of that State*. Carlisle, WA: Hesperian, 1993.

Notes

1 This paper was given at the Australasian Drama Studies Association Conference, University of Waikato, Hamilton, New Zealand, 2 July 1998. The newspapers and journals used here are held in the Battye Library, Perth, Western Australia.

2 A Geraldton correspondent to The Victorian Express (12 May 1880) wrote that a local amateur theatre would 'accomplish good among the members of Society by cementing good feeling, [and would] do a vast amount of good among the youth of our town.'

3 The Perth Gazette and West Australian Times (30 April 1869). See also Nicolay, Rev C. G: 'From the earliest days of the Colony horses of the best blood from England has been introduced into Western Australia, the necessities of life, and the pleasures of kangaroo hunting, especially in the country districts, made women as well as men at home in the saddle (sic)' (208-209).

4 *West Australian Times* (25 June 1880). See also the *Victorian Express* (30 June 1880).

3.
Performing animal, becoming animal[1]

David Williams

Animal Others

> *Do you know which animal you are in the process of becoming and in particular what it is becoming in you [...] a whole mob inside you in pursuit of what ...?*
>
> (Deleuze & Parnet 76).

My current research focuses on interactions between humans and animals in performance contexts in the broadest terms. From the performative bestiaries of Borges, Broodthaers, Beuys, Burroughs, butoh, Bausch and Bartabas, to the recent spate of animal hunting computer games in the wake of GT Interactive's notorious *Deer Hunter*. From Steve Paxton's so-called 'gland dance' improvisations with his dog, to Nipper the quizzical terrier in the celebrated HMV logo, listening to His (dead) Master's Voice on an Edison phonograph. From the aleatory choreography of the seagulls in Australian performance artist Jill Orr's *Lunch with the Birds* (1979) on St Kilda beach, to the perpetually frozen *mises en scène* of taxidermy and Damien Hirst's formaldehyde-borne animal sculptures. From the Russian clown Vladimir Durov's pig-Kaiser and their banishment from Germany in 1907 for 'treason', to the metamorphic theatricality of inter-species blurrings and couplings in contemporary fiction.[2]

At the heart of this research is a constellation of questions. How might one articulate the nature of an animal's 'performing', and what models of performance would this propose? What is the animal-body/intelligence/eye so beloved of certain performance theorists, practitioners and others (Jerzy Grotowski, Steve Paxton, Wim Vandekeybus, Deleuze and Guattari, Gaston Bachelard, Elias Canetti, John Berger, James Hillman, etc.)? And in what ways are 'animality' – and 'humanity' – being constructed in the animal discourses of, for example, performance, criminality and social conflict?[3]

Here I am indebted to Michel Foucault's post-humanist archaeologies of the 'broken dialogue' (Foucault x) effected through the disciplinary separation of those 'bestial' others deemed criminal, sexually deviant, diseased, insane. His explicit critique of the 'anthropological sleep' in philosophy ('What is man?') ghosts much of what follows, as does Judith Butler's perception of the potentiality of the 'constitutive outside' of the 'human':

> The construction of the human is a differential operation that produces the more and the less 'human', the inhuman, the humanly unthinkable. These excluded sites come to bound the 'human' as its constitutive outside, and to haunt those boundaries as the persistent possibility of their disruption and rearticulation (Butler 8).

Perhaps above all, my concern is with inter-subjectivity as ethical enquiry and tactical praxis. How might one interact with an-other whose difference is re-cognised as an active event, rather than a failure of plenitude? What are the *productive* qualities of alterity? In what ways might one work (in) an existential in-between and perceive other-wise? Bakhtin's notion of 'answerability' and its relational architectonics, and Levinas's articulation of 'responsibility' in the encounter with an-other he calls the 'face-to-face', have been of continuing stimulus in this context.[4] Each of them conceives of identity as act, verb, multiple, becoming. Each conceives of alterity in terms of unrealisable surplus: that which exceeds the cognitive emprise of the selfsame, an outside necessitating an opening towards a performative, dialogical response. And as Michael Gardiner points out, each of them argues that '[E]thics is constitutively linked to corporeality, the direct experience of "lived" time and place, and our effective and meaningful relations with concrete other' (Gardiner 122). Can Bakhtinian and Levinasian models of (human, all too human) inter-subjectivity and sociality be opened up to concrete animal others?

Finally, Deleuze's conception of ethics as a pragmatic and evaluative micro-politics is invaluable in this context. In his cartographies of the assemblages, lines of flight, molecular becomings and black holes of 'man [sic], *deterritorialised animal*' (Deleuze & Parnet 134, italics in original), his recurrent disposition towards immanent vitality – his affirmation of attempts 'to make life something more than personal, to free life from what imprisons it' (Deleuze, *Negotiations*,143) – continues to provoke enquiry into the persistent possibilities of 'Life' as a processual, *event-based* ontology, traversing 'both the livable and the lived' (Deleuze, 'Literature' 1):

> Making an event – however small – is the most delicate thing in the world: the opposite of making a drama or making a

> story. Loving those who are like this: when they enter a room they are not persons, characters or subjects, but an atmospheric variation, a change of hue, an imperceptible molecule, a discrete population [...] Everything has really changed (Deleuze & Parnet 66).

In this context, my concern is with horses. Horse play. Horse flesh. Horse power. Horses for courses.

Animal acts: a flying and falling list

> *List.* n. A border; a boundary (obs.); a destination (Shake.). A catalogue, roll or enumeration. Desire; inclination; choice; heeling over.

Pegasus, the Vedic *gandharvas* and the five kinds of Chinese celestial flying horses. Centaurs, ichthyocentaurs (centaur-fish), hippogriffs and sea-horses. Alexander the Great and Bucephalus, El Cid and Babieca, Napoleon and Marengo, Roy Rogers and Trigger. Mr Ed. The nomadic horseback warriors of Scythians, Mongols, Tartars and Huns. The centrality of horses to the Islamic prophet Mohammed's *Jihad.* The wind-drinkers of the crusades. The fifteen horses Cortés took to the New World in 1519. The Iron Horse. The Suffragette Derby Day suicide. The twenty ponies who accompanied Scott on his ill-fated expedition to the South Pole in 1911. The estimated 375,000 British horses killed in the First World War. Red Rum opening shopping centres. The game of *buzkashi* played by Afghan tribesmen. The padded mounts of picadors in the corrida. The privileged roles ascribed to horses in Siberian, Korean and American Indian shamanism. Ocyrrhoe's becoming-horse in Ovid's *Metamorphoses.* Jonathan Swift's equine Houyhnhnms and human Yahoos in *Gulliver's Travels.* The Italian trainer Grisone, author of one of the sixteenth century's most influential equestrian treatises, *Gli Ordini di Cavalcare,* who recommended persuading a 'nappy' horse to go forward by tying flaming straw, a live cat or a hedgehog beneath the horses's tail. The Horse Latitudes and the *Gulfo de Yeguas* (Gulf of Mares), areas of the Atlantic Ocean so named because of the numbers of horses who died and were thrown overboard during early crossings from Europe to the New World. The apocryphal terror of the Aztecs when one of Pizarro's riders fell from his horse; it is said the Aztecs had believed rider and horse to comprise one indivisible creature. Mr Green's equestrian balloon ascents in nineteenth-century century London, astride his favorite pony. Géricault's death from a horse fall. The flogged horses who (appear to have) triggered psychological crises in Nietzsche and Little Hans. King and Queen, turn of the century diving horses who performed ten-metre head-first drops into a lake at Captain Boynton's Coney Island pleasure grounds. Jerry Brown, Cocaine, Kilroy: three of Hollywood's best-known 'falling horses', all winners of the Craven Award for humanely trained animal stunt performers. The dead white horse suspended from the raised Leningrad bridge, then dropped into the river, in Eisenstein's *October*. The horse who s/tumbles down a flight of stairs in Tarkovsky's *Andrey Rublev*. Maurizio Cattelan's dead chestnut horse spinning slowly above the heads of the gallery-goers, its spine arched unnaturally around the harness support under its midriff – like those horses shipped live from England to the abattoirs of France, for human consumption. The direct descent of all thoroughbreds in the modern world from one of four Arab stallions brought to England in the early part of the eighteenth century: the Darley, Byerley, Godolphin and Helmsley Arabians. The New Zealand stallion Sir Tristram's recent ritual burial, with his tail pointing to the rising sun. The continuing struggle over Phar Lap's remains. The disappearance of Shergar. The White Horse of Uffington. The silver brumby. The equine chronophotography of Etienne-Jules Marey and Edward Muybridge. Byron's *Mazeppa*. *The Misfits*. *A Man Called Horse*. Jean-Louis Barrault's centaur in *Around a Mother*, as described by Artaud. Joseph Beuys's shamanic action with a white horse in *Iphigenia/Titus*. Lucy Gunning's video work *The Horse Impressionists*. Forced Entertainment's panto horse. Monty Roberts, the 'horse whisperer'.

Horses and fertility, divinity, warfare, prestige, commodity, the instinctive, the irrational, an elemental force, the apocalypse, the natural and free. Horses as ideograms of energy, life-fulness, speed, sexual drives, the disorderly, explosive danger-fear-nightmare-madness, abject 'beastly' suffering, kinetic and energetic event.

The gallery as stable: Jannis Kounellis

> The poet, therefore, is truly the thief of fire. He [sic] is responsible for humanity, even for the animals; he will have to have his inventions, smelt, felt, and heard (Rimbaud 103).[5]

In response to an invitation to exhibit at the Galleria L'Attico in Rome in January 1969, the Greek-born artist Jannis Kounellis brought twelve horses, of different breeds and colours, into the gallery and stabled them there, tethered to three of the walls. The work was called *Senza Titolo (12 Cavalli)*. The horses were to be viewed frontally within a formally symmetrical pictorial framework; they remained there for three days. The space of the encounter was carefully controlled as *theatron*: on one side the horses, restrained but not absolutely immobilised; on the other, milling spectators contained within a demarcated area.

Kounellis was allied with a disparate group of artists who called their work 'Arte Povera': poor or impoverished art. The term was coined by the Milanese critic Germano Celant in the late 1960s:

> What has happened is that the commonplace has entered the sphere of art [...] Physical presence and behaviour have become art [...] *Arte Povera* is a refreshing phenomenon that tends towards 'deculturation', towards the regression of the image to the pre-iconographic stage. (Godfrey 178)

For Celant, Kounellis's provocation lay in his recuperation of 'a popular language, that of the senses', and his emphasis on the 'critical presence of materials'.

Kounellis has suggested that his installation endeavoured to redirect the assisted ready-made – animating, theatricalising and poeticising it. Furthermore, it proposed a critique of the commodificatory imperatives of commercial art (the object is unsellable), as well as of the antiseptic neutrality of the white-walled gallery. It aimed to amplify the gallery's diminished sensorium, in particular in terms of the olfactory and auditory. In short, for Kounellis it dramatised the contradictory relations between animate, dis-orderly, corporeal sensibility and the bourgeois, social structure of galleries (Kounellis 668). Shortly before creating this work, Kounellis had articulated, in explicitly theatrical terms, his desire for what he called *'basic authenticity'*:

> By basic authenticity, I mean the continuous 'gesture' which rebels against its pigeon-holing within a 'product', rebellious both as 'material' and as 'expression'. A rebellious, 'material' and 'expressive' gesture which puts the actor – as a permanent disturbance [...] – in contact with the viewer, who is also a permanent disturbance [...] [T]he 'real' and the 'living' as driving elements in performed actions ... must shake off both technicality and convention. (Christov-Bakargiev 248)

Most contemporary responses to the installation propose readings in terms of text and context, and almost all of them are determinedly post-iconographic (*pace* Celant). For the installation seems to have activated a dense field of personal, cultural and poetic intertexts, ghostly equine 'elsewheres' that visit and canter through the herenow

– war, heroic painting and statuary, freedom and the natural, the indomitable patience of herd animals, and, to borrow the ambiguous title of Jérôme Garcin's meditation on horses, *La Chute de cheval* (1998) – the fall from or of the horse, its reduced status in contemporary culture. Here, for example, is Rudi Fuchs:

> Yes, they galloped through history before they arrived in that gallery in Rome, for *us* to see. At each individual moment art is the allegory of its troubled past. [...] No more temple, no more hippodrome, no more battlefield: the gallery as stable. (Fuchs 33)

Invariably, however, the *aesthesic matter* of the horses' 'basic authenticity' as live presences, and the disturbance of *their* conventions (rhythms, habits, environments) generated by them being installed in a gallery for three days, are wholly ignored in favour of *aesthetic* effect and interpretation. The horses are authentically displaced (aesthesically disturbed); and their concrete presence serves to trigger virtual displacements (aesthetic disturbances). Evidently, as signifiers, the horses were construed as 'hot', mobile, auratic, animistic. In themselves, of course, they did not signify any elsewhere; they were simply there, both near and far in the same space, in the process of doing what dis-placed horses do: an aesthesic event, rather than a sign.

In this context, the vectorial desire of signification is pasted on to the other without implicating power in the scene of the other; and the self-referentiality of the gallery context constitutes a kind of closed loop. In the process, of course, all sorts of other signs are glossed over by aestheticist reifying gazes; the animals' dumbness merely reflects the perceiver's deafness. Anyone familiar with horses looking at the published photographs (see for example, Fuchs, Kounellis, Christov-Bakargiev) will immediately recognise the palpable signs of animal 'dis-ease' in the puritan propriety of this interior. Some horses have their ears back; one is pulling against the rope, its head up. Their ropes are tethered at the wrong height for comfortable movement and are too short; over a long period of time without free head movement, the action of a horse's lungs may be constricted. The floor is too slippery for shod hooves, and too hard for long periods of standing immobility. It affords no cushioning, and the impedence of blood flow would eventually lead to swollen legs; for without the movement of grazing, the pump in the hoof – the 'frog' – is not adequately activated. The floor is an inappropriate surface for pissing; horses dislike being splashed. Horses prefer to shit in given areas, contiguous with others in the herd. Enclosed horses prefer to have their backs to a wall, looking out, as in any stable. Their predicament here allows no possibility of rolling, lying down, mutual grooming, and so on. In short, this is a potentially traumatic site for horses; it stinks. Social herd animals alone together, without the possibility of their own forms of interaction. So much for inter-species communication.

I am wary of the little tyrannies within the aesthetic frisson of an urban gallery-goer transported by the smells of horse sweat, shit, piss / by the percussive *musique concrète* of metal shoes on the tiled floor, and the vibratory, tactile sounds of nicker, blow, whinny, neigh / by the unfamiliar intimacy of an exchange of gazes with 'others' looking back from the place of their looked-at-ness / by the surprising transposition of a familiar if distanced everyday to a claustrophobic, enculturated interior. But what happens if you reverse the terms, disturb the viewing positions, make the gallery *un-stable* in search of what Mireille Calle-Gruber perceives in Hélène Cixous's writing: a 'poethics' of the two-way '*passage de l'une l'autre*' (Cixous & Calle-Gruber 10,79)? Rather different smells and sounds – and the unflinching eye contact, from eyes set forward in the skull, close together, stereoscopic, like all predators in nature. Horses are unsettled by being stared at.

Horse sense

> [Man] was bound to fear the eye of the animal as *the carrier of a view of himself over which he had no control* (Berger, 'Animal World' 99: italics in original).

Animals – 'trapped in a place of endless misrecognition', like women,[6] like *Terra Australis*, like all of patriarchal humanism's others – are often defined in terms of lack: of reason, memory, imagination, free will, conscience, language, and so on. Furthermore the mapping of an animal's body, the naming of many of its constituent parts, is effected through an anthropomorphic lens; for example, the 'points' of a horse include forelock, jowls, throat, shoulders, breast, elbows, forearms, knees, heels, belly. The Empire of the Selfsame.

But what can a horse's body *do*? Let's take two examples. Firstly, horses are often homogenised as a species, despite the enormous array of forms and types of *equus caballus*, and the particular qualities of individual horses; and, like ballet dancers, their bodies are often defined in relation to an abstract ideal (conformation). The Akhal-Teke, a golden-sheened desert horse from Turkmenistan highly prized by desert nomads, is all 'wrong' in terms of this ideal; in addition to its notorious disdain for humans, its back is too long, its hind legs marred by sickle hocks and lacking the 'second thigh' so valued by Western riders, its chest too narrow, its rib cage too shallow, its withers too high, its head held impossibly high 'above the bit', that is, above the level of the rider's hands, and therefore uncontrollable. In (classical Western) theory, an Akhal-Teke should be unrideable. Yet as a long-distance endurance horse its resilience remains unparalleled. In 1935, in a journey lasting eighty-four days, Akhal-Tekes were ridden from Ashkhabad to Moscow, a distance of over four thousand kilometres, almost one thousand of which were over desert; they covered four hundred kilometres through the arid Karakoum in just three days. The Olympic gold medal winner for dressage in Rome in 1960, a stallion called Absent, was an Akhal-Teke. At present, there are Akhal-Teke performers in Bartabas's equestrian operas with Théâtre Zingaro (see below).[7]

Secondly, like the early Christian philosophers, Plato, Aristotle, Descartes, Hegel and others constructed hierarchies of the senses, categorised according to degrees of 'humanity' and 'animality'. They tell us nothing about the particularities and differences of animal senses and perception – they homogenise animals, and privilege human vision and its connections with the *cogito* (eye/I) above all else.

A horse's 'surplus of seeing' in Bakhtin's phrase (Holquist 36) is humanly unthinkable. Its eyes are the largest of any land mammal. Set laterally on the head, they have a field of vision of approximately 357 degrees, of which only about 60 degrees frontally are binocular. A horse holding its head level has two narrow blind spots: one directly behind its rump, one a few centimetres directly in front of its nose. In a horse's eyes active receptivity and blindness coexist. The placement of the eyes permits a panoramic view in the horizontal plane of vision; but with only limited accommodation in its lenses (about one fifth of the diopters of human eyes), a horse has restricted focusing ability. Its relatively fixed focal length is set at some distance, where it has a high degree of visual acuity – but without a fovea (enabling the tight, 'grasping' area of focus in human vision), a horse's vision remains planar, largely undifferentiated: that is, peripheral throughout the panoramic vista, *tactile*. Like many mammals horses are dichromates; they have red-blue colour vision, analogous to colour-blindness in humans. Like many mammals, and unlike most humans, however, they have excellent night vision (Budiansky).

The art work as un-stable: Mark Wallinger

> We know what is really out there only from the animal's gaze; for we take the very young child and force it around, so that it sees objects – not the Open, which is so deep in animals' faces. Free from death. (Rilke 193)

In the early 1990s, British artist and horse-racing aficionado Mark Wallinger created a series of painted and constructed pieces inspired by horse-breeding reference books and the history of racing. Then in late 1993, in an action he described as 'a self-inflicted dare' (Bonaventura 46), he purchased a yearling racehorse for 6,600 Irish guineas: Lot 44, a thoroughbred chestnut filly yearling 'by the miler Keen out of an unraced dam Nememsha by Roberto'. Wallinger had never seen the horse before purchase; acting on his behalf at the sale in Ireland was Newmarket trainer Sir Mark Prescott, who had agreed to purchase, then train and campaign a horse through the 1994 flat season. In a gesture self-consciously reminiscent of Marcel Duchamp, Wallinger named the horse A Real Work of Art.

As Mark Bonaventura points out, Wallinger's choice of 'a flesh and blood ready-made, a speedy found object which remained as blissfully unaware of its role as a work of art as it was of its role as a racehorse', was a reaffirmation of an artist's right to name anything as 'art'. Furthermore, '[t]his designation builds upon Duchamp's original gesture by embracing the *unpredictable* not only in the process of selection, delegated to the infinitely more experienced Prescott, but in his inability to influence the filly's latent talents, either as breeder or trainer, or determine the course of her future career '(Bonaventura 46). The horse itself represents not only a displacement of the material art object, but an abdication of volition and artistic/'authorial' control over representation in favour of the unpredictability of her performative becomings as a 'real work of art'. This 'immediate relation with the outside, the exterior' is one of the attributes of what Deleuze has called 'nomad thought' (Deleuze, 'Nomad Thought 144). It encourages an unravelling of the self-contained identity of an art work, a dynamic in-stability akin to what John Cage has called 'silence' – in Nick Kaye's words, 'that which is always in occurrence beyond what would be the pre-determined parameters of the work' (Kaye 3).

To help finance the horse's training and racing costs, Wallinger exhibited a range of materials constituting traces of the absent Real (let's call her 'Real' for short): vet bills, letters from Prescott, race-sheets, hoofprints, and an edition of fifty rather kitsch die-cast metal statuettes, co-funded by his agent and a network of curators/dealers. So, the commercial art world and/as horse-racing: surreptitious deals and alliances, commodificatory tradings in 'horse flesh', competitive play with-in preordained but uncontrollable event-structures, unpredictable intensities and lines of flight. In Deleuze and Guattari's terms, machinic assemblages of desire ...

The right horse: Théâtre Zingaro

> One does not conform to a model, one straddles the right horse (Deleuze & Guattari 286).
>
> The animal eye perceives and reacts to the animal image in the other (Hillman in Moore 68-9)

Over the past fifteen years, Théâtre Zingaro have created six different productions: three versions of *Cabaret Equestre* (1984-90), *Opéra Equestre* (1991-3), *Chimère* (1994-6), and *Éclipse* (1997-99), as well as two films, *Mazeppa* and *Chamane* (Velter, Garcin 99-114). This body of work, characterised by an aesthetic heterogeneity and the centrality of animal-performers, has its roots in new circus, street theatre, the corrida and, above all, Spanish high school dressage forms. However although company director, trainer and performer Bartabas is an *écuyer* of exquisite finesse, his project is minoritarian; he is a foreigner in his own tongue. Here the machinic assemblage[8] of classical dressage stutters (repetition) and stammers (suspension), and produces impossible lines of flight; so, for example, he is only the second known rider this century, after James Fillis, to have realised the ('unnatural') reverse canter. At the same time, each of the productions has been conceived scenographically and musically in terms of a particular horse-/traveller-culture; the company's stylistic trajectory has traced an itinerary of increasing sobriety from *Mitteleuropean* gypsies, to Berber and Caucasian nomads, to Rajasthani itinerant musicians, to Korean shamanism. Above all, Bartabas structures every show – and every day at their communal base in Aubervilliers, north-east of Paris – around the primacy of encounters with horses. As well as being core performers, the horses constitute a kind of *anima(l) mundi*, the cornerstone of a way of life for these contemporary nomads. But in what ways do these animals perform?

Ethologists have written extensively about animal display, their so-called displacement or redirected activities, and ritualized behaviours, in terms of performance. However Richard Schechner suggests that, because most such behaviour is 'hard-wired, genetically determined', animals lack one of the defining qualities of theatre:

> [A] great difference between human and non-human performers is the ability of humans to lie and pretend [...] Although a few species specialize in 'deceit', most animal performances are automatically released, fixed, and stereotyped. There is no irony, no pliable back-and-forth play between the role and the performer, no trilogical interaction linking performer to performer to spectator. (Schechner 225, 248)

In a more comic, anecdotal vein, Laurie Anderson has articulated a similar perception:

> We built a big platform in my loft to do the 'angry dogs' film I needed for a song I was writing [...] Captain Hagerty, their trainer, promised: 'They're vicious! Really vicious!' But he could only get them into attack mode for a few seconds at a time before they began to smile those happy dog smiles they've all got. That's what I love about dogs: they're such lousy actors. (Anderson 73)

If one shifts the model of performance and its interactions, it may be possible to conceive of this lack or inability in rather more affirmative terms. So, for example, the performances of Théâtre Zingaro seem to me to inhabit the space of an unpredictable play between task or 'work-game',[9] horse-performer and human-performer, where performer is conceived in Grotowski's terms as 'an *organism-channel* through which the energies circulate, the energies transform, the subtle is touched [...] Everything is in lightness, in evidence. With Performer, performing can become near process' (Grotowski 375-6). The 'lousiness' of the 'actors' in terms of their inability to sustain fictive bodies, and effect a consciously ironic meta-braiding of a not-self with a not-not-self, makes for a particular quality of attention, conductivity and present-ness in the face-to-face.

Each Zingaro performance is structured around a series of encounters, dialogues, singular interactional events ('*haecceities*'):[10]

> An encounter is perhaps the same thing as becoming, or nuptials [...] an effect, a zigzag, something which passes or happens between two [...] intermezzi, as sources of creation. (Deleuze & Parnet 6, 28)

These encounters, 'doings in the now moment'[11] in which the saying takes precedence over the said, offer the possibility of what Deleuze calls 'becomings-animal':

> In an animal-becoming a man and an animal combine, neither of which resembles the other, neither of which imitates the other, each deterritorialising the other [...] A system of relay and mutations through the middle (Deleuze & Parnet 50)

Each of these encounter-events emerges from Bartabas's training processes, his pragmatic re-cognition of the particularities and differences of individual horses, what is 'quick' in them as opposed to dead: their music, qualities of energy, intensities, sensitivities, dis-abilities; their *affects* and their circulation in relation to an-other.

> Like Deleuze with reference to Spinoza, he asks, 'What can a body do?' You have not defined an animal until you have listed its affects. In this sense there is a greater difference between a race horse and a work horse than between a work horse and an ox (Deleuze & Parnet 60).

So, for example, Bartabas never obtains a particular horse to realise a specific activity (as in equestrian sports: a thoroughbred for speed, an Arab for endurance, a *Selle français* for jumping etc.). He works with horses of many different kinds: Andalusians, Lusitanians, Hackney ponies, Anglo-Arab crosses, Percherons, Friesians, Akhal-Tekes – many of them bought cheaply because they were injured or unable to do what their owners required of them. At present, and for the first time, he is working with nine Portuguese/Lusitanian horses, all of them blue eyed, through herd (choral) interactions in the same space. In general, however, he trains each horse individually over a long period of time through an interactive floor technique sometimes called 'tackless' training, or 'free lungeing': a *listening* 'beyond the ear' (Cixous) rather than a 'whispering'. He shares a space with them, a close-up, haptic, 'smooth' or 'nomad' space, with its imperative for a 'tactile' or 'animal' eye.[12] With them he explores very fine improvised dances of the im/possibility of contact; riding vectors, negotiating thresholds, sometimes dynamically, sometimes with an almost imperceptible slowness. He listens, watches, calls, attends to or provokes an impulse-based dialogue through a step, a shift in the angle of the head or gaze, a tension in the shoulders, a run, a sound.

The aim of these inter-subjective encounters – which are event-based rather than structural, like much contemporary science and like Lyotard's 'dissemiotic' theatre of energetics – is to elicit trust and confidence, and to both encourage and witness the flaring into appearance of each horse's particular differences. The ideal is that self-generating, forward-moving impulsion and centredness that equestrian theorists call 'self-carriage': a practised and decided body rather than a docile body. For behavioural scientists, the horses' actions are simply hard-wired, the causal and instinctive manifestations of dominance/submission, flight/fight, reward-based imprinting. Bartabas, on the other hand, talks of learning through a common 'birthing' (*co-naître*), while in the same breath insisting that 'The more one knows (*connaître*), the less one feels'. These interactions are the means and material function of a choreographic devising process that takes about two years per performance. They represent a kind of tact-ical singularity, a possibility, an exchange. A delirious provocation to qualities of attunement, of answerability, of an 'animal eye'/'I'. A becoming for both parties that is always 'in the middle'.

References

Anderson, Laurie. *Stories from the Nerve Bible: A Retrospective 1972-1992*. New York: HarperCollins, 1994.

Auster, Paul. *Timbuktu*. London: Faber, 1999.

Berger, John. 'Why Look at Animals.' *About Looking*. London: Vintage, 1980. 3-28.

— 'Animal World.' *Second Nature*. Ed. Richard Mabey. London: Jonathan Cape, 1984. 96-100.

— *King: A Street Story*. London: Bloomsbury, 1999.

Bonaventura, Paul. 'Mark Wallinger: A Real Work of Art.' *Locus + 1993-1996*. Newcastle-upon-Tyne: Locus +1996. 44-7.

Boyd, William. *Brazzaville Beach*. London: Penguin, 1991.

Budiansky, Stephen. *The Nature of Horses*. London: Weidenfeld & Nicholson, 1997.

Butler, Judith. *Bodies that Matter*. London & New York: Routledge, 1993.

Christov-Bakargiev, Carolyn, ed. *Arte Povera*. London: Phaidon Press, 1999.

Cixous, Hélène. 'Aller à la mer.' *Modern Drama* 27.4 (December 1986): 546-8.

Cixous, Hélène & Mireille Calle-Gruber. *Rootprints: Memory and Life Writing*. Trans. Eric Prenowitz. London & New York: Routledge, 1997.

Deleuze, Gilles. 'Nomad Thought.' *The New Nietzsche: Contemporary Styles of Interpretation*. Ed. David B.Allison. New York: Delta, 1977. 142-9.

— *Negotiations: 1972-1990*. Trans. Martin Joughin. New York: Columbia UP, 1995.

— 'Literature and Life'. *Essays Critical and Clinical*. Trans. Daniel W. Smith & Michael A. Greco. London: Verso, 1998: 1-6.

Deleuze, Gilles & Félix Guattari. *A Thousand Plateaus*. Trans. Brian Massumi. Minneapolis: U of Minnesota P, 1987.

Deleuze, Gilles & Claire Parnet. *Dialogues*. Trans. Hugh Tomlinson & Barbara Habberjam. London: Athlone Press, 1987.

Edwards, Elwyn Hartley. *The Encyclopedia of the Horse.* London: Dorling Kindersley, 1994.

Foucault, Michel. *Madness and Civilization: A History of Insanity in the Age of Reason.* Trans. Richard Howard. London: Tavistock, 1969.

Fuchs, R.H., ed. *Jannis Kounellis* (catalogue). Amsterdam: The Van Abbemuseum, 1981.

Garcin, Jérôme. *La Chute de cheval.* Paris: Gallimard, 1998.

Gardiner, Michael. 'Alterity and Ethics: A Dialogical Perspective'. *Theory, Culture and Society* 13.2 (1996): 121-43.

Godfrey, Tony. *Conceptual Art.* London: Phaidon, 1998.

Griffin, Susan. 'The Show Horse'. *Made from This Earth.* London: Women's Press, 1982. 88-93.

Grotowski, Jerzy (1990). 'Performer'. *The Grotowski Sourcebook.* Ed. Richard Schechner & Lisa Wolford. London & New York: Routledge, 1997. 374-78.

Hillman, James. 'Bachelard's Lautréamont, or Psychoanalysis without a Patient.' *Lautréamont by Gaston Bachelard.* Trans. Robert S. Dupree. Dallas: Pegasus Foundation, 1986. 103-23.

— *Dream Animals.* San Francisco: Chronicle, 1997.

Hoeg, Peter. *The Woman and the Ape.* London: Harvill Press, 1996.

Holquist, Michael. *Dialogism: Bakhtin and his World.* London & New York: Routledge, 1990.

Kaye, Nick. *Art into Theatre: Performance Interviews and Documents.* Amsterdam: Harwood Academic/OPA, 1996.

Kounellis, Jannis. 'Structure and Sensibility: Interview with Willoughby Clark.' *Theories and Documents of Contemporary Art: A Sourcebook of Artists' Writings.* Ed. Kristine Stiles & Peter Selz. Berkeley: U of California P, 1996. 666-71.

Levinas, Emmanuel. *Ethics and Infinity.* Trans. Richard A. Cohen. Pittsburgh: Duquesne UP, 1985.

— 'Philosophy and the Idea of Infinity.' *Collected Philosophical Papers.* Ed & trans. Alphonso Lingis. The Hague: Martinus Nijhoff, 1987. 47-60.

Lyotard, Jean-François. 'The Tooth, the Palm'. Trans. Anne Knap & Michel Benamou. *Sub-Stance* 15 (1976): 105-110.

Moore, Thomas, ed. *A Blue Fire: The Essential James Hillman.* London: Routledge, 1990.

Rilke, Rainer Maria. *The Selected Poetry of Rainer Maria Rilke.* Ed. & trans. Stephen Mitchell. London: Picador, 1987.

Rimbaud, Arthur. *Complete Works.* Translated by Paul Schmidt, London: Picador, 1988.

Self, Will. *Great Apes.* London: Penguin, 1997.

Schechner, Richard. *Performance Theory.* London & New York: Routledge, 1988.

Schutzman, Mady. 'A Fool's Discourse: The Buffoonery Syndrome.' *The Ends of Performance.* Ed. Peggy Phelan & Jill Lane. New York: New York UP, 1998. 131-48.

Silver, Caroline. *Guide to the Horses of the World.* London: Elsevier Phaidon, 1984.

Velter, André. *Zingaro, suite équestre.* Paris: Gallimard, 1998.

Williams, David. 'Working (in) the In-between: Contact Improvisation as an Ethical Practice.' *Writings on Dance* 15 (Winter 1996): 14-37.

Zarrilli, Phillip B. 'What Does it Mean to Become the Character: Power, Presence, and Transcendence in Asian In-body Disciplines of Practice.' *By Means of Performance: Intercultural Studies of Theatre and Ritual.* Ed. Richard Schechner & Will Appel. Cambridge: Cambridge UP, 1990. 131-48.

Notes

1 An earlier version of this paper was given in April 1999 at the Performance Studies International Conference 'Here be Dragons' in Aberystwyth, Wales. With sincere thanks to Manolo Mendes, Bartabas, Barry Laing, Sarah Gray, Mark Minchinton and, above all, Rachel Ireland. This paper is dedicated to these animal others, to BJ, and to the memory of Zingaro; *Non olvidaré la luz de los caballos* (Pablo Neruda).

2 See, for example, three recent 'becoming-ape' novels: Boyd, Hoeg and Self, or two recent 'becoming-dog' novels: Berger and Auster.

3 The number of animal appellations in para/military contexts (relating to strategies, weaponry, individual combative 'styles', propagandist bestialisations etc.) is remarkable. In recent times, for example, 'Operation Desert Fox' was an attempt to 'shut Saddam Hussein back in his cage', according to British Prime Minister Tony Blair. The Milosevic regime's genocidal 'cleansing' of Kosovo was codenamed 'Operation Horseshoe'; one of its most infamous agents was the Serb police chief at the Smrekovnica jail, Vukcina (Wolfman). One of Britain's most shadowy white supremacist groups calls itself the White Wolves, in hommage to a Nazi SS group.

4 For extended discussions of the 'face-to-face' and 'answerability', see for example. Levinas (*Ethics and Infinity,* 'Philosophy') and Holquist. For a discussion of the relations between the face-to-face and contact improvisation, see Williams.

5 Arthur Rimbaud, from a letter to Paul Demeny, 15 May 1871 (author's translation).

6 'Women and animals are represented as cohabitants of similar symbolic space – a kind of amorous disciplinary laboratory in obedience, tricks, and often bizarre balancing acts. [...] Women and animals are seemingly trapped in a place of endless misrecognition where they cannot gain access to symbolic space or to a re-cognition that proffers verification in a discourse of power' (Schutzman 136). For a comparison of the disciplinary regimes of equestrianism and patriarchy, see Griffin.

7 For further details of Akhal-Tekes, see Edwards (74-5) and Silver (178-80).

8 '"Machine, machinism, machinic": this does not mean either mechanical or organic. Mechanics is a system of closer and closer connections between dependent terms. The machine by contrast is a 'proximity' grouping between independent and heterogeneous terms (topological proximity is itself independent of distance or contiguity). What defines a machine assemblage *is the shift of a centre of gravity along an abstract line*' (Deleuze & Parnet 104, my italics).

9 Veterinarian and horse authority Andrew Fraser has suggested that equestrian sport may activate a 'residual inclination toward play' in some adult horses, for it may offer 'analogs' to natural play. He suggests the enthusiasm horses display for such activities might be better understood if one conceived of the activities 'more as "work-games" from the horse's point of view'. (Qtd. in Budiansky 101). Whether this is an anthropomorphic projection or not, some

horses' pleasure in such contexts is undeniably manifest; and the notion of 'work-game' is reminiscent of task-oriented performance practices, or Steve Paxton's conception of contact improvisation as an 'art-sport'.

10 Deleuze and Guattari describe 'haecceity' as 'a mode of individuation' consisting 'entirely of relations of movement and rest between molecules or particles, capacities to affect and be affected [...] the entire assemblage in its individuated aggregate that is a haecceity [...] It is the wolf itself, and the horse, and the child, that cease to be subjects to become events, in assemblages that are inseparable from an hour, a season, an atmosphere, an air, a life. [...] A haecceity has neither beginning nor end, origin nor destination; it is always in the middle. It is not made of points, only of lines. It is a rhizome' (261-3).

11 This phrase is used by Phillip B. Zarrilli to describe the goal of Asian performer training regimes in which performance techniques are 'encoded within the body': 'the state of accomplishment (Sanskrit, *siddhi*) in which the doer and the done are one [...] a state of stillness in motion [which] frees the martial or performing artist from 'consciousness about', preparing him for a state of 'concentratedness' [...] doings in the now moment' (Zarrilli 131,134). Such bodily enculturation and its holistic accomplishment is wholly pertinent to, for example, both horses and riders in classical equitation/high shool dressage.

12 'The first aspect of the haptic smooth space of close vision is that its orientations, landmarks, and linkages are in continuous variation; it operates step by step. [...] The eye that beholds them [has] a function that is haptic rather than optical. This is an animality that can be seen only by touching it with one's mind, but without the mind becoming a finger, not even by way of the eye' (Deleuze & Guattari 493 -4).

4. Fleshed, muscular phenomenologies: across sexed and queer circus bodies

Peta Tait

Theoretical warm-up

Club Swing performed three short daylight shows in Melbourne for casual bystanders in January 1998.[1] They rigged trapezes, a small chrome ring, and tissu (hanging lycra cloth) apparatus off the exterior of the Victorian Arts Centre, from about three storeys in height. In the first show the performers wore short, tight-fitting, zipped-up uniforms, a retro-1960s space-age look, with short fake blue and pink wigs. Robyn Laurie, a director of new circus and adviser on these shows, recounted overhearing a male bystander identify Club Swing's Anni Davey, wearing all-pink, as a woman. After Davey, standing on the ground, lifted Celia White into the air, Laurie heard the bystander comment: 'No, it's a man in drag'. A response in words can be expected from a spectator – audiences talk freely during traditional circus. Clearly this comment presumed that male bodies are strong, capable of lifting and holding the weight of another body easily. Muscular actions of strength, traditionally associated with maleness, outweighed the visible significances of the body surface signing femaleness aligned with femininity.

The musculature of this performer was viewed within a prescriptive social language of sexed body identity (Grosz). While the sexing of body surfaces might be predicted with public viewings, technical knowledge about the muscularity of the upper-body shape of female aerialists cannot be expected. Instead the performance text of a strong muscular body in action read as a parody of femininity, a signified excess. Importantly, in this type of performance it is a performer's body doing muscular action that underscores the impression of costumed drag. Since the muscular action is conventionally delineated as male, the female body has become invisible (inert) in the act. Surely this heightened display of muscularity could also suggest a parody of masculinity, alternatively, muscular drag. In this instance, however, redesignation of the female body in reception as male denies both female muscularity in action and ambiguous sexing. It denies the queering of a specific performer's body in its reception. While this example confirms a regressive viewing of bodies, one blind to the strength and muscularity of female circus bodies, it also reverses and/or doubly sexes the performing body according to its inaction or action.

I am considering how bodies in the forms of traditional circus and its recent derivatives of new circus and physical theatre perform across multiple bodily spaces. In these forms, performing bodies usually without speech do extended muscular actions and extraordinary tricks that produce meaningful cultural spaces which are socially symbolic as well as phantasmically evocative. They produce muscular spatialities. A discussion about spectators and performing bodies in circus underscores our fascination with looking at bodily difference by observing musculature and, in this instance, its fast motion. This entails viewing performance spectacles where the excessive 'action' of bodies, muscularity in action, thrills and amazes because it exceeds expectations of a body's capacity for movement.

This chapter asks whether viewed muscular bodies doing physical actions might potentially reinforce as well as resist their bodily reception as socially symbolic. It stretches out speculatively, theoretically, from outdoor shows by the Australian all-female aerial groups, Club Swing and Airated, to consider how sexed identity arises with but overlays muscular appearances. While accepting that (in)substantial energies also co-exist with observed spatialities, desire and desiring are not specifically discussed here. An example of muscular drag in performance expands but challenges a theoretical presumption that the material properties of bodies might be socially received as ambiguously sexed. (I am following up the possibility of viewing resistances that contradict my desired readings of performing bodies in physical theatre.) Ambiguous identity in action, a strongly muscular female body (a graceful male body), may or may not impact on its social identification in reception. Instead, the theoretical re-viewing in this chapter recognises a potential for a reversing or double-sexing of musculature. In the spaces between and of bodies, a performing muscular body might be recognised as female only to have this identification reversed to that of male, overriding a theoretical expectation of a queer zone; the space between sexes exists only as a momentary hesitation. If muscular circus bodies need to be explicitly known, that is, socially labelled, conversely, does thinking and imagining changes to social ideas of bodies and their hierarchical positioning also require ongoing interventions with their physicality, the patterning of muscular action?

Since the delineation of Foucault's docile bodies, the symbolic body delineated with words has produced discursive sites for repeated tracings and imaginings that ironically seem to circumvent engagements through and between fleshed physicalities. Theory desires imagined bodies – unified or fragmented, dispersed across surfaces – to be mediated with words, and assumes that socially progressive changes in materialities can be effected with thoughtful words and arguments; thus, languages are interchangeable. Yet even ideas of a self that is 'becoming' or unfolding implies flesh in motion. Somatic knowledges such as those accumulated in actor training, rehearsal techniques and in theatre's reception are barely mentioned: theatre's mimetic 'action' is narrativised rather than perceived as physicalised. In actuality theatrical and circus bodies – like bodies on the sports field – would seem to be popular attractions because of the immediacy of speechless exchanges between bodies even where they continue after the event framed as worded entities. As this chapter illustrates, such live body action spectacles are designed for and become conceptualised in commentaries from viewing positions that usually follow the action, if only by split-seconds.

Three types of nonverbal visual language are presented in circus at one time: technical, a trained body doing skilful actions; theatrical, aesthetic codes of and surrounding bodies created with lighting, costuming, sound and stylised movement forms such as balletic poses; and cultural, the configurations of visual nomenclatures signing social identity whether fabricated or not, that is, gender, race and sexuality – sexuality by the interactions between socially defined bodies. Even if spectators cannot interpret the specific technical languages or theatrical ones, performing bodies are recognisable as social ideas within broad categories of gender and race. Nevertheless, in the absence of words about the action (the rules of the game), I suggest that spectators often find it more difficult to interpret physical theatre bodies in action for complex or unpredictable meanings than they might find it to absorb (read) words in a (spoken) text or even (repeatable) images.

I propose that we see/observe performing bodies as visible and invisible bodily. Moving eyes see moving bodies bodily. I wonder though if it is habitual physical patterns that interpret (other) bodies as social entities in conjunction with conscious and unconscious responses. Here, I am considering how to think about social acts of viewing bodily. These suggest possibilities for politically re-reading body-specific phenomenology while rejecting originating presence, in order to frame politics of phenomenologies across unstable spaces and misfitting bodies.

In theorising about the cultural and physical appeal of a body in action, it is necessary to acknowledge that kinaesthetic maps exist in relation to shared and phenomenological spaces in sensory kinetic fields. I contend that theorising the reception of bodies doing tricks in circus and physical theatre texts prefigures ideas of lived bodies as live entities in a phenomenal field. Circus performance engages with bodily knowledges over other languages, although cultural theory seems largely to avoid discussing how knowledges are expounded (or deleted) bodily. The application of Maurice Merleau-Ponty's ideas of the phenomenologies of a body-subject – either focused on outwardly observing or inwardly thinking in words, since he implies that one precludes the other – to the reception of circus is not to imply a pre-existing natural or essentialist body or a unified subject position in the world.[2] Instead, his ideas, invigorated with the bodily languages produced by circus, can be used to evoke multiple skilled, theatrical and social bodies in continuous positioning and re-positioning that vanishes neutrality and unity. While admitting that sight dominates circus reception and acknowledging feminist philosophical objections, intercoporeality arises within sensory spaces created by culturally material bodies, inclusive of hugely variable physicalities and their differences. In theorising that the surface phenomenologies produced by performance contribute to a social ordering of bodies, the risk is that destabilised binary categories are not received as such – as performative theory proposes for the phantasmic perception of bodies – but viewed as material entities binary categories are re-imposed. Muscular materialities are stabilised as meaningful in reception according to habitual patterning. Therefore changes to ideas of bodies cannot be simply rethought, they must be also physically re-staged in full view. Political interventions that expand cultural ideas of bodies need to impinge (as they do already) on the habitual patterns of bodies, in their flesh-to-flesh engagements with muscular action.

A live performing body's subjective experience of doing physical action in circus should be distinguished from a spectator's perception of the colliding surfaces of a performing body as an object/text.[3] A performer's subjective experience of his or her body is often one of working with muscular pain,[4] but this is imperceptible in a surface text of carefree ease, daring action and joyful exuberance, of pleasure. (Circus acts are repeatedly rehearsed and deliver a different type of theatrical text due to this extreme physical repetition.) Viewing perceptions bounce back off these textual surfaces, scattering into spectatorial bodily sensations and visceral imaginings. The covert danger that thrills spectators is the risk of a circus body suddenly visibly mangled or even dead. Ironically, the aerialist knows that in the muscular effort of doing the act, he or she risks the loss or failure of bodily motion. Circus bodies perform an illusionary ease of musculature as part of their fleshed identity.

Speechless bodies cite identity

The word and image might be axiomatic (Phelan 2), but it cannot be assumed that bodies doing athletic and acrobatic actions is axiomatic to speaking and thinking, beyond perhaps crudely allocating social identity. This is particularly evident with performances of extreme exertion. It is my experience that spectators at circus can be 'lost for words' after the event while professing their enjoyment.[5] If words help costume muscular bodies for social recognition, regardless of whether this identity originates in a performed or spectatorial body-text, the absence of words can present gaps in visual language that are redressed as much by habitual convention as imagined invention (Tait, 'Wrestling').

In physical theatre, performers with specialist body skills enact bodily movements which spectators probably cannot do. A specialist viewer, however, whose body can replicate comparable movement can dissect an action-specific body-text more easily and translate it into words. By inference, the viewing of performing bodies for their reviewing in words, might become suspended for some non-specialist viewers. This difference raises a more fundamental question about the theatrical reception of bodies. In what ways does bodily awareness, the accumulated movement of physical bodies with their kinaesthetic and phenomenological knowledges, contribute to theatrical spectatorship? If body-texts are received bodily – underpinning aesthetically – is this awareness habitually reinforced to be conventionally sexed in ways that inhibit rather than expand definitions of cultural identity despite changes in social thinking?

The spectator's identification in the example of muscular drag would seem to be a response determined by beliefs about habitual patterns irrespective of other possible interpretations of performance fictions. In another example given by Alisa Solomon of a female bodybuilding show, Solomon, although she is making a different argument, recounts seeing a male audience member pre-empt a female bodybuilder's entrance during a rescue scenario by rushing up to the stage to rescue a second woman calling for help (15-16). Under such circumstances women would be expected to show biceps, to act masculine, to do heroic actions, but the man's habitual physical response would seem to have been overpowering despite the context. Ideally, in a phenomenal field, the social identities of bodies constituted through visible languages might be constituted as more fluid; particularly where they are speechless, without labels. Therefore to produce a gender politic of phenomenology would require, in many instances, challenging habitual seeings that establish the social order through engaging bodily perceptions of action – muscular and physical motion – in the phenomenal field.

Stanton B. Garner writes that 'theatrical watching' is about 'the spatial conjunction of bodies, objects and other performance elements that constitute at once the object of such watching' (1). Is a performer's body observed differently, however, if it is acrobatic and/or extremely mobile rather than moving in a life-like way? The spectator cannot avoid watching the action of a performing body. In circus and physical theatre, performing bodies are objects in motion that frame the larger text as an object, its boundaries defined by the outer parameters of their motion. Furthermore, acrobatic bodies present fast extraordinary actions so that the visual field changes rapidly. This physicality requires focused viewing, a sensory absorption with the action.

This argument suggests that speaking bodies without extreme movement in performance are also seen in part with words (the pre-determined expressions of familiar scripts), and overt social languages have the capacity to disrupt pre-existing beliefs, at least as far as social identity can be spoken. If performing bodies habitually exist within a field of words, then the cultural meanings of wordless muscular body surfaces are opaque rather than transparent and must be independently explicated for their cultural significances. This might also apply to social bodies. Certainly circus and physical theatre offer a useful sphere of cultural representation with which to explore the heightened languages of muscular bodies in action.

Feminist and postmodern criticisms of Merleau-Ponty's framing of a (male) totalising, universalising I-subject-body with an all-encompassing subjectivity are valid, especially since his subject-body perceives its external visual world with an unquestioning spatial dominance of it (Grosz 105). Nevertheless Merleau-Ponty's ideas about knowledges accruing from a lived subject-body, a responsive mind-body, in a phenomenal field offer a useful theoretical springboard (a theoretical equivalent to an acrobat's teeter board) for recalling viewed bodies in circus and physical theatre. Firstly, Merleau-Ponty's proposition that a subject-body observing the phenomenal field will be momentarily disengaged from thinking (theorising) seems pertinent to an experience of viewing circus bodies. It undermines assumptions that bodies are viewed indistinguishably, inseparably and interchangeably as social ideas, as aesthetic objects and as physically skilful (within technical languages). Secondly, Merleau-Ponty argues that there is an openness of movement from a sensible phenomenological body towards what is not in ourselves; a reversibility in seen visibility. There is an openness and orientation to the action of other bodies. While accepting the argument that the physiology of seeing is culturally but unconsciously structured (Krauss), I believe that there are resistances in the seeing of fast and strong muscular action – in its reversibilities – that reside throughout the muscular body as well as in the psyche, itself potentially dispersed in muscularities. This has significance for how gendered and social bodies perceive other bodies as phenomenon within categories of sameness and difference. Reception theory explores how what is seen in comparatively slow-moving bodies in performance reflects the ideological positioning of the viewing subject, and delineates the objectification of performers as and within social ideas (Dolan, Bennett). Such social seeings must also be located in a body-subject's sensory responses that habitually internalise and remap its kinetic field. Nonetheless it cannot be assumed that unspoken bodily responses will compliantly and subordinately follow on from thinking and speaking about the hierarchical ordering of bodies, white and black, male and female. Habitual patterning would seem to need repeated contestation in the viewing of muscular actions.

In considering dramatic representations of embodiment, Garner noted the repudiation and dismissal of phenomenology by poststructuralism (22). As he points out, the criticism relates to phenomenological origins in (Husserlian) transcendental subjectivity rather than the recent unfolding of phenomenological thinking about embodiment in the writings of, for example, Lyotard and Butler (*Bodies* 22-3). Garner discerns an 'antitheatricality that runs through much poststructuralist criticism, an attitude symptomatic (like all antitheatricality) of a deeper uneasiness with the body – in this case, with the body as a site of corporeal and subjective elements that always resist reduction to the merely textual' (26). What is resistant to reduction if it is not the body in action, its unfolding live fleshed physicality? (Is it acceptable to allocate this to the unknowable Real?). Garner analyses symbolic bodies in the written play and avoids the vexed issue of how the subjectivities of speaking bodies produce or at least override visible material surfaces in theatre, or challenge their orthodoxies.

Judith Butler (*Gender Trouble*) argues that, socially, bodies in performative acts produce seamless citations of gender identity. A performative social identity is constituted in an embodied doing. While conventional theatre presents spoken and visual citations of identity, nonverbal circus bodies deliver identity as they move so that textual ambiguities are also visible actions. The example of how a performance of muscular drag was negated in a category reversal in reception confirms the theoretical presumption that speechless bodily identity is habitually viewed as a citation, although this is not necessarily seamless. It suggests, however, that citations of identity arise from responsive habitual physicalities that potentially counteract other knowledges.

The embodiment of familiar social identities is implicit in conventional theatrical performance. For example, the visual coding of a female body remains unquestioned unless the female performer performs otherwise with her speech and/or costume and/or gesture. In physical theatre and circus, however, the muscular female body might sign towards femininity in a costume and balletic movement, while performing physical actions delineated as masculine. In traditional circus, gender difference is reinstated at the end of the act through gesture and stance. In some postmodern physical theatre, however, bodies are staged to be transgressively defiant of such binaries.[6] Where spectators respond from bodily knowledges and phenomenologies in entrenched patterns, these would need to be engaged in provocative ways in order to refocus habitual patterning and facilitate changed viewing.

Lived spectatorial bodies

Melbourne's Victorian Arts Centre's street forecourt, where Club Swing performed, and the glass-roofed atrium at the adjunct Southgate complex during successive Melbourne International Festivals facilitate a random gathering of audiences. Despite a long history of Australian circus as popular entertainment and twenty years of women's circus in Melbourne, these gravity-defying outdoor circus acts still seem extraordinary viewed from the ground by standing bodies. Does this physical positioning also invite a watching spectator to respond bodily according to pre-existent phenomenological engagements?

Anna Shelper's exciting and complex solo trapeze routine in Airated's 1997 *O My Gorgeous* was set high in the glass-roofed atrium at Southgate – Club Swing's Kathryn Niesche had previously performed up there on a cloud swing (rope swing). Shelper's extremely fast, dynamic motion included a fall from a standing position on the swinging trapeze bar to hang upside down by her ankles.[7] The glass roof high above meant that, in daylight, Shelper seemed a distant blue-green figure; at night under lighting she became incandescent. This was an exceptionally good demonstration of aerial skills. Allocating a social identity to the distant body during the act, however, was virtually impossible. At the end the performer descended closer to the viewers on her safety line. Although lessening the perception of risk – there is a greater perception of risk where the safety line remains invisible – it allowed social identification of the performer.

Michael Balint argues that the viewers' thrills increase with the performers distance from them (25), while fixing the safety zone of the ground as belonging to the feminine partner of a daring masculine aerialist (47). Perhaps this gendered demarcation corresponds with Balint's phenomenological body reception as much as his thinking, but it seems at odds with observations of circus. The cultural idea of a circus in the scholar's imaginary contains the danger of making the specificities of performing bodies invisible and inactive (Tait 'Circus Bodies'). In Balint's framework the metaphoric thrills of viewing acrobats and aerialists to explain the psyche and its regressions excludes observed bodies in action, the muscular visibilities of female aerialists. Yet it is apparent that within cultural binaries a muscular body in action is masculinised but, contradictorily, an aerial body is also symbolically feminised producing oscillations across socially symbolic spaces.

Identification with the performing body in action in a visible phenomenal field of reversibility implicates phenomenologies that are inclusive of kinaesthetic body-schema of motion and imaginative imagery. While this opens up the possibility of an ongoing reversibility, logically it must be asked if same-sex identification or other dominant patternings in relation to bodily difference predominate within this process of reversibility. How does variability across bodies function within bodily knowledge to expand binaries of identification?

Merleau-Ponty claims it is not simply that perception is subjective or corporeal (*Visible* 7). He writes that 'it emerges in the recess of a body' (9); 'perception, which perhaps is not 'in my head,' is nowhere else than in my body as a thing of the world' (10). In claiming that the knowing of what we see seems to be unattainable because of the continual 'forgetfulness' about phenomena (*Phenomenology* 58), Merleau-Ponty explains that while a body is not an object it is regarded as an object so that its experience becomes an idea and acquires an artificial sameness (*Phenomenology* 71). The lived body moves with what Merleau-Ponty calls its postural or corporeal schema, its 'body-schema' of accumulated sensory experiences, a schema of and in motion and in movement, rather than posture or pose. Its 'I can' is derived from the spatiality of a moving body as distinct from a static composition, an inertness, and it exists in movement that is continual and to a large extent happens without conscious execution, that is without focused thinking. Body-schema and body images are 'tactile, kinaesthetic and articular' (*Phenomenology* 99) and 'dynamic' (100). A 'corporeal schema' based on habits (142) which are culturally caught creates 'motility' but also requires 'intentionality' (137) and these habits are derived from the 'motor and perceptual' (152). A body is of the space not only in it (148), and produces the space. It must be pointed out that this mobility sets up more than one entity.

Merleau-Ponty claims that observing and perceiving what is being looked at requires deliberate focus and this must be constantly renewed, while consciousness in intellectual thinking requires withdrawal from the visual field (*Phenomenology* 240-1). When Rosalind Krauss contests the modernist vision of a fast ball in motion as pure instantaneity and presentness, she is challenging its denial of seeing without thought and language (7), and the corollary in its rejection of visuality as arising in the intellect (111). She argues that images are received culturally, inclusive of physiology (123), and structured in the unconscious without separations. But automatic bodily responses to the action of phenomena may diverge from focused deliberate thinking and unconscious responses. Since a body is not a ball, the seeing of a circus body in fast motion (an aerialist, ideally a flier) might be supposed to connect more immediately with seeing bodies even while they are thinking. Seeing and thinking are culturally determined but may remain distinguishable from bodily observing, especially if this is dispersed throughout the body. What if a bodily observing is implicated in pre-existing beliefs and languages?[8] In addition to Krauss' understandings, it might be argued that seeing/observing is from within and across symbolic languages and the habitual physical patterns of phenomenological bodies.

If, as Merleau-Ponty argues, it is moved action that allows bodies to become intelligible to themselves (*Phenomenology* 102), he implicates the sensory reception of other bodies, a sharing of relational spatialities applicable to viewing moving bodies including those in performance. In an application of his framework to the reception of physical theatre, active performing bodies engage watching spectators whose muscles are not in movement but whose body-schemata retain motion. This is not to claim a pre-existing 'I' subject but one located within constantly active phenomenal bodies traversing languages.[9] (Merleau-Ponty's approach contrasts with the idea of phenomenology as transcendental perception that reveals itself in expressions of consciousness rather than living.) Although he frames his ideas from the position of a singular subject-body, when Merleau-Ponty writes of 'intercorporeity', this can be expanded beyond a single entity consciousness unifying the multiple sensory states, to denote clusters of consciousnesses across bodies (*Visible* 141). This is an unfolding multitude of sensory spaces across and around bodies.

Therefore, if perception of the dynamism of a physical body is dependent on body-schemata and, as they come into sensory existence, these exist and produce cultural languages, then phenomenological perception is both socially defined and viscerally thought and unthinkingly visceral. Viscerality functions in the reversibility of the social identity of the body-subject. A visceral body in/of the phenomenal field is constantly active and unpredictable, unstable and indeterminable. Merleau-Ponty proposes ideas of motility with a consciousness that is dispersed in a body of vision so that it is erratic, peripheral, watching and observing but not always reflecting on that observing. If this locates self-knowing in a Deleuzian nomadism of selfness engaged in surface flows, it also prefigures not so much disruptions as hesitations (a pause to focus before a leap) in its continuing motion.

For a spectator whose stomach jumps in an involuntary physiological response to an aerialist leaping away from a swinging trapeze towards a hanging rope, there is an almost imperceptible delay in the conscious after-thought that the leap must be part of the act. According to the argument here, physiological and sensory responses take place because a spectator is phenomenologically receptive to languages of motion and movement in the reversibility of his or her visible field as well as unconscious and conscious perceptions and knowledges, the latter slightly delayed.

To summarise Merleau-Ponty's proposition: the 'I' (eye) consciousness within a body is not immersed in thought and observing the phenomenal world simultaneously, but oscillating in awarenesses circulating in and around bodies. If my lived body is focused on observing the circus body in a phenomenal field then I am not simultaneously intellectually theorising. Observing may be automatic or focused, but in Merleau-Ponty's analysis it would seem that thinking requires focus and is linked more to words than images. While images facilitate both conscious and unconscious imaginings, sensory kinaesthetic bodily knowledges are not contained by images; expanding from dispersed trajectories they foreshadow alternative spaces for cultural knowledges.

I would argue that cognitive understandings of bodies in action in physical theatre can be learned like grammatical languages – it seems that perceiving a body doing actions might become momentarily separated from reception of its social meaning. This gap provides an opening for rethinking. If, as Merleau-Ponty argues, thinking in relation to words and bodily observing the phenomenal field are distinguishable, then phenomenologically perceiving a physical body in action might bring about oscillations within recognition of its social identity. Therefore, it might be argued that a spectator seeing the social identity of a (performing) body in pre-determined ways might not simultaneously observe its physical action but resist or override this with ways of habitually observing. Where spectatorial reception is especially attuned to socially defined bodies, that is, bodies as ideas, there might be selective forgetfulness of responses to muscular physicalities and actions or vice versa. Given languages' (disfiguring) absences and losses, viewing acrobatic movement might well elude the process of conscious thinking and yet still intervene across body phenomenologies. The difficulty remains one of cohering thinking and muscularity.

Significantly, Merleau-Ponty claims that there is flesh between the seer and the thing, that is, the visible world is flesh (although he does not refer to matter here) as it is bodily received. He suggests that 'the gaze itself envelops them, clothes them with its own flesh' (*Visible* 131). Merleau-Ponty writes of the 'bond between the flesh and the idea' (149). But 'the reversibility of the visible and the tangible' (142-3) also brings about a 'sublimation of the flesh' (145); of female flesh in particular (Irigaray qtd in Grosz 105-6).

Circus bodies in action are fleshed in their reception. Club Swing performers were costumed in underwear in their second show, maximising exposure of skin; these performers sometimes wear body paint in dance part acts rather than costumes (see the cover of *Body Show/s*). Perhaps such a perception cannot be replicated theoretically when, as Merleau-Ponty argues, thought and its ordering in social languages deny phenomenological bodies, their flesh and circularities, and dispersal in body spaces. At least in the domain of cultural representation, traces of bodies in circus and physical theatre seem to prefigure the tangled continuities of visible, sensible and lived processes. Acrobatic and athletic bodies heighten and reflect back ideas of the liveness of bodies. They appear as metonymic exaggerations of Merleau-Ponty's dynamism of 'flesh in the world'; bodies capable of doubling back over fleshed patterning.

Performing deadness with liveness

If aerial acts seem to confirm what Alphonso Lingis argues are the outer limits of a body in an exposure to death (89), triumphant acts by aerial bodies also signify liveness with risk taking. In Club Swing's third short show based on a Sleaze Ball act (see Chapter 14 'Animated Suspension'), Simone O'Brien and Kareena Oates were costumed as vampires on a trapeze above Niesche and White as an acrobatic duo working from inside a slightly raised coffin while Davey stood behind, cross-dressed in suit-tails as a Dracula imposter. This show parodied the feared spectre of the body that defeats death by sucking the life-blood out of other bodies, with a form that performs a heightened text of liveness. The coffin, symbolic of deadness, served to exaggerate the liveness of aerial and acrobatic bodies. When the two performing bodies in the coffin moved they were seen, and when they stopped moving they become invisible, lying in the coffin in textual deadness before rising up again. Clearly this show also parodies spectatorial thrills of viewing a performing body risking death. At the same time it parodies the cultural idea of circus where the aerialist's sublime action contrasts to the comic grotesque clown moving on the ground.[10] In flaunting cultural fears, Club Swing's act also prefigured a different idea of grotesqueness as deadness arising from the inertness of a live body because it cannot be observed. Thus, grotesqueness equates here with the loss or absence of motion, of liveness, in phantasmic (imagined) spaces.

Circus bodies have become synonymous with Bakhtin's ideal of classical spectacle as well as the comic grotesque of carnivalesque. Yet circus as a cultural idea is also claimed to evoke anxieties of a fearful repressed grotesque, which Mary Russo explains is personified as female, ultimately conflated with the fear of death. She notes that the classical sublime manifests most explicitly as an 'aerial sublime' (11) but she discerns in this a latent grotesqueness, akin to Freud's ideas of the uncanny. Russo discusses how such cultural manifestations evoke the interiorised grotesque, subjectivity's feared and repressed (phantasmatic) other, while the freedom and liminal possibilities of aerial acts also suggest the pre-symbolic (Mulvey qtd. in Russo 36-7). Does this phantasmatic grotesque or sublime arise from seeing/observing aerialists in action or does it come from an imagined seeing of them in motion? Certainly, the trick effects of observing/seeing trigger symbolic associations as aerial bodies repeatedly evoke comparisons with both birds and angels, the spaces of seen and imagined flight.[11] Traditional circus, however, can be observed to materially enact and restage the cultural separation of grotesque from sublime through the visible actions of muscular bodies in performance. Leaving aside animal bodies – the cultural staging of nature – circus' sublime spectacles triumph over the clowning grotesque.

Most circus acts (inside the ring) present highly disciplined bodies in physical action. I would argue against the notion that seeing/observing skilful moving body spectacles evokes a sense of grotesqueness as fearful deadness through their risk taking (Russo 22). On the contrary, these acts confirm liveness with their action. Even the moving grotesque identified by Russo suggests liveness. The comic grotesque of clowning, however, includes acts where clowns join but fail doing aerial tricks, a skill in itself, as they appear to stall leaving the ground. The observed spectacle of distant aerial bodies taking risks might encourage body-schemata to leap with them engaging phantasms of motion, and this potentially might open out from pre-existing (and pre-symbolic) imaginary and habitual patterns of muscular and sensory spaces. That is, unless phantasms mimic the clown as it stalls in the act, in a failure of motion.

Sublime musculature performing doubly sexed nomenclature might evoke a cultural unconscious fear of queerness, of freakery as grotesque. While distinguishing body images from body-schemata, Merleau-Ponty would contend that 'the imaginary is not an absolute unobservable; it finds in the body analogues of itself that incarnate it' (*Visible* 77). Therefore the imaginary body and its images exist in relation to body-schemata that are always unfolding, capable of movement and action. When it is constantly unfolding and reshaping in relation to the instability of phenomena, it mimics acrobatic bodies in action. In Club Swing's show, performing circus bodies prefigure inertness as grotesque in relation to liveness. In this show grotesqueness is a body without action or movement, but this is one that cannot be observed.

For phenomenological bodies, liveness is an engagement of visceral sensations, kinaesthetic trajectories and imaginings in motion and movement. Spectatorial phantasmic ideals that arise in relation to the defiant triumph of fleshed muscular action fly away from embodied inertia. A fearful grotesque of a live phenomenal body in action unfolds as lived bodies fearing loss of movement, the failure of the motion of body-schemata.

Focus on political phenomenologies

Circus bodies and in particular aerial bodies remain distant, in marked contrast to the more intimate invitations of performers who can look back from conventional stages. However, the effect of distant bodies is localised through a 'palpation of the eye' (Merleau-Ponty

Visible 133). It might be argued that the eyes watching the circus body are attuned by habitually viewing other bodies in action in social contexts; the danger is that these bodies are motionless ideas, gendered and grounded, unable to move beyond inertness in social identity.

Although Merleau-Ponty is criticised by feminists for the dominance of sight in his phenomenology about lived bodies, sight is nonetheless central to experiences of this type of circus performance. Feminist interrogations of performing bodies expose the ideological implications inherent in spectatorial seeings (Dolan) and visibility (Phelan) and feminist performance challenges to gender orthodoxies about bodies (Schneider). As Peggy Phelan explains: 'Sight then is both imagistic and discursive' (15). Jill Dolan, exploring gender power relations in theatre, exposes how the male gaze is potentially offset by the feminist spectator. While this has encouraged different ways of thinking and seeing bodies, to a large extent this thinking remains detached from a body-subject's sensory perceptions in and observations of the phenomenal field of motion. Racial and sexed identity arise from lived bodies as active spatial entities in constant action. There is a theoretical 'forgetfulness' about lived bodies as actively physical entities in relation to social ideas. Bodies are lived as sexed, so that the social identity of a performing body surface comes as much from the imperatives of spectatorial bodies as it does from the coding of bodies in the text. The performing body-text functions as a site of divergences as much as congruences of identity.

It might be presumed that spectatorial bodies sex a performing body through correspondences with habitual actions. Muscularity in action by male and female bodies might be perceived to masculinise a performing body, although this is doubled by the way such performers are objectified and therefore feminised. Given theories of subject-object relations and the gaze, then phenomenally lived bodies see according to historical and social imperatives, but this confirms lived bodies will see/observe differently. It would seem that the subserviences imposed on the lived female body and/or the racially dominated body mean that they might perceive fleshed bodies in the phenomenal field differently to dominant bodies. If objectified subserviences are embedded in the actions of habitual body-schemata, while it is presumed that thinking will negate the social order of body-subjects it is necessary also to think through seen/observed phenomenologies. Subserviences residing in body-schemata that bring about social inertness need to be challenged by muscular bodies in action.

Exposures to muscular action by bodies might potentially realign bodily viewings. While acknowledging infinitely variable intersections in bodily living of culture, race, sexuality, eroticism and physical movement and degrees of forgetfulness in specific bodies, performing bodies are also seen within social histories of movement and action. They confirm pre-existing bodily knowings as they move towards revoking them.

In the example above of negated muscular drag, it is the action in the performance that results in spectatorial imperatives to sex the performing body as female then male. This reiterates a sexually differentiated body-schema in which the other sex becomes invisible and phantasmically inert. But sex-specific inertness has the potential to be reversible when visible motion is reinstated and re-viewed. Where a spectator envisages a phantasmic body-schema of its own making across the surfaces of viewed performing bodies it can become re-imagined fleshed entities of motion. The speculative logics inherent to gender theories of reception suggest that some dexterous spectators engage more readily than others with the motion of doubly sexed acrobatic and aerial bodies to offset socially limited body-schema habits. Moreover, changes to pre-set body-schemata necessitates engagement with phenomenological muscular bodies in differing ways. Words and images describing ambiguously marked bodies may impact on thinking while not on muscular bodies or vice versa. The multiple possibilities of phenomenological interpretation become like acrobatic bodies in motion; somersaulting, back flipping, shifting shape and meaning in a rapid succession of moves in and out of the fixed poses of social categories.

Although relations between embodied words and flesh seem circular, if the capacity for body-to-body exchanges remains subordinate to spoken and thought exchanges and/or in turn gives way to written ones, the physical body is still an absent spectacle of liveness. Retrospective re-viewings of a live body in action such as here allows for a repeated phenomenological engagement with liveness (this thinking, writing body/ your reading body). Focused thinking through words, however, cannot substitute for focused bodily observation of bodies in the phenomenal fields of circus and performance.

References

Balint, Michael. *Thrills and Regressions*. New York: International Universities P, 1959.

Bennett, Susan. *Theatre Audiences*. London: Routledge, 1990.

Butler, Judith. *Gender Trouble*. London: Routledge, 1990.

– *Bodies That Matter*. London: Routledge, 1994.

Dolan, Jill. *The Feminist Spectator*. Ann Arbor: Michigan UP, 1988.

Garner, Stanton B. *Bodied Spaces: Phenomenology and Performance in Contemporary Drama*. Ithaca: Cornell UP, 1994.

Grosz, Elizabeth. *Volatile Bodies*. Sydney: Allen & Unwin, 1994.

Krauss, Rosalind. *The Optical Unconscious*. Cambridge, Mass: MIT Press, 1994.

Lingis, Alphonso. *Foreign Bodies*. New York: Routledge, 1994.

Merleau-Ponty, Maurice. *The Phenomenology of Perception*. Trans. Colin Smith. London: Routledge, 1996.

– *The Visible and the Invisible*. Trans. Alphonso Lingis. Evanston: Northwestern UP, 1995.

Phelan, Peggy. *Unmarked*. London: Routledge, 1993.

Russo, Mary. *The Female Grotesque*. London: Routledge, 1994.

Schneider, Rebecca. *The Explicit Body in Performance*. London: Routledge, 1997.

Solomon, Alisa. *Re-Dressing The Canon: Essays on Theater and Gender*. New York: Routledge, 1997.

Tait, Peta. 'Defying Gravity: Trends and Meanings'. *Real Time: 24 Theatre, Performance and the National Arts* (April-May 1998): 31-32.

– 'Wrestling Body Translations of *Whet Flesh*'. *TheatreForum* 15 (1999): 4-11.

'Circus Bodies as Theatre Animals'. *Australasian Drama Studies* 35 (October 1999): 129-44.

Notes

1 Club Swing performers for these three shows were Anni Davey, Kathryn Niesche, Kareena Oates, Simone O'Brien and Celia White, and their shows were part of the outdoor Victorian Arts Centre's program of activities to celebrate circus. I am discussing these performances because these were not paying, self-selecting audiences. I viewed these three shows first on 21 January 1998 and discussed them with Robyn Laurie at that time.

2 Merleau-Ponty (*Phenomenology*) critiques both scientific objectivity and the relativism of subjectivity. I encountered Merleau-Ponty initially through Philipa Rothfield, 'Points of Contact, Philosophies of Movement.' *Writings on Dance* 11/12 (1994): 77-86.

3 Ideas of gaps in the embodied reception of circus somersault into assumptions that performed body surfaces can deliver the performer's subjective experience, albeit as that of a character, within more conventional theatre texts. Circus exaggerates how theatrical bodies are opaque.

4 This statement is based on numerous comments made by physical theatre performers in conversation with the author, and information communicated about performers working with injuries since 1992.

5 This comment is based on my experiences of viewing this type of work since 1991 with friends and colleagues, and sending groups of students to review it who generally seemed to find it harder to review than other theatre forms. I have noticed how a number of spectators attending Australian new circus/physical theatre performances, whom I know to be fairly articulate about conventional spoken theatre, express their enjoyment of the show and then struggle to discuss it (the theatrical texts). Words seem to fail them, even though the shows are rich in nonverbal theatrical, technical and cultural languages. Conversely, over the same period, I observed how physical theatre performers become uncharacteristically talkative after viewing the shows of other performers as they dissect each bodily move, gesture and action (the technical language). In addition, some of my students have queried and researched the entrenched gendered responses of spectators to comedy and other types of performances that seem to confirm the difficulty of shifting habits of perception through viewed and spoken exchanges, where the surface of the performing body is not impinging on the muscularity of the viewing body.

6 In performances by Club Swing, The Party Line, Acrobat, Rock 'n' Roll Circus and Jeremy Smith, the muscular acts are recognised as queered flesh at dance party and club performances by a self-selecting gay and lesbian audience.

7 I viewed this show first at 6 p.m., 26 October 1997. See Tait, 'Defying Gravity'. Anna Shelper worked with Circus Oz and Canada's Cirque du Soleil.

8 Unconscious responses that manifest bodily repression as hysteria may not be the same as a phenomenologically receptive and perceptive but unthinking body. As Merleau-Ponty implies then, can mental processes become distorted by malfunctions and interventions in the spatial motility of phenonemological bodies?

9 Certainly, Merleau-Ponty can be criticised for his ideas of a 'natural generality' of 'my' body, seeming to universalise bodies as singular (152) and objectify their seen world, even perhaps essentialising phenomenology as neutral and implying that it has an a priori naturalness.

10 It should be noted that Celia White and Simone O'Brien are familiar with Mary Russo's writing and ideas of the uncanny from their work with The Party Line.

11 There is a scene in Wim Wenders' film *Wings of Desire* in which the female aerialist costumed in wings is watched by the film's wing-less male angel as she trains on a trapeze in the circus ring. She verbally refers to a chicken, while her coach on the ground refers to a dove then a sparrow.

Part II

Sightings

5. Staging seduction: the Sydney Front and the postmodern geopolitics of theatre's bodies and spaces

Kerrie Schaefer

> *Our work is about excess, about a gesturing that goes far beyond that necessary for any reasonable discourse. The superabundance of our work has the paradoxical aim of releasing the spectator from false complicatedness. We continually collapse our own rhetoric and bring the focus back to the body's fleshy organs. By thus returning to where meaning is embodied, we aim to protect ourselves and the spectator from the terrorism of grand abstractions that cannot be lived out (*Sydney Front, *25 Years* 54*).*

In seven years the Sydney Front[1] created seven major performance pieces including *Waltz* (1987), *John Laws/Sade* (1987), *The Pornography of Performance* (1988), *Photocopies of God* (1989), *Don Juan* (1991), *First and Last Warning* (1992) and *Passion* (1993). In this body of work the Sydney Front staged a relentless interrogation and playful manipulation of the rules and conventions of theatrical representation (see above). One Sydney Front member[2] has described the company's work in the following way: 'it's work that takes as its basic subject the moment of performance, not the script that precedes it' (Waites 7). Writing on the discourse of representation in the theatre, Herbert Blau asserts that the subversion of the authority of the dramatic text has shifted critical focus onto the live performance in such a way that the audience has taken the stage (27). The locus of the Sydney Front's mischievous exploration and testing of the limits of theatrical representation is the relationship between performer and spectator in live performance. This was expressed by a member of the Sydney Front in a radio interview previewing *Don Juan*: 'All our work is about the relationship between the performer and the spectator and that relationship takes different forms ... that's the essential relationship of theatre so often lost in the naturalistic tradition which pretends the audience isn't there' (2SER-FM).

In an introductory discussion of theatre audiences, Susan Bennett remarks that 'the intensity of interest in the audience sparked by the rejection of naturalist practice has, in the latter part of the twentieth century, become an obsession' (7). The Sydney Front share this obsession, a self-admittedly excessive preoccupation with the spectator and the dynamic of the performer/spectator relationship in live performance. The short history of the Sydney Front's work represents different stages in the development of their ideas concerning the performer, the spectator and the relations of power and knowledge between these different kinds of bodies in the theatre space. In their first show, *Waltz*, the Sydney Front performed extreme physical actions in an attempt to possibly exceed the spectator's appetite for spectacle. In *The Pornography of Performance* the performers offered up their bodies to the gaze *and* touch of the audience in order to demonstrate literally the spectator's insatiable desire for flesh. Ushered into the performance space by a member of the company, the audience was encouraged to place their hands through holes punched into large cylindrical shaped objects standing in the space. Standing inside each tube was a naked performer. In *Don Juan* the performers changed tack and required that the spectator place his/her body equally in the theatrical frame of the performance. The Sydney Front asked and paid an audience member to take their clothes off and then to stand naked on stage for two minutes.[3] During this time the performers disappeared, leaving the audience in a circle around the naked spectator. The performers returned only to receive the audience's applause. In *First and Last Warning* the audience was required to undress and wear black negligees given to them by the performers for the entire performance. In *Passion*, the performers disappeared themselves almost completely, appearing only at certain strategic moments on the margins of performance. The performance script for *Passion* – a set of written instructions for the audience to perform – was delivered to an audience member chosen by a small girl in a Holy Communion dress.

The subject and object of this paper is the Sydney Front's fifth major production, *Don Juan*.[4] The Sydney Front's *Don Juan* did not follow the conventional plot or characterisation of works based on the legendary seducer, including Tirso de Molina's morality play *The Joker of Seville and the Guest of Stone* (1630), Lorenzo Da Ponte's libretto to the Mozart opera, *The Punished Libertine or Don Giovanni* (1787), or Molière's *Don Juan* (1655). Displaying an irreverence matching the mythical libertine's roaming infidelities, the Sydney Front poached the theme of seduction from the legend of Don Juan[5] and employed its dynamics to interrogate the relationship between performer and spectator in theatrical performance. The Sydney Front's *Don Juan* was the first major show produced after the company's 1989 European tour of *The Pornography of Performance*. It marked a significant change in direction for the group. This was articulated in the publicity for *Don Juan* where it was announced that 'Having allowed the public to fondle our bodies in *The Pornography of Performance*, the members of the Sydney Front now intend to redress the balance'. In an interview, a company member explained that 'In *The Pornography of Performance* we didn't challenge the roles between the performers as exhibitionists and the spectators as voyeurs. In *Don Juan* we play with this relationship throughout the show. We take the idea of seduction in the Don Juan myth and apply it to the theatrical relationship between the actor and spectator' (Waites 7). The Sydney Front's use of the audience in *Don Juan* was notably more considered and proficient than in the early work. This level of complexity was carried through into later work, which is why *Don Juan* is a key performance piece in the Sydney Front's oeuvre and worthy of significant critical attention.

The Opening Scene[6] of the Sydney Front's *Don Juan* began as the double doors of The Performance Space (TPS) slammed open. The sound of the doors hitting the walls of the theatre was amplified by two resounding chords which, in Mozart's opera *Don Giovanni*, announced the appearance of the ghost of the Commendatore, the avenging stone statue, come to dine with Don Giovanni on his impudent invitation. The solemn mood invoked by these notes and the associated thematic undertones of revenge and divine retribution – in this case, the performers getting their own back – were almost immediately overturned by a baroque soundtrack composed by Raffaele Marcellino. Marcellino' s composition played the entire Mozart opera continuously at twenty times its normal speed. This highly embellished soundscape accompanied the audience's entrance into the performance space. At the box office each spectator was supplied with a black mask and asked to wear it for the duration of the show. At the door to the theatre, the spectator was supplied with a small plastic cup of wine. With the mask affixed and glass of wine in hand, the spectator entered the black box theatre to find the performers sitting in the audience seating.

Six performers, attired in white wedding gowns with white powdered faces, were positioned randomly throughout the tiered audience seating which was secured against the audience by a rough barricade on three sides. The entire fortification was covered in barbed wire. Barricades also blocked easy access into the performance space. Each spectator was forced to walk in single file before the performers. The performers eyed the spectators seductively; they looked and smiled, licked their lips, and at times noted down personal details in small black books. At the end of the line, the audience assembled together in the empty space on the opposite side of the barricade, facing the performers.

The movement of the audience milling in the theatre, accompanied by an extravagant musical score and lit by medium bright lighting that covered the entire space – including both performers and spectators – created the illusion that the audience was performing for the performers. This reversal was underlined by Marcellino's score which sampled dance tracks into the opera mix so that recognisable lines from commercially popular dance tracks by well-known artists, such as Madonna and the artist formerly known as Prince could be distinguished over and above the gibberish. The spectator was alternately interrogated – 'What are you lookin' at?' – and entreated to actively participate in the performance – 'Get up on the dance floor' – by the voices of the singers sampled into the sound mix.

In a discussion in the rehearsal process, a performer stated that the Opening Scene of *Don Juan* was pivotal to the performance as a whole. Another performer asserted that the whole show should refer back to this scene, that is, 'to the relationship between the watching performers and the watched audience'. It was remarked that 'this concrete relationship is the essential dramaturgy for the entire piece'. Given these comments, it would be possible to read this scene as simply a reversal or inversion of the conventional relationship between performer and spectator in the theatre space, which was how one performer in rehearsal characterised the scene; 'the audience are putting on a show for us'. While the Opening Scene was in some ways a reversal of the conventional relationship between performer and spectator, making the passive viewing audience active, I want to argue that it was not entirely reducible to such a reading. Firstly, the audience's activity in *Don Juan* was strictly controlled and directed by the Sydney Front. Secondly, the performers were not converted into wholly passive viewers. Located in the audience seating, they watched and actively recorded and responded to the appearance, actions and behaviours of the audience filing into the theatre one by one. The performers, in fact, actively re-asserted their presence to a present and fully visible audience. This situation is designed to be most unsettling or agonising for the spectator drawn into the soft glare of public focus and away from the power and privilege of invisibility. In other words, the front-on, face-to-face physical arrangement of the performer and spectator in the Opening Scene of *Don Juan* establishes an encounter of two-way gazes which is, I want to argue, of the order of seduction. I am drawing here on a notion of seduction described by Baudrillard, a critical source in the rehearsal process. According to Baudrillard,

> In seduction we are not dealing with a new version of universal attraction. The diagonals or transversals of seduction may well break the opposition between terms; they do not lead to fused or confused relations but to dual relations. It is not a matter of a mystical fusion of subject or object, or signifier or signified, masculine and feminine etc., but of a seduction, that is, a duel and agonistic relation. (105; emphasis in original)

The Sydney Front name seduction as one of two major themes in their work.[7] Seduction is defined as 'a game of identity for adults' and as 'mastery of the strategy of appearances against the force of being and reality' (*25 Years* 54). This definition makes direct reference to Baudrillard, who writes that seduction stakes ' mastery of the strategy of appearances, against the force of being and reality' (10). He states 'There is no need to play being against being or truth against truth; why undermine foundations, when a *light* manipulation of appearances will do?' (10). For Baudrillard, seduction is a mode of action that operates outside of and as a foil to the forces of power that perpetuate belief in truth, reality and/or identity. The attributes of seduction are not those of the real, the true or the self-identical, but are, instead, those of play and gaming, challenges and duels. As seduction cannot take on the terms of power directly, it plays on the surface appearances of things, denying them their truth and turning it into a game. Through this game or play, seduction thwarts all systems of power and meaning. Seduction is, in other words, a triumph of seeming over meaning, of representation or the lie over the real or the true. In this sense, it is possible to compare seduction characterised by Baudrillard as mastery of the arts of trickery, deceit, subterfuge, disguise and deception, to what de Certeau calls a tactic:[8] 'ways of operating' which are 'clever tricks, knowing how to get away with things, 'hunter's cunning', manoeuvers, manipulations' (37).

It is precisely this mastery of illusion over reality that is celebrated by Julia Kristeva in her writing on the mythical figure of Don Juan. Kristeva, another critical source referred to by the Sydney Front, examines the 'wicked yet laughable and compelling' (191) mode of masculine seduction portrayed in Mozart's opera buffa *Don Giovanni*.[9] She claims that in Mozart's music, the figure of Don

Giovanni is transformed into a being without an inner (psychological or moral) self: 'His polytopicalness, his combinative pleasure, his lack of attachment, his laughter with and at prohibitions, turn him into a being without internality'(197). Don Giovanni lacks, in other words, what might be called a psychological subjectivity, an authentic sense of identity. Attracted to secrecy and disguise, he asserts himself 'through a play of inconsistencies, seemings and fascinations' (198). He is, in other words, 'an artist with no authenticity other than his ability to change, to live without internality, to put on masks for fun' (199). Implicit in Kristeva's description of Don Giovanni's lack of character is the assertion that what he lacks he makes up for in other ways. She states, 'He has no internality but, as his roamings, his flights, his many as well as unbearable residences show him to be, he is a multiplicity, a polyphony. Don Giovanni is the harmonisation of the multiple' (193). In other words, the figure of Don Juan asserts an alternative yet still affirmative, or positive and desiring, mode of being which is more akin to what Deleuze and Guattari would call 'becoming' (232-309). The presentation of a positive and productive alternative to a conventional mode of existence as ego-based subjectivity is, as Kristeva notes, a great achievement. She states, 'Don Giovanni succeeds ... He succeeds in conquering women, challenging God, putting together an existence just as one puts together an opera, for instance. Don Giovanni is able to. Don Juanism is an art, as have been, during given periods, aristocracy or the dandy's stance' (194). Such accomplishment, Kristeva suggests, demands that we therefore understand the libertine attitude as a 'longing to change existence into a form, a game, jouissance' and that we view the libertine outlook as an 'extraordinary claim to change life into art' (197-198).

Kristeva' s examination leads her to conclude that the mythical master of seduction depicted in Mozart's opera offers a radical alternative to the dominant theatrical mode of narrative-based representation centred on revealing the psychological interiority of a character. She asserts that the myth of Don Juan should be read allegorically in so far as it represents a challenge to psychological realism as an aesthetic, and signals its replacement by a baroque aesthetic. Don Juan is, she says, 'a myth transformed into an aesthetics':

> Baroque aesthetics induces the audience to dream and to hallucinate while pointing out that it is only a game never to be confused with reality. Such exhilaration through seeming does not become for baroque man any more than for Don

> Juan a 'second nature' (as nineteenth century realists were asking actors to have) ... The fire that engulfs Don Juan is the same as the one that swept away the baroque set. It is a triumph of the seeming, which after having captivated its amorous victims and enthralled us, the hallucinated audience, allows itself the luxury of expending itself ... Beyond baroque art, is not all art essentially baroque, that is, Don Juanistic? (198-199).

Following Kristeva, the Sydney Front read the legend of Don Juan allegorically, taking seduction as a key theme and using it as a tactical ploy to destabilise a series of binary oppositions underpinning the workings of theatrical representation: for instance, stage and auditorium, performer and spectator, active and passive, doer and viewer, body and mind, visible and invisible, public and private, enslaved and free. The seduction of the spectator in their *Don Juan* cannot be reduced to an attempt to lead or draw a putatively passive or disinterested spectator into the performance, to actively engage them in a participatory way with the action onstage. The Sydney Front did not seek to furnish the spectator with a complete or undivided experience of collective action, a communicative synthesis through performance called *communitas* by Victor Turner. Rather, the Sydney Front targeted the machinery of theatrical representation itself, to show how individuals are transformed into spectators through a specifically theatrical making and doing, or disciplining. Through seduction, a play on distance and proximity, alienation and attraction, the Sydney Front demonstrated that the spectator's 'critical distance' from the performer on stage is the product of an institutional practice, a 'panoptical' machinery (Worthen 21), which works to conceal its productive operations by distributing and positioning individual's bodies within a differentiated space.

The value given to critical distance, that is, to distance *and* proximity in critical and other spaces, is a key issue for postmodernism which Edward Soja describes as 'a theoretical discourse and a periodizing concept in which geography increasingly matters as a vantage point of critical insight' (62). Soja attributes to Jameson's account of postmodernism as the cultural logic of late capitalism, 'an ability to see in the cultural logic and forms of postmodernism an instrumental cartography of power and social control; in other words a more acute way of seeing how space hides consequences from us' (62-63). Marrying Jameson's postmodernism of resistance and Foucault's critical analysis of disciplinary technologies, Soja asserts that postmodernism is 'an expressly geopolitical strategy in which spatial issues are the fundamental organising concern, for disciplinary power proceeds primarily through the organisation, enclosure, and control of individuals in space' (63). The tactic of seduction in the Sydney Front's *Don Juan* dramatises the rhetorical conceit, or rather deceit, of the critical distance on which the performer/spectator relation in theatrical representation is based. At the same time, seduction insinuates an element of play and in(s)anity into the theatre relation, as did the dandy's interruptions of theatrical performance, to stave off the 'boredom and stolid indifference experienced in the stalls' of private commercial theatres after 1850 (Booth qtd. in Bennett 3-4).

The Sydney Front's manipulation of the spectator in *Don Juan* effects multiple transformations in the organisation of bodies in space in order to underline, and to introduce some play into, the relations of power/knowledge instituted by the particular arrangements of these semiotic elements in the theatre. As I described earlier,[10] on entering TPS the spectator was corralled in single file in front of male and female performers in white wedding dresses (expectant brides?) sitting in the rostrum of audience seating roped off with barbed wire. As the masked spectators filed into the auditorium they gathered on the opposite side of the barrier, face to face with the performers. The spatial arrangement, soundscape and lighting effects institute the challenge and game of seduction. To reinforce this, the Opening Scene comprised a number of different actions that played on the motif of seduction. In one piece, for instance, three performers took fishing rods and cast their bait of red plastic roses into the audience. The roses landed on the floor at the feet of various spectators. They ignored these offerings, which were slowly reeled in by the dejected performers.

At the end of the first scene, one performer left the barricaded rostrum and ventured into the audience. He was directed by the other performers to choose one spectator, a man. This man was singled out from the rest of the audience. He was seated on a chair in the centre of the floor space directly in front of the performers. The audience around him formed a semi-circle to better view the performer's verbal seduction of the man. They asked the man a set of leading questions from a pre-written script: for example, 'did you come here alone tonight?' 'do you have a lover at home?', 'are you looking for a change?', 'do you have any un-nameable desires?' The scene was tagged Seduction Victim in rehearsal because the idea was to humiliate this one person or to make them, at least, feel extremely uncomfortable, singled out from the rest of the audience for the pleasure and enjoyment of the performers and spectators. The position of the lone spectator was potentially a horrible and agonisingly painful one as he was subject to the gaze of both performers and spectators. For the rest of the audience I suspect that the feeling was, at first, one of immense relief at not being chosen. Then it's likely that a creeping sense of uneasiness arrived with the realisation that any individual spectator could be singled out and seated alone in the middle of the space, left to sweat and squirm under the stage lights and salacious questions of the performers. The spectator's enjoyment of the spectacle of the performers seducing the lone spectator was designed to be tempered by this awareness.

At one point a performer from the back of the rostrum said to the seduction victim 'I think I'd like to touch you.' He stood and began to walk down the stairs toward the spectator. At the same time, the barbed wire covered bar blocking the audience's entrance to the rostrum of seating lifted (the stage manager operates the mechanism that raises the bar). The way is made clear for the performer to have his way with the spectator. At this point, the rest of the performers rose from their seats, one saying 'I think we all want to touch you' as they proceeded down the stairs and into the auditorium behind the leading performer. The leading performer walked right up to the seated audience member as the other performers fanned out behind him. This moment was designed to produce intense apprehension, to make the audience wonder whether the performer would, in fact, 'touch' or fondle the spectator. At the same time as this was happening, the other performers targeted and closed in on the audience standing in a semi-circle around the seated spectator. I noted that at this point laughter from the audience was transmuted into silence as the situation appeared to turn back on the spectator. The Sydney Front, having created what I perceived to be a moment of intense anxiety, then let it go and, asking spectators to move to the side for the next part of the performance, moved onto the next scene.

As directed by the performers, the audience divided into two groups standing on opposite sides of the performance space, leaving a passageway down the middle for the performance. This was the spatial configuration for several pieces to follow including Java Dance, Dick Lecture, Thump Rump and the Pavan/Fuck Me scene. The first three scenes were parodies of different kinds. Java Dance, for instance, parodies the dance of seduction, while Dick Lecture ridiculed male sexuality. The tone of the Pavan/Fuck Me scene was opposite to that of the preceding scenes. Against the background of a slow, stately court dance, a female performer made rough sexual advances toward her male counterparts. Her advances were violently rejected by the men. At the end of the scene the woman lay sprawled on her back, legs splayed apart, in the middle of the space. She was naked and exposed to the audience on either side of the space. The theatre at this point was silent and still. I found this moment to be an extremely uncomfortable one, a feeling intensified by the sudden change in tone from the previous scenes, a series of humorous parodies. At this moment, as the audience was left to take in the extreme gravity of the sexual violence depicted in the Pavan/Fuck Me scene, their voyeurism was exposed by the open arrangement of the audience on both sides of the space, both watching and watched.

To begin the next scene, the performers walked purposely back into the space carrying two chairs each. They sat on one chair and placed the other opposite them, motioning the audience to take a seat. A spectator accepted the invitation and took a seat opposite a performer. The performers ask questions such as 'how are you feeling?', 'have you had any problems lately?' and so on to draw the spectator into and engage them in a conversation. This scene was called Audience Counselling. As the performer counselled the spectator, the remainder of the audience rearranged itself around and in between the chairs to better hear the conversation. The space became full of spectators as they milled around the five pairs of chairs, getting in close to listen to the intimate conversation of the performer/spectator. At this point, the tone of the scene changed suddenly. The performers frown and then begin to cry until they are quite hysterical, at which point the performer pushed the spectator out of the chair and exited the stage taking the chair.

Audience Strip[11] began with the space in black-out. The audience was still occupying most of the performance space in a random fashion after Audience Counselling. Suddenly a male performer appeared under a spotlight in the middle of the space. He asked the audience to gather round him in a circle. He then announced that he had a request to make: 'We would like one member of the audience to take their clothes off'. The performer explained that the audience member will be required to stand naked for two minutes. He reassured the group that 'nothing further will be required of them'. A spectator stepped forward (always).[12] The performer asked the man to remove his clothing. While the spectator did that the performer found someone in the audience with a watch and asked the person to time two minutes. When the spectator was fully undressed the performer asked that the count begin and disappeared, leaving the naked spectator in the middle of a circle of spectators.

In the final scene of *Don Juan*, the Sydney Front achieved their ultimate aim, to seduce a spectator into becoming the spectacle. The willing compliance of the spectator to assume the 'role' prescribed by performers at this and other points in performance, for example, as masked party revellers, victims of seduction, voyeurs, patients/clients or strippers, raises a question concerning the power of seduction in the theatre. The Sydney Front did not reflect on or resist the power of seduction in their performance of *Don Juan*. They used seduction as a tactical ploy and, through a combination of intimate and distancing modes of performance, both inveigled and alienated the spectator. The simultaneous solicitation and frustration of the spectator's involvement and engagement in performance is meant to be intensely unsettling and discomforting, in a way that is designed to dismantle the spectator's ability to take something away from the event. What is left over, or what remains, is a sense of wonder at the intolerable indeterminacy of performance. That is, it is left for the spectator to reflect on their experience of the spectacle or, rather, what they were seduced away from and what they, willingly or not, were led into.

References

Baudrillard, Jean. *Seduction*. Translated by Brian Singer. London: Macmillan, 1990.

Bennett, Susan. *Theatre Audiences. A Theory of Production and Reception*. London & New York: Routledge, 1990.

Blau, Herbert. *The Audience*. Baltimore & London: John Hopkins UP, 1990.

de Certeau, Michel. *The Practice of Everyday Life*. Trans. Steven Rendall. Berkeley: U of California P, 1984.

Deleuze, Gilles & Guattari, Félix. *A Thousand Plateaus. Capitalism and Schizophrenia*. Trans. Brian Massumi. Minneapolis: U of Minnesota P, 1987.

Kristeva, Julia. *Tales of Love*. Trans. Leon S. Roudiez. New York: Columbia UP, 1987.

Morris, Meaghan. *Great Moments in Social Climbing. King Kong and the Human Fly*. Sydney: Local Consumption, 1992.

Soja, Edward. W. *Postmodern Geographies. The Reassertion of Space in Critical Social Theory*. London & New York: Verso, 1989.

Sydney Front. *Don Juan*. The Performance Space, Redfern, 11-28 April 1991 and 10-28 May 1992.

– Radio 2SER-FM, (April 1991).

– In *25 Years of Performance Art in Australia*. Paddington: Ivan Dougherty Gallery, University of New South Wales College of Fine Arts, 1994.

Van Kerkhoven, Marianne. 'On Dramaturgy.' *Theaterschrift* 5-6, 1994.

Waites, James. 'Treading a Fine Line. The Sydney Front and *Don Juan*: Exploring the Actor-Audience Nexus.' *The Sydney Review* (April 1991).

Whitton, David. *Molière: Don Juan. Plays in Production*. Cambridge: Cambridge UP, 1995.

Worthen, W. B. *Modern Drama and the Rhetoric of Theatre.* Berkeley: U of California P, 1992.

Notes

1 Formed in November 1986 and disbanded in December 1993, the Sydney Front was Andrea Aloise, John Baylis, Clare Grant, Nigel Kellaway, and Christopher Ryan.

2 In this paper I will not identify the statements of individual members of the company in order to preserve the sense of collective creation fundamental to the Sydney Front's work. I only wish to note that the collective organisation of the Sydney Front is best described as 'many-voiced'. In stating this I wish to include the work of the Sydney Front within the new dramaturgy central to contemporary European and American companies. This dramaturgy is essentially a collective one but, as Maryanne Van Kerkhoven states, the collective 'has a nature different from the one we remember from the seventies: at that time the groups all tended to rally themselves behind one single political conviction; these days the collectives (cf. The Wooster group, BAK-Truppen, Theatre Repere-Robert Lepage, De Vere etc.) are, rather, ... expected to provide many voices' (21).

3 A cash amount of up to $50 was put aside each night to bribe spectators into performing naked. The Sydney Front always managed to bribe an audience member into performing naked, often for less than the $50 amount set aside. Occasionally a bribe was not required at all.

4 In making *Don Juan* the Sydney Front collaborated with Elise Ahamnos, singer/performer Annette Tesoriero and composer Raffaele Marcellino. I was invited to join the company to document the rehearsal process for *Don Juan*. My analysis is based on a casebook of rehearsals which records the entire process from November 1990 to April 1991. First performed at TPS, Redfern, in April 1991, *Don Juan* was reworked in 1992 for a second season at TPS before it toured nationally and internationally. I saw numerous performances in both the first and second seasons. Some of these performances were video recorded for later analysis.

5 Here I refer to the legend of Don Juan in acknowledgement that the story, first plotted by a Spanish monk in the seventeenth century, is largely based on medieval legend. Tirso de Molina's *The Joker of Seville and the Guest of Stone* (1630) combines medieval folk legend, tales telling of statues of the dead coming to life to exact retribution from the living, with the story of an unrepentant womaniser. As David Whitton notes, Molina unwittingly created a mythical archetype in the figure of Don Juan. He explains that the combination of the stone guest motif with that of a fiercely non-believing or unrepentant master of seduction proved extremely popular and the play travelled quickly to Italy and France (2). In Italian and French re-workings of the play in the seventeenth and eighteenth centuries, the focus shifted from the moral lesson to the central character's motivation, leading to the emergence of Don Juan as a modern psychological type rather than the Everyman of a morality play (2).

6 In rehearsal the Sydney Front gave names to the scenes they devised for example, the Opening Scene, Seduction Victim, Java Dance, Dick Lecture, Thump Rump, Pavan/Fuck Me, Audience Counselling and Audience Strip. In this paper I use these titles when discussing particular scenes.

7 The second major theme is sacrifice: 'the one magnificent gesture that would put an end to games once and for all, every night, again and again' (*25 Years* 54)

8 I characterise seduction as a tactic after Michel de Certeau's distinction between two different types of action: strategy and tactic. According to de Certeau, strategy is 'the calculus of force relations which becomes possible when a subject of will and power (a proprietor, an enterprise, a city, a scientific institution) can be isolated from an "environment". A strategy assumes a place that can be circumscribed as proper (propre) and thus serve as the basis for generating relations with an exterior distinct from it (competitors, adversaries, "clientèles", "targets", or "objects" of research)' (xix). Tactic, on the other hand, is defined as 'a calculus which cannot count on a "proper" (a spatial or institutional localisation), nor thus on a borderline distinguishing the other as a visible totality' (xix). Tactical actions are, as Meaghan Morris explains, a way of operating or making do available to people displaced or excluded as Other by the bordering actions of strategy (1992, 27). She notes, most importantly, that a tactic maintains an active relation to place by means of what de Certeau calls an *art of insinuation* (27; my emphasis). As seduction is strange to the terms of power, yet actively related to power through deceit and trickery raised to an art form, it can be likened to what de Certeau calls a tactic. Seduction therefore shares the same capabilities as a tactic, that is, 'a mobility that must accept the chance offerings of the moment, and seize on the wing the possibilities that offer themselves at any given moment. It must vigilantly make use of the cracks that particular conjunctions open in the surveillance of the proprietary powers. It poaches in them. It creates surprises in them. It can be where it is least expected. It is a guileful ruse' (37).

9 According to Kristeva, it was not until the 1787 Prague production of Mozart's *Don Giovanni* that the 'fearsome seduction of the Spanish nobleman was freed from the moral condemnation that accompanied it, probably from its beginnings, ... and found within music the direct language of amoral eroticism' (191).

10 I approach the work of the Sydney Front as a spectator and as a participant in the performance-making process. Thus my analysis of the Sydney Front's *Don Juan* is informed by reception of various performances and by knowledges from the process. When I do speak as a spectator I speak from my own experience of the Sydney Front's *Don Juan*, without attempting to generalise my response to that of the audience as a whole entity. At the same time, I do try to outline the ways in which the Sydney Front attempted to position the spectator in relation to the performer and in doing this they did refer to the spectator as part of a single entity, the audience.

11 In the Sydney Front's second season of *Don Juan* the performance concluded at the end of the scene called Audience Strip. One of the reasons for ending the show with this scene in the reworked version of *Don Juan* was that the set required for the final scene was considered too unwieldy and difficult to tour. At the same time the Sydney Front's decision to end the show with Audience Strip was readily apparent. In this scene the Sydney Front achieve their main aim which was to seduce the spectator into making a spectacle of themselves, into taking responsibility for the workings of the spectacle (the performers disappeared into the dressing rooms). In this sense, the performance concludes with the ultimate seduction of the spectator.

12 Here, I am referring to a particular production recorded on video in which a male spectator did step forward at this point.

6.
Catalogue notes: independent female artists at The Performance Space 1991-97

Angharad Wynne-Jones

The Performance Space (TPS) in Sydney, founded in 1982, has provided for over twenty-five years much-needed physical and conceptual space for performance and art that challenges and infiltrates conventional and heritage arts practice.[1] Literally, it provides venues for visual and performance artists whose work reflects contemporary intellectual discourses, and metaphorically it operates as a site for the exchange of new ideas. Importantly, it has been consistently funded and supported by the Australia Council and the New South Wales Ministry for the Arts, perhaps to their relief that a tangible structure exists (able to be assessed and monitored within institutional frameworks) which nurtures and supports the hybrid practices typical of contemporary performance and visual arts. This work is fluid, dynamic and experimental but apparently hard to name as the changing terminology testifies: cross art form/hybrid/ new media /new form. TPS as an organisation reaches beyond its architectural confines across the country, and it has done and continues to make a major and unique contribution to the development of Australian culture.

After seven years of observing, facilitating and making performance around TPS, first as an artist and venue manager, then as the Artistic Director, I find it impossibly hard to organise the activities and many performances of those years into any kind of hierarchy of significance. Although I know I witnessed a formative movement, a cultural wave of new ideas and artistic expression across the decade, its lasting impact only becomes clearer as this decade merges into the next one. Regardless of the level of skill and experience of the hundreds of artists who worked there, the effort, the vulnerability, the energy, the fear, the thrill and the innate exhibitionism arising from performance seems common to them all. If each work was especially important for the artists who created it and the audiences who witnessed it, this was due in part to the way it reflected ongoing debates, controversies and histories, and the artists' capacity to communicate their curiosities, to expand networks and relationships, to pick up on fashions; and, practically, to market and budget in order to reach audiences.

The well-known ensemble companies, whose work became synonymous with TPS as they subverted notions of performance throughout the 1980s and early 1990s, began to reconstruct as different organisms by the mid-1990s. Sydney Front, with more integrity and intelligence than they knew what to do with, self-combusted (see the Chapter 5 'Staging Seduction'); its fragments reconstituted themselves into individual life forms that continue to delight and provoke through performance. Longstanding groups like Entr'Acte, One Extra and Theatre is Moving all reconfigured or moved on, creating spaces for others to move into. Yet they also left an awareness of the emptiness and the vacuum of the contemporary performance vista without those groups, often built around long-term personal relationships and their extended families. Perhaps ironically Sydney groups, long associated with TPS's performance style but usually performing elsewhere, remain although with very different strategies: Death Defying Theatre (See Chapter 15) relocated to western Sydney; Sidetrack resistant and intransigent, Legs on the Wall adaptable and opportunistic.[2] Open City's audiences distilled like a good stock to a few fine fellow artists, who sought out and appreciated the reflective spaces created by the nimble wordsmithing moving away from the vigour of physical performance. Ultimately their medium shifted and the paper *Real Time: Theatre, Performance and the National Arts* beckoned to Open City's Keith Gallasch and Virginia Baxter as a more potent space, and it consistently provides insight and context for the work of contemporary and independent artists often sidelined in mainstream media.

New ensembles emerged around an artist or a project, but were short-lived. These produced shows like *Stages of Terror* (1993), *Tales of Mad Women* (1993), and Safa's *The Politics of Belly Dancing* (1994). It might seem that once the idea was worked through in performance, the motivation to remain together disappeared. However, none of this happened in a vacuum. There were high and low pressures and hot and cold fronts that interrupted movements and gatherings, blew out the establishment of an interesting formation and blew in some new forms. The 1990s saw the 'rationalisation' of the arts culture and the establishment of the Major

Organisations Board (now the Major Organisation Fund) by the federal government that privileged the large companies and shored up their funding, while unlocking the support of smaller companies, requiring them to compete for funds first on a program basis and subsequently on a project-only basis. The demise of many important smaller companies became inevitable. Perhaps there were some cobwebs to blow away, some old wood to burn, but more significantly, there was the clear message that smaller groups without a strong management and commercial know-how were unsustainable as a permanent or even long-term structure. This is the environment we continue to inhabit, with outcomes-based policies engendering the language of business, so that work becomes termed 'product', ideas become strategies, and those that cannot be reduced to bullet points are considered not worth saying, let alone doing.

Artists are the most adaptable, reflexive and responsive of creatures and are not afraid to take risks; perhaps they should be called futures traders. Women artists have had to be that much more adaptable. Female practitioners have always been strongly represented in contemporary performance. If pragmatically they want to enter a domain where there are many like-minded female collaborators and fewer men, artistically these practitioners want to explore the territory of performance beyond the conventional forms.

Weather/ing patterns

A cold front, crisp and clear, and so articulate one could see the clouds form and move across the sky: 1992. This year brings individual artists that seem outside the known context as if operating on a different ampage, not always comfortable or resolved, but distinctive and attracting others around them.

Sarah Cathcart performed *Walking on Sticks*, co-written with Andrea Lemon, in February 1992. She depicted Nicaraguan, Australian and North American characters who told stories about Nicaragua using dynamic physical actions that enhanced a narrative full of political insight, personal reflection, and almost evoked the smell of the country. Sue Ellen Kohler presented *BUG*, April 1992, as a performance by herself and Sandra Perrin with film. Kohler used her own extraordinary yoga-release technique to explore a realm of movement that is part animal, and impossibly human. Filmed by Mihalya Middlemist with lighting by Margie Medlin, sound by Ion Pierce, it showed Kohler endlessly rolling towards us, the audience, her sharp hip bones, her sloping buttocks rolling until she finally fell.

She stood on one leg, the other wrapped around her body, thrashed in water; the show's lights slung so low they almost touched our heads, and we seemed to move underground.

Tess De Quincey (see Chapter 10 'Liminality and Corporeality') directed and choreographed *Infinity Squared* in October 1992, with Barbara Allen as executive producer. The dancers were Peter Fraser, Leah Grycewicz, Claire Hague, Nikki Heywood, Stuart Lynch, Russell Milledge, Philip Mills and Leike Mueller; cinematographer, Roman Baska; music by Rik Rue, Jim Denley, Stevie Wishart, Jamie Fielding; sound engineering, Shane Fahey; lighting, Geoff Cobham. De Quincey in a vivid silk frock stepped out, stamped out, eccentric and focussed; the set consisting of plumb lines hanging in a familiar European aesthetic crossed with the unfamiliar physicality of Butoh in a heady mix.

Then came a warm front, drawing more clouds; it was darker, harder to see, not knowing whether to rain or shine: 1993. This brought a damming up of frustrations that needed to be articulated, but with no sense of horizon and brooding, internal spaces.

Rachel Rosenthal came to Australia as *filename: FUTURFAX*, February 1993. We were so excited to see the woman herself, the doyenne of hard-core performance art in the 1970s, but disappointed with the simplistic Californian eco message of that performance from this beautiful bald old woman. If this reinforced the view that our performance was cutting edge, the host of Australian artists and academics contributing to the same event exemplified innovative approaches, especially those concerned with electronic media; Margaret Trail, Zoe Sofoulis and Virginia Barratt. The only ongoing all-female ensemble, The Party Line, produced *Appearing in Pieces* in May 1993, exploring ideas of gender as bodily gesture informed by a feminist politic, the first of these incursions into theory.[3] It set up a space of confusion, of being caught out, one in transition between feminisms and forms, processing forward with ideas about the body.

The barometric pressure drops and the rains fall: 1994. In the only patch of blue sky Leisa Shelton and Theatre is Moving were cutting out a pair of cat's trousers in *Steps 1*, February 1994. This season of short works included Anna Sabiel in collaboration with sound artist Peter Baxter and resonated like a clear chiming bell. Sabiel's focus was very strong, her task so specific as she unloaded the readings of her body by privileging the sound it made. Her body was suspended between suspended drums, suspended form, moving ladders, all subterranean, underneath articulation.

The 'girls' get caught out once again! In May 1994 there was a conference festival, '25 years of Performance Art' in collaboration with the Ivan Dougherty Gallery. A timely event: a summary of the great moments of performance art in Australia. Certainly, it was an extraordinary survey but its nostalgia for performance art's history seemed to be at the expense of its futures. Bizarrely, we all sat quietly when told that performance art had stopped happening when Mike Parr stopped doing it. I remember Barbara Campbell crying quietly at the forum table, silenced, despite her work's intense articulation (an installation of domestic objects connected to a female murderer). After Penny Thwaite completed her performance (a small dinghy on the floor, with Penny gripping the sides, feet splayed and rocking it, hard), someone from an earlier decade trivialised the work with supreme confidence, unable to appreciate all the complex resonances of the female hysteric's silence subverted in rockings and escapes, and symbolic drownings defeated by physical endurance. This disappearing act was redressed somewhat by an inspiring one-day conference, 'Performing Sexualities', convened by Peta Tait in July 1994, involving a number of presenters and introducing North American theorists Peggy Phelan on performance, Susan Bennett on audiences and Lynda Hart on lesbian identity.

The Post Arrivalists appeared in a storm and took over with their adolescent energy and focus. The mostly male group members expressed formidable confidence, and unquestionably the group marketed their shows brilliantly with stickers on every lamp-post. They locked us in and threw away the key. It became clear that year that things would never be the same again, as if versions of Australia's performance history were too different to co-exist in the same room and that we should go our own ways.

The winds come: 1995. The artists gathered momentum, rode the impetus and let it rip.

Nikki Heywood's *Creatures Ourselves*, January 1995, with the musical talents of Tony Backhouse and Garry Bradbury. Heywood boldly sets herself up as the mother of all mothers in a monumental costume with a cast of several nameless men which included performers Alan Schacher, Denis Beaubois, Ari Ehrlich, Tim Rushton and Jeffery Stein. Without rancour she places matriarchy in the middle. She sings and I squirm because her voice is so loud and her mouth is so big and she has so flagrantly, deliciously abandoned herself to it.

Four on the Floor involved four independent but known performers. Joel Markham, Dean Walsh, Deborah Pollard and Rosalind Crisp had all consistently been creating short performance works for Open Season, TPS's annual mid-year season open to newcomers. I remember Crisp's body work as a tantrum, a lunging, effortful, falling sequence. She was dressed in a strange linen trouser suit with padded shoulders that rose up as she moved. She finished with a dramatic footslam and a flourish as if wanting applause. She demanded it and she kept repeating the final sequence until she had it. Perhaps in another culture these four would have formed their own companies, buoyed up by the support of audiences and presenters, if not funding; but in Sydney, temporarily locked in an eddy of reduced expectations, this was the first time they had been able to get together – they toured the country.

The eye of the storm, the epicentre: 1996. This was the year of the solo female performer.

Club Bent, a two-week cabaret program of short rotating performances with lesbian, gay and queer appeal was held annually at TPS to coincide with the Sydney Gay and Lesbian Mardi Gras Festival in February. In 1996 Barbara Karpinski performed 'I'm Too Beautiful to be Lesbian'. The 'girls' in the audience went wild as Barbara stuffed her large breasts into a too-tight black corset, and became a moll doll with a fetish for dogs. She pastiched every bad American soapie with a quintessential 'take no prisoners' Aussie comic style. I cannot remember what she said now, but she made me laugh with relief that she could do it, and be that smart and we could enjoy her intelligence. Moira Finucane from Melbourne, assisted by Jackie Smith, started her one-woman monologues as Romeo in a transgender drag act. She was skilful and confrontational in her immaculately tight embodiment of males and females. Azaria Universe did a naked drag with her pearls, but with an energy in performance that was trance like – she was so loose she fell off the stage and into our open arms. There were unsung hero/ines at all these evenings who made them possible: our production manager Sherridan Green, in see-through black lace ruling with an iron fist; stage manager, Annette Dale; and sound and everything else, Mark Mitchell.

At 'A Progressive Dinner', TPS's seventh conference event, Catherine Fargher was a southern belle in a quaint, pretending way.

She led us gently into her story and then put the knife in as it twisted into a tale of abuse and incest. Sugar-sweet coatings with politics on the inside.

In *Fish out of Water*, July 1996, Deborah Pollard wrapped herself in an Indonesian sari, balanced wicker baskets on her head and teetered across a floor strewn with cups and saucers. Working with Margaret Bradley, Suhandi Kosasih, Nigel Kellaway, Simon Wise and Joel Markham, she gabbled her anxieties to the audience, her excruciating awareness of her position as a white woman in an Asian country, repelled and repulsive, terrorised and terrorising, in a post-colonial era. She puffed exhaustingly on clove cigarettes and as her anxiety level rose her speech broke down into a series of squeals and shrieks that betrayed the collapse of her inner world.

In *Face Value* October 1996, Kate Champion collaborated with artistic consultants Chris Ryan and Ros Hervey to create a slice of life. Designed by Russell Way with Mark Blackwell and Olivia Hines and lit by Neil Simpson and Geoff Cobham, the show set a cross-section of a house, where we saw Champion wonder what to wear, check the fridge, and get confused. I was bowled over that she had made her house, literally, and seemed so at home. This was dance theatre unafraid to finish the narrative.

Deborah Leiser was *Hungry* in September 1996. The show's music was by Elena Kats-Chernin and directed by Tanya Gerstle, with digital images from Michael Strum and set design by Tom Moore. Leiser tracked her Jewish histories, finding a place for herself in all. She was speaking from the set as a scroll and from her heart's unfolding.

The storm blows over, the winds lessen: 1997. This brought dispersal as performance became performative and mobile.

Lynette Wallworth dreamt up 'Big New Sites' which put performance artists on the cinema screens in front of big audiences. Vicki Spence was at the helm of those fantastic public arts events, the 'Solstice Suppers', which were ritual without the quackery, employing the culinary skills of Gay Bilson, the installations of Anne Grahame, the hard graft of Francesca Cathie. Julianne Pierce drew together extraordinary events from 'A Progressive Dinner' to 'Pacific Wave'; importantly, the first Australian contemporary performance event for performers with South Pacific Island backgrounds.

These are some of the extraordinary independent female artists I particularly remember making their mark, their move, during my time at TPS, although there were many more and there are so many more to come.

References

Burvill, Tom. 'Sidetrack Performance Group and the Post-Modern Turn'. *Our Australian Theatre in the 1990s*. Ed. Veronica Kelly. Amsterdam: Rodopi, 1998: 182-194.

Allen, Richard & Karen Pearlman, ed. *Performing the Unnameable: An Anthology of Australian Performance Texts*. Sydney: Currency/Real Time, 1999.

Notes

1 Artistic Directors/co-ordinators of TPS: Mike Mullins 1982-84, founding director Nicolas Tsoutas 1983-85, Barbara Campbell and Sarah Miller 1985, Allan Vizants 1986-87, Noelle Janaczewska 1987-89, Sarah Miller 1989-93, Angharad Wynne-Jones 1994-97, Zane Trow 1998, Fiona Winning 1999-.

2 For artistic statements and partial scripts for Entr'Acte, Sidetrack, Legs on the Wall and other groups like Kinetic Energy Theatre Company, see Allen & Pearlman, Burvill.

3 See The Party Line's *Appearing in Pieces* in Allen & Pearlman 87-92. It was directed by Gail Kelly, dramatist Peta Tait, composer/musical director Christine Evans; performers Edwina Entwisle, Brigid Kitchin, Kathryn Niesche, Simone O'Brien, Barbara Totterdell, and Celia White; visual design Elvis Richardson; costume design Amanda MacNamara; lighting designer Efterpi Soropos.

7.
Of fears and violent fantasies: performance and responsibility in Open City's **All That Flows**

Edward Scheer

> *In the dark I smell, my father, sweat and liniment. I'm four ... violets and piss and vanilla and shit and ... roses ...* (Gallasch, *All That Flows*)
>
> *It is the connection of desire to reality (and not its retreat into the forms of representation) that possesses revolutionary force.* (Foucault xiii-xiv)

What did Artaud mean when he said of Van Gogh that there was a state of consciousness in which there was nothing more to do except to 'pile up bodies'? (148). Perhaps he meant that we can only continue to talk of theatre in terms of terror, in the context of endless violence against bodies, in the name of politics and in the name of pleasure. Perhaps he was directing us to look at the intersection of these issues both in the theatres of war and in the theatres themselves; in the endless varieties of human and other bodies and how they are represented; to think at the same time of the tortured bodies piling up in the Balkans and the toned sleek bodies of the Australian image factories which theatre sometimes feeds. If one can speak of an Artaudian ethics it might consist of an ecstatic quest to stand outside oneself and one's culture and to root out what Foucault calls 'the fascism in us all, in our heads and in our everyday behaviour, the fascism that causes us to love power, to desire the very thing that dominates and exploits us' (Foucault xiii).

But how can we talk of performance and of fascism at the same time without sounding hysterical (remembering that this is now referred to as Histrionic Personality Disorder) or at least vaguely retrograde?[1] How can any performance deal with an issue without falling into didacticism or the superfluity of representations (narrative and character), let alone these issues of bodies in crisis and threatened collectivities? If we need to tell ourselves reassuring narratives then we will miss the potency of this interaction. Narrative is still the great aesthetic of disappearance of our time. It leads astray. It seduces but it is theatre without issue. Instead, I will look at a type of performance which allows a real-time confrontation between bodies to occur without the aesthetic distance of narrative or character-based theatre. We are, however, still talking about the 'in between' energies of a kind of entertainment (*entre-tien*), but above all we are talking about a theatre of 'interest', of *inter-esse,* situated between beings. A performance which implies the active presence of an audience and calls forth its response in a way which Samuel Weber, quoting Benjamin, refers to as the construction of 'groupings of interest' ('Scene and Screen' 31), suggests provisional transitional collectivities in crisis connected not in identity but through affinities and through the specific space/time of a performance: their own.

In the sense that an issue is political it concerns the possible and the communal, but perhaps for performance, it is not a thing. To take an issue as a thing is to represent, in other words to lose interest, the essential in-betweenness; it is to fetishise and eventually to seduce. It is to have one's mind made up on the substance of the issue in advance of the real-time confrontation with it that constitutes the performance. But we can say instead that in performance an issue derives from bodies, flows from them. The *Oxford English Dictionary* offers us outflows, outgoings, discharges, proceedings as issues. We might see that an issue for a performance flows from a body.

Responsibility

For Open City, namely Keith Gallasch and Virginia Baxter and their collaborators,[2] the primary flow is language. Language in its verbal, physical and gestural forms is an issue which has been of central importance to Open City in more than fifteen productions and various pieces for radio since their first performance at The Performance Space (TPS) in 1987. From early work like *Tokyo/Now/Thriller* (1987) and *Photoplay* (1988),[3] to their recent works *Talk Studio* (1996), *Promiscuous Spaces: Table Talk* (1996) and *Joke Joke* (1996) – the latter three comprise *Mondolingo,* a work exploring the state of Australian languages at the end of the millenium – Open City explores language through the articulations of conventional verbal exchange but also through antiphonies, the brushing of sound against word, the disjunction of a kind of secular catechism, calling forth a response. Open City relies on their audiences to be able to formulate a response ... to be responsible.

Does the verb 'to respond' have an opposite, Derrida wonders in 'Passions'? (15). Would this be not responding? Would this be silence? The performance persona[4] Virginia, says 'In fact you might note the variety of silences you'll hear tonight in *Tokyo Two*. Here's one now ...'[5] Open City opens these spaces in language, poses questions, invokes responses, releases a radical irresponsibility of language. In *Sum of the Sudden* (1993) obsessing about the name of a Hitchcock film, the performance persona, Keith, says 'I feel giddy. Let's forget it. It'll come back to you as soon as we stop talking about it.' This is followed by 'PAUSE'. Virginia says 'That doesn't work for me, I just stop breathing' (Open City, *Sum* 67). Later an injunction to 'stop talking!' closes the scene (68) . Silences were abreacted, called forth in a never-ending control exercise as if to reassure us that the dialogue can continue in the absence of a shattering truth, or that the interlocutor is still there on the other end of the line, or even that the self is still there at this end. For example, Keith: 'Hang up or I'll never speak to you again! ... Hello. Still here. Hello? All right don't talk ...' (69). It is a performing language rather than a communicating language. Consider the way Gallasch and Baxter's dialogues seem to question the dialogue itself, exerting no authorial responsibility for meaning but content to play language games, like Wittgenstein, but shifting the goalposts as they go. They construct the performance in the shape of a question about language and the body and suggest that bodies like language are also full of gaps, holes, noise and silence.

All That Flows

The performance *All That Flows* was an important early piece addressing the male body: its inner tides and moods; its hard contours and soft articulations; its screams and murmurings; its silence and responsiveness.[6] It considered the politics of the abject body in performance. In the program notes Gallasch describes the approach:

> Although drawing on myth and inspired by [Klaus] Theweleit, *All That Flows* comes primarily from the lives of its contributors and from the juxtapositions and intersections of their contributions, from male and female experiences of the male body ... It is a work for you the audience/guests at this performance/soiree, to wander through and take in. You can move through the design and the photographs, listen to recorded stories, follow the action closely or at a distance, take a break at any time and return to pick up the anecdotes, jokes and criss-crossing narratives of *All That Flows*. As

> always, Open City invites you to stay on after the performance to talk with us over a drink. (*All That Flows*)

So what happened to aesthetic distance; what happened to the character, the commodity, the text fetish, the oeuvre, the compulsory sedentary voyeurism of the theatre spectator? What have they done with the theatre? Victor Turner uses the notion of 'flow' to determine that state in theatrical performance in which the performers are in a kind of primary process, dreaming that they are in fact the roles they are playing. He insists on the essential value of 'flow' to the performance genre itself, arguing that 'the actors do not take part in the formulation of the author's messages; what they do is activate those messages by the "flow" quality of their performance – a flow that engages the audience as well, impressing on its members the "message" of the total production' (107). Ironically, in *All That Flows* nothing flowed in this sense of the term. The audience was constantly reminded of the secondary process involved in generating significance from events in reading and responding to them.

It was a Cagean approach to theatre based on looking and listening, and consists of broken vignettes, fragments of narrative and interrupted jokes. (Keith) Gallasch played 'Keith', who deals with his own physical presence by trying to make it disappear in a lather of jokes and truncated musings on the world of men and their bodies: 'having difficulty keeping the inside in and the outside out. But you don't want to hear any of that, do you? You wouldn't want to be within a mile of me if all that personal shit came rushing out ...' (*All That Flows*). He then launched into the one about the two oral hygienists at a funeral ... His jokes set up an aesthetic of disappearance, causing him to appear insubstantial in the world of the performance. Keith's stage presence, like Virginia's, was radically contingent. It was a pastiche of the persona, but unlike Virginia, whenever Keith allowed himself to be heard it must be ironic or not at all: 'Like to hear something profound? The whole world has become a gymnasium where men give the appearance of putting themselves back together again'.

How can such an irresponsible approach do justice to these issues and, more generally, to cultural demands tinged with a fascistic insistence for the perfect body? The title of Open City's piece was taken from a chapter in Theweleit's chilling two-volume study on the psychology of fascist murder, *Male Fantasies*. In the *All That Flows* program notes Gallasch articulates his interest in this text which:

> although it might not be great history, strikes responsive chords in the male reader. He [Theweleit] argues that men's fear of suppressed emotion is externalised into a fear of 'all that flows', especially of women who are seen as fluid, cyclical, emotional and therefore dangerous to male rectitude. This fear of the flood of emotions within oneself ['personal shit'] and without [women, homosexuals, foreigners] yields a simmering defensiveness or a violent hostility and a fear of eruption. (*All That Flows*)

This suggests that the piece is itself in the form of a response to Theweleit, rather than a reading of it or an attempt to embody it, for these issues represent only one particular strand of the argument in these books. *All That Flows* can be seen as an attempt by Open City to bring Theweleit's historicised observations into contact with quotidian Australian life in a way which both constructs a critique of modern (Australian?) male behaviour but also, and probably inevitably, attenuates some of the horrors in the books which relate to the specific history of pre-fascist Germany. I will sketch some of these and point to the way they might still be brought into contact with the Open City project.

Male fears and fantasies

Consider the Freikorps' fantasies that Theweleit describes:

> the fascist has two distinct and different masses in mind, two masses that stand in mutual opposition. The mass that is celebrated is strictly formed, poured into systems of dams. Above it there towers a leader (Fuhrer). To the despised mass, by contrast, is attributed all that is flowing, slimy, teeming. (*Male* II, 4)

The fascistic fear of all that flows is an interior realisation projected explosively onto the other. While the focus of *All That Flows* is on the variety of experiences – neurotic, athletic, erotic – of the male body, this essential message about the constituent elements of fascistic violence is preserved in the piece which makes it an important work, not only for the zeitgeist of the late 1980s and early 1990s with the intensification of debates around maleness and physicality in the age that claims to be post-feminist, but for the current political context which has seen a re-emergence of fascist rhetoric and brutal violence on a large scale. We can all think of the Balkans but Open City invite us to look closer.[7]

> KEITH: She'll be right. She'll be right. Maybe you did it. Maybe you bumped me off! It all falls into place. Not the women. Not the Asians ... you! The enemy's on the inside.

> Mate versus mate. You're opening the floodgates ... (*All That Flows*).

This text was addressed partly to himself, partly to the audience and partly to Zoran Kovic, a male dancer who has been manipulating Gallasch's body through this section of the piece. Kovic's actions shift between different registers of male comportment, from aggressive martial arts moves to graceful, fluid gestures. Kovic, as the dancer, represented the various possibilities for an expanded repertoire of male behaviours, the re-awakening of the male which the piece explored and which Keith nervously deferred by denouncing Kovic as a 'traitor' and a 'woman'. Eventually Keith broke away from Kovic and relocated his abjection in another false object:

> Its OK, mate. It's not you. It's them – the Asians, the endless flood of overpopulating immigrants. Don't go. You'll never make it. Tide's up. Keep calm. She'll be right. She'll be right. (*All That Flows*)

All That Flows raises a number of questions that contemporary Australia still needs to answer if we are to become responsible, to develop a capacity to formulate a response to our fears and the events which they trigger.

Australian fears and fantasies

In Pauline Hanson's notorious opening speech to Parliament in 1996 she used the phrase 'swamped by Asians' to express the fear of an undifferentiated mass which threatens to engulf an entity which must be, but no longer can be, clearly defined. This entity is the notion of middle Australia as an ethnically homogeneous constituency of disinherited battlers, underdogs and strugglers, suburban and ex-urban. The problem is that this is one of the spongiest referents around. Somewhat belatedly, Ernst Bloch says of the rise of 1930s fascism in Europe that 'Not all people live in the same Now' (Foster 188). The One Nation movement has realised that there is a crisis of representation and social evaluation for elements of Australia's constituency. This realisation has triggered a petulant discourse of damaged community – Bloch's 'primitive-atavistic 'participation mystique' (Foster 188) – to reconfirm a validity and identity denied by history and menaced by the immigration program drawing upon the Asian 'swamp'.

In the litany of anathematised substances which Theweleit lists the swamp figures prominently: 'someone was already lying in every morass or swamp you sank into. And since swamps became peaceful again afterward, since you couldn't tell how dangerous they were, it was easy for them to be seen as embodiments of deceptiveness' (*Male* I, 409). The swamp deceives, hiding the changes it makes to the geography, concealing the bodies it consumes without itself betraying any change: 'after they spill over a man or allow him to sink into themselves, their surfaces become calm again' (409).

To bring this imagery a little closer to home, think of the familiar uncanniness of the final scenes in Martin Scorsese's remake of *Cape Fear* when a demented Robert De Niro reappears from the swamp he has sunk into to threaten the family unit all over again. In a way, the primal fear of the oedipal triad, that it will sink into the undifferentiated swamp of anti-social criminality, is also the fear of Oedipus himself: *aphanisis* the disappearance of the 'I', the terror of a history that does not include the self that one thinks is one's own. One's own life has been lived by an imposter who failed to recognise his own parents, his own country, etc. And if, in the tradition of Freud's uncanny and the tradition of the theatre, one is more than one and is hybrid, as Sophocles suggests, then the possibility of the hybrid must be extinguished in symbolic castration, as in Theweleit's white terror, in permanent war.

Hybridity

Samuel Weber has argued that truly hybrid forms caused the Greeks considerable consternation in Aristotle's time, and that the mixing of genre and media in certain performances provoked a state of 'theatrocracy' in which the audience riotously took control of the event. The type of theatrocracy which Open City invite is not an anarchic or Dionysian explosion but a transferred power to interrogate and question, to reflect and to respond.

Open City's work consciously constructs the hybrid form with a mix of text, choreographed movement, photography, video, sampled noise and live percussive music. It is a hybrid with aerated spaces and imaginative rooms in which an audience may get lost and find itself again. It constructs an imaginary audience as there are multiple points of focus; audience reactions are not necessarily linked to individual acts or moments. In the gaps between scenes, the audience can bodily recover and breathe again. In this aspect of the work Open City produces a writing event of bodies which supposes that breaks in the habitual/quotidian perception of an event, and provokes heightened states in which bodies can be re-acquired in new ways. The silences in Open City's work operate as an aesthetic which is strategically and not accidentally produced, such as in the pauses between movements in a music recital in which members of the audience cough and blow their noses.

Hybridity, disappearance and the empowerment of the audience are the keys to an expectation of a performativity of response and interest, and to the generation of a general responsibility which breeds something other than the production of death, perhaps even the production of desire. To turn again to the images of hybridity in Theweleit is to return to a theatre of death articulated through the most banal forms of production, the most natural forms turned monstrous. Theweleit's anathematised substances were defined by 'their ability to flow and their hybrid status' (*Male* I, 409). He notes 'the soldier male's intense fear of the hybrid' and suggests that this springs from an experience of the soldier's own body:

> At some point, his bodily fluids must have been negativized to such an extent that they became the physical manifestations of all that was terrifying. Included in this category were all of the hybrid substances that were produced by the body and flowed on, in, over and out of the body.' (409)

He lists some of these effects in a manner which tries to convey a sense of how they were experienced by the soldier males. This is one of the most disturbing aspects of these books, the way he tries to bring these horrors closer to the reader, to provoke the realisation that these crimes, however historically specific, were not committed by monsters or freaks, not by the Other, but by people not unlike ourselves.

The criminal violence which spatters the pages of Theweleit's books is diffused in *All That Flows* into the neurotic murmurs of low-level guilt. In either case, the level of violence is not reducible to loss of language – the Freikorps diaries and journals that form the archive for Theweleit's study attests to that – though it is a killing language, a way of paralysing the world through the signifier. But a certain type of language, what we might call the language of laughter or unbinding, is nowhere in evidence in Theweleit.[8] These playful unbinding energies were alive in the words of the players in *All That Flows*. Towards the end of the text, stage directions tell us that:

> Keith's desire is suppressed. He rattles off a list of masturbation terms: Pull your rope. Shine your pole. Shoot the tadpoles. Slam your hammer. Slam your spam. Spank the monkey. Strike the pink match. Stroke the dog. Stroke your poker. Talk with Rosy Palm and her five little sisters. Tickle your pickle. Unclog the pipes. Varnish your pole.

Wank. Wonk your corker. Yank your yam. Yank your crank.
(*All That Flows*)

Language flows into the blockage and unleashes laughter rather than violence. Given the subject matter it is both a balm and, as Kristeva says 'an irruption of the drives against symbolic prohibition' (222). Language is used to remind the body of its impulses, not to bury them as in Theweleit. It puts the senses into communication again.

Short talk: for fear of the news

For fear of the news
He has become afraid
Of the television
and the telephone

The daily dead
Flicker by, shock by shock
soulless on the TV

The disembodied
Address him on the 'phone
With 'Is that you? Did you hear ...?'

He has enough Bosnias of his own he says
He too, he says, is an innocent victim
(although not a woman or a child)

He has learned, like you, to keep his finger on
the remote at all times,
Like you he has learned, when the phone rings
At all times, to answer: 'I can't come to the
'phone right now but if you leave your name and
number I'll get back to you.' (*All That Flows*)

Walter Benjamin (217) attempts the rescue of both technology and the senses from the fascist aestheticisation of politics and its spectacles of seductive power. This is essentially about the uses of film which Benjamin links to '[m]an's need to expose himself to shock effects' as a form of 'adjustment to the dangers threatening him' (252). He argues that 'film has taken the physical shock effect out of the wrappers in which dadaism had, as it were, kept it inside the moral shock effect'

(240). Benjamin calls for a critical use of technology to counter the crippling 'self-alienation' of mankind which he says has 'reached such a degree that it can experience its own destruction as an aesthetic pleasure of the first order' (244). As the smart missiles with cameras attached rained down on Belgrade, who has not been implicated in this thrill of the destruction of bodies?

These images need a new context, but I wonder if we have not become used to the cinematic medium? The performance art of the 1960s and 1970s was a reaction to just this problematic outlined by Benjamin, but inverted so that it is film, even with its animation of the optical unconscious, which has diminished the shock effect in a moral wrapping and performance and returned it to the audience. (The shock effect was inaugurated by the Dadas and, ironically given Benjamin's critique of their war mongering, by the Futurists as well.) The question was and is: how to shock the senses back into a state of alertness, of awareness? How to counter this self-alienation which enjoys its own destruction and which, in Benjamin's time and again in our own, fascism is rendering aesthetic?

Susan Buck-Morss has tried to answer this question with her notion, through Benjamin, of the reinvention of the 'synaesthetic system' where external sense perceptions come together with the internal images of memory and anticipation as the basis for an analysis of aesthetic experience. This could operate as an antidote to the 'alienation of the corporeal sensorium' that fascism 'manages' (3). Buck-Morss calls for *Aisthesis* or the sensory experience of perception to be restored to the field of Aesthetics and that thereby the construction of modern man as 'an asensual, anaesthetic protuberance' may begin to be undone (8). She registers this rethinking of the aesthetic dimension as a 'discourse of the body' and notes that while the body's experience of cinema is often anaesthetised, it is also the case that the instinctual power of the body's senses can be restored through the experience of cinema. This latter potential of the cinematic image to reactivate the senses I would argue, is even more strongly evident in the real time confrontation between bodies that constitutes performance.

As in Benjamin, Open City's performances can be read as a return to the 'synaesthetic system', to the discourses of the body as the ground upon which all our aesthetic reflections are constituted. But their work is not an anachronistic search for a pre-technological experience of the body, or for an organic unity. *All That Flows* exhibited a multimedia approach, merging photographic images with video and sampled digital sound, dance with dialogue and percussive live sounds. It produced the essential disjunctions in the space but also established connections through a plethora of mirrors, springs and frames with the bodies in the audience and called forth their responses. Flowing around these shock effects are the signifiers of the synaesthetic. In *All That Flows*, photographs by Sandy Edwards and Pam Kleeman showed naked fathers and sons embracing one another. The penultimate scene in this piece staged the merging of the senses and the touching of multiple bodies, imaginary, sensual, bodies of interest, between beings. The script recalls:

> KEITH: In the dark I hear your eyelids, ears, armpits, anus, lips, nipples whisper their smell, vanilla, sweat, violets, roses, rose, warm roses...
>
> VIRGINIA: Around your toes, sweet animal smell. Whoops! dark in here. Parsley and piss. There's a pulse running through your body just under the skin.
>
> KEITH: In the dark I touch your afterglow. I shed my old skin under the new moon. My new skin is warm, moist, electric, the little circuits tick electronic again, each cellular memory ticking over, ticking over, over, over ...
>
> VIRGINIA: ... A woman is swimming around inside the lining of your coat and then, out through a seam and close as she can get, under the cool, between your legs, sticky sweet, around, under in and out ...
>
> KEITH: I rise up, a faint glow, thirsty for you, hungry for roses ...
>
> VIRGINIA: And while for her you are smell and touch, she can't see you. She's like a ribbon pulled smoothly and lightly through the arm of your coat, wrapping around your body, her head at your head, her tail at your foot. And then ... she's out through the top of your collar, across your mouth, around your neck and out, eye to eye.

References

Artaud, Antonin. 'Van Gogh: The Man Suicided by Society.' Trans. Mary Beach & Lawrence Ferlinghetti. *Artaud Anthology*. Ed. Jack Hirschman. San Francisco: City Lights, 1965.

Benjamin, Jessica & Anson Rabinbach. Foreword. In Klaus Theweleit, *Male Fantasies* II: 1-xxiii.

Benjamin, Walter. *Illuminations*. Ed. Hannah Arendt, & Harry Zohn. Schocken Books: New York, 1968: 217-252.

Buck-Morss, Susan. 'Aesthetics and Anaesthetics: Walter Benjamin's Artwork Essay Reconsidered.' *October* 62 (Fall 1992): 3-42.

Derrida, Jacques. *'Passions' in On the Name*. Ed. Thomas Dutoit, trans. David Wood, John. P. Leavey Jr. & Ian McLeod. California: Stanford UP, 1995.

Foucault, Michel. Preface. *Anti-Oedipus: Capitalism and Schizphrenia*. By Gilles Deleuze & Felix Guattari. Trans. Robert Hurley, Mark Seem & Helen Lane. Minneapolis: U of Minnesota P, 1983.

Foster, Hal. *Compulsive Beauty*. Cambridge, Mass: MIT Press, 1993.

Kristeva, Julia. *Revolution in Poetic Language*. Trans. Leon S. Roudiez. New York: Columbia UP, 1984.

Open City. *Sum of the Sudden. Performing the Unnameable*. Ed. Richard Allen & Karen Pearlman. Sydney: Currency Press/Real Time, 1999: 61-68.

— *All That Flows*. Unpublished ts., 1990.

Silverman, Kaja. *Male Subjectivity on the Margins*. London: Routledge, 1992.

Theweleit, Klaus. *Male Fantasies: Volume I. Women, Floods, Bodies, History*. Trans. Stephen Conway, Erica Carter & Chris Turner. Cambridge: Polity, 1987.

— *Male Fantasies: Volume II. Male Bodies: Psychoanalysing the White Terror*. Trans. Stephen Conway, Erica Carter & Chris Turner. Cambridge: Polity, 1989.

Turner, Victor. *The Anthropology of Performance*. New York: PAJ, 1986.

Weber, Samuel. 'Scene and Screen: Electronic Media and Theatricality. Unpublished ts. University of Sydney, 1998.

— Lecture. School of Theatre, Film and Dance, University of New South Wales, Sydney. 20 August 1998.

Notes

1 I want to take Benjamin at his word when he says we should take seriously the image of the angel of history walking backwards into the future. Nor should we flinch from the pile of detritus forming at its feet. In this article I invoke Benjamin as the angel and the detritus of fascism as two polarities of a discourse on male violence, performance and responsibility.

2 Open City are a Sydney based performance entity founded by writer/publisher/performers Keith Gallasch and Virginia Baxter. A number of their performances involve collaborations with a changing team of performance-makers. Gallasch and Baxter have also created award-winning works for radio and since 1994 have been the publishers of the national bi-monthly arts tabloid *Real Time*.

3 This was a solo work by Gallasch and was in some ways a prelude to the piece I am looking at here, although it approaches the masking of masculinity in different ways.

4 References to Keith and Virginia indicate their performance personae.

5 *Tokyo Two* (1992) was a revised performance of *Tokyo/Now/Thriller* (1987). Quotes are taken from unpublished texts made available to the author, except for *Sum of the Sudden*.

6 *All That Flows* artistic production team at TPS, August 1990. Writers and performers, Keith Gallasch and Virginia Baxter; musician/composer of 'Moon Stories', 'Telling Time by Passing Clouds', and 'Boo Bam' music, Robert Lloyd; black and white photography, Sandy Edwards; colour photography, Pam Kleemann; dancer, Zorah Kovic; choreographer, Julie-Anne Long; jackets,

Frances Joseph; musician, Leigh Giles; Downing Men Stories, Tony MacGregor, Audiodrift (Virginia Madsen and Tony MacGregor), sound; designer, mixed media constructions, Michael Geissler and Stefan Kahn; lighting design and technical co-ordination, Simon Wise.

7 Also see Silverman. She provides one way of explaining the different registers of these works by pointing out that the war situation in which the Freikorps operated constitutes a specific 'historical trauma' in which the threat of dissolution which terrified these men can be contextualised to a certain extent. However Silverman also acknowledges 'the centrality of the discourse of war to the construction of conventional masculinity' (62). This is an argument which accords with Gallasch's use of Theweleit's text in *All That Flows*.

8 'The purpose of this writing is to combat the aliveness of experience, to turn it into something lifeless.' See Benjamin & Rabinbach (xxiii).

8.
Real men don't wear shirts: presenting masculinity in professional wrestling

Sharon Mazer

'I want all you Pillsbury doughboys out there to shut up and take a good long look at a *real* man.' This, give or take a few choice insults, was Ravishing Rick Rude in the late eighties and early nineties, accosting the audience before dropping his brilliantly sequined robe to reveal a perfect bodybuilder's body, and lycra tights painted with the image of his opponent's face over his crotch. Rude, in his self-presentation at least, was a 'real' man, even or perhaps especially when he resorted to cheating in order to win. His performances in the World Wrestling Federation were paradigmatic of professional wrestling's celebratory and hyperbolic, yet often contradictory, messages about masculinity. They conflated burlesque with force and juxtaposed his hyperdeveloped 'hard' body with feathers and sequins reminiscent of Gorgeous George. His body was presented as an artifact of maleness, embodying the results of years of hard work, at once disciplined and excessive, and his poses were presented simultaneously for admiration and contempt. He marked his victories first by one 'rude awakening' – in which, after choke-holding his opponent into unconsciousness, he gyrated his hips over the other man's face – and then another, in which after kissing a woman into unconsciousness, he gyrated over her face. As a 'cock of the walk' Rick Rude displayed his mastery over men and women alike in an aggressive conflation of the masculine and feminine, of straight and gay aesthetic, of power and obscenity. He was a 'heel' with heat. Fans hated him and debated his performances with astonishing vehemence, but they came to the arenas in droves expressly to see him as well as his peers in the days when the World Wrestling Federation was hot, and the World Championship Wrestling was not.

What is a 'real' man? In professional wrestling as in life, the signs by which one can recognise a 'real' man and the differences between men are not necessarily fully visible or stable. It's not as clear as it first appears. The wrestling event is built upon assumptions of irreconcilable differences between men, but what one man ultimately faces in the ring is an 'other' man more like himself than not. What underlies and belies the rhetoric of difference – the wrestlers' challenges and grudges, femme and butch performances – is a mirror effect which reflects essential sameness between opponents and spectators. What distinguishes and divides two men in the ring is ultimately superficial, the difference between a flip of the hip and a flick of a toothpick. In the ring, any man can be a 'real' man, no matter how superficially feminine or lacking in virtue. A 'real' man may break the rules of the game or the society, or he may attempt to uphold them; for that matter, he may appear not to take the conflict – or rather, his opponent – seriously at all. Regardless, he will appear to struggle to prove himself to the bitter end, even if it appears to cost him the contest and a bit of machismo.

In wrestling the 'real' man is not necessarily the good guy (or babyface) who stands for the community against the bad guy (or heel). Nor is the 'real' man necessarily the one who wins. He's not even necessarily the man who performs the masculine ideal against a more feminised opponent. Even the first and most famous femme wrestler, Gorgeous George, was a 'real' man, at least when he momentarily dropped the drag to drop kick his opponent into oblivion. And Ricky Starr – a little guy in ballet slippers who consistently defeated his much bigger, brutish opponents as much with sexual taunting as with his fast moves – was much loved by his audiences, male and female alike, despite or perhaps because of his camp performance. All wrestlers swagger, strut and show, boast and bully. All eventually get down to all-out wrestling, hitting and being hit, climbing and falling, apparently struggling to the limits of their endurance regardless of the apparent wear and tear on their bodies. Once it is understood that the finishes are fixed – what wrestlers perform is a conflict in which the outcome has been predetermined by the promoter – it becomes possible to read in the wrestling performance a conflict in which belts and titles are not so much contested and affirmed as are definitions and expressions of masculinity.

Professional wrestling's first transgression is that it violates the sporting principle of a fair fight, that is, what is performed is not 'real' wrestling. Its next is that, while appearing to pit 'real'men against 'not-so-real'men, the wrestling performance is underscored with an idea that all men – at least in the ring – are potentially 'real'. There is, after all, always a new challenge to be issued, another chance for a wrestler to reclaim his claim to the masculine ideal. Every professional wrestling event thus offers every man, whether performer or fan, a test of his manliness. The wrestler takes the opportunity to prove himself directly in action, while from the stands, the fan has the chance to see himself mirrored in the range of masculinities presented, to participate in judging the relative masculinity of other men, and to reassure himself of one certainty: at least he is not a woman.

The conventional signs of femininity and masculinity are both medium and message in the wrestlers' closet, visibly encoded into everything from the wrestlers' names and costumes, to their bodies and signature moves. To some degree, a professional wrestler is always in drag, always enacting a parody of masculinity at the same time that he epitomises it. Professional wrestling is often accused of selling its audience – particularly the young pre- and just-adolescent men who are its most fervent fans and target consumers – a model of manhood which is at once vulgar, violent, and sexually suspect in its sometimes lurid heterosexism and barely suppressed homoeroticism: elements which are abundantly apparent at the more pornographic end of the wrestling economy.

With its extravagant displays of feathers and fights, professional wrestling does indeed appear to pit an anti-masculine, or at least an ambivalently masculine, aesthetic and ethos against one that is hyper-masculine. Its excessive male-body-centered performances confront and confound prohibitions limiting such displays to women, and as a result, appear simultaneously to subvert and to legitimise the very idea(l) of the American man. Yet, despite its apparent transgressions – and even though women are always visible in the margins and in the audience – professional wrestling is always a performance by men, for men, about men. Both its aesthetics and its ethos are explicitly centered on the idea of masculinity as something at once essential and performed.

From cute to brute, the types of man represented in the squared circle are, at first glance, extraordinarily diverse and by no means mutually exclusive or discrete. The flamboyant parodic femininity of a Gorgeous George or a Goldust intersects with the comic-book drag of an Undertaker or a Mountie or a Kamala or an Ultimate Warrior, and collides with the rocker/outlaw machismo of a Randy Savage or a (post-Rockers) Shawn Michaels or a Rowdy Roddy Piper or a Razor Ramon, all of which doubles back and confronts itself more or less out of drag in the apparently earnest masculinity of a Tatanka, a Hulk Hogan, or even a Vince McMahon. And then there are the Bushwackers – Kiwi blokes American style, gap-toothed, hairy and dirty, swilling beer and shovelling food into and at each other, little guys who overpower their opponents with apparently clumsy oddball moves, cheerful mates whose performance is always the most apparently stupid the moment before they get smart and win.

Superficially, it appears that the truth about men is that they are so antagonistically individuated that, despite extolling the virtues of a brotherhood of men, in practice they cannot come within sixteen or eighteen feet of one another without coming to blows. Superficially, it appears that 'real' men are American patriots – or the foreign equivalent – who, when they fight for a title also fight for truth, justice and the American way. They don't fight selfishly, only for themselves – as Lex Luger put it during his radical face turn in the early 1994 – but for 'all of America.' Superficially, it appears that the only certain thing is that 'real' men – or at least masculine versions – wear fewer sequins and less makeup than 'not-so-real' men – or feminine versions – and they tend not to worry about their hair so much.

But for all that wrestling displays the antagonism of difference, it also, and I believe more importantly, affirms what it is these men have in common: that is, that they are men. What is at stake in the squared circle in each individual performance, and what is sold to as well as celebrated with the audience, is nothing less than an underlying idea(l) of a community of men whose differences are always to be understood as superficial, a kind of drag overlay on an essential masculinity. Wrestling fan and cultural critic Angela Carter recognises: 'The "mask" or persona of the wrestler bears no connection at all to his actual prowess' (228). That is, the proof of the man is not in his appearance, which he manipulates for his own and our pleasure. The proof of the man is in the force and skill he applies, whether he wins or loses, with and against other men. When Gorgeous George stops patting his hair and grapples with Larry Moquin, when Ricky Starr stops his pirouettes and rides Karl von Hess until the apparently more powerful man squirms helplessly on the floor, when Mr Perfect pursues Lex Luger out of the arena and takes a beating from the waiting gang, when Hulk Hogan raises himself bleeding from Randy Savage's chokehold, when Shawn Michaels pulls himself from the floor in a last, futile attempt to avert Razor Ramon's reach for the championship, what is made visible is nothing less than manliness itself, the will and spirit of a 'real' man as it underlies and transcends both character and circumstance, latent (if not immediately apparent) in all men.

In professional wrestling, masculinity is presented and contested in a way that appears to mirror and affirm American ideology about 'real' men. The babyface represents the real man, earnest standard carrier for the rules and the community's dominant values. The heel is the rule-breaker who plants himself in opposition to the crowd, and as such literally and visibly the cheat and the fake, the not-so-real man. That is, superficially, the babyface is a kind of literal embodiment of the masculine ideal, which the heel parodies, critiques and ultimately exposes as impossible. As in the medieval carnival that Bakhtin idealises, professional wrestling celebrates an idea of communality alongside the rogue's

> right to be 'other' in this world, the right not to make common cause with any single one of the existing categories that life makes available; none of these categories quite suits them, they see the underside and the falseness of every situation. Therefore they can exploit any position they choose, but only as a mask (*Dialogic* 159).

What the wrestlers celebrate with the audience is the freedom as men to create themselves anew with every match, to act the hero or the villain, the purist or the cheat, the manly or the not-so-manly man at will. Even the performance of emasculation is ultimately just that, a performance.

Professional wrestling's play of masculinity is thus profoundly carnivalesque as it affirms and mocks, celebrates and critiques prevailing definitions of what it is to be a 'real' man in contemporary American culture. Because it is centered on, and always returns to, the display of male bodies, and because the action is both a simulation and a parody of violence between men, the performance is always highly ambivalent and profoundly transgressive, at once hypervisible and hyper-masculine. They are simultaneously like real men – those watching, for example – and larger than life. Wrestlers are often simply enormous, big of body and loud of voice. They proclaim unyielding enmity, yet their apparently fierce blows rarely cause serious injury and seem, in the end, as mocking of themselves as their challenges are of each other. They flaunt their enlarged and excessively developed bodies in exaggerated costumes which are drawn from, and elaborations of, cultural stereotypes: the Macho Latino, the Boy Toy, the Ghetto Blaster, the Native American, the Nature Boy, the Biker, the Surfer, the Dancer, the Trucker, the Preacher, the Professor, the Tax Man and the Undertaker. Often their names insinuate an exaggerated sexuality and imply the type of sexual insults more appropriate perhaps to the burlesque stage than to the sports arena: Gorgeous George, Rowdy Roddy Piper, Ravishing Rick Rude, Brutus Beefcake, Jake the Snake, and so on.

The action at the heart of the wrestling event is simple and predictable, as ritualised as Sunday Mass, as temporal and celebratory as Mardi Gras, and as much a rite of passage as a Bar Mitzvah or, perhaps more to the point, the kind of primal masculinist rites envisioned by Robert Bly in which 'older men welcome the younger into the ancient, mythologised, instinctive male world' (15); literally in many cases, given that wrestling has a high proportion of older wrestlers, and its fans are predominantly younger. One after the other, men appear to test their strength and wits against each other in a highly codified pattern of give-and-take, which requires a period of loss and humiliation regardless of outcome. Professional wrestling's spectacle of domination and submission offers its audiences a ritually circumscribed and performed test of manhood that is resolved in a climactic scene of reversal and recognition in which one man holds another (apparently disabled and as such at least temporarily emasculated) man to the floor while he is judged the victor. What is at stake is more than the immediate loss or victory. The stability of the world order is embodied by these men. When they confront each other, the world is temporarily cast into disorder. When the good guy wins, the world – or at least the fans – celebrates with him.

In his discussion of what he calls 'carnival culture' James Twitchell recognises the medievalism in wrestling's contemporary joust: 'True, the knights and giants have been democratised and unionised. They no longer play the parts of princes-in-training and ersatz giants but are street-smart working men, bellowing braggarts, trend-setting macho fashion plates, and greedy capitalists – all images drawn from the day-to-day world of the audience' (226). As in the Middle Ages, however, in the world of wrestling the surfaces of a character may be all, but it is not as it seems. A hero may reveal himself as a villain over time. An apparent 'sissy' may indeed demonstrate his moral and physical fortitude under duress. Like Bakhtin's rogues, clowns and fools, the wrestlers 'create around themselves their own special little world [which is] connected with that highly specific, extremely important area of the square where the common people congregate.' (*Dialogic* 159). They are simultaneously real and not-real:

> one cannot take them literally because they are not what they seem .... Their existence is a reflection of some other's mode of being – and even then, not a direct reflection. They are life's maskers; their being coincides with their role, and outside this role they simply do not exist (159).

What the wrestling performance offers the audience is both recognition and license, in Bakhtin's words:

> In the struggle against conventions, and against the inadequacy of all available life-slots to fit an authentic human being, these masks take on an extraordinary significance. They grant the right not to understand, the right to confuse, to tease, to hyperbolize life; the right to parody others while talking, the right not to be taken literally, not to 'be oneself' ... the right to act life as a comedy and to treat others as actors, the right to rip off masks, the right to rage at others with a primeval (almost cultic) rage – and finally, the right to betray to the public a personal life, down to its most private and prurient little secrets. (*Dialogic* 163)

Despite – or indeed because of – wrestling's exaggeration and exploitation of cultural stereotypes, what the event celebrates is not a reiteration but rather an unleashing of social inhibitions on masculine and masculinist expression, from the hyper-masculine to the apparently feminine. The wrestling event is transgressively ambivalent, a carnival performance that – again in Bakhtinian terms – is simultaneously 'gay, triumphant, and at the same time mocking, deriding. It asserts and denies, it buries and revives' (*Rabelais* 12-13). The masculinity represented therein is likewise both idealised and mocked, disrespected and valorised. As it is essentialised, located in his body, and as its potential is realised and elaborated upon in action, a man's masculine identity is not constrained by the social order. Because he is a man, any man from Gorgeous George to Hulk Hogan can play the man, if, when and how he chooses.

Instead of offering fans a presentation of masculinity that is singular and conservative, each wrestling match presents two or more contradictory possibilities poised against and co-existing with one another. Masculinity is both a choice and an essence, simultaneously an option and an imperative. While the professional wrestling performance always presents a version of masculinity that is sanctioned by the dominant culture, its presentation of alternative masculinities as concurrent proposes a community of men that is inclusive of a wide range of identities and behaviours, and as such heterogeneous rather than homogenous. Rather than prescribing limitations to masculine behaviour – as is the case with other more 'real' sports practices – professional wrestling recognises the official version at the same time that it acknowledges and, it might be argued, even encourages the unleashing of masculine expressivity in all forms. It is no wonder, then, that professional wrestling is remembered so fondly by so many American men as a key part of their adolescent transition into adult masculine expression and sexuality, a step toward understanding themselves as men among other men. When documentary maker Clifton Jolley remembers his fourteen-year-old self's fascination with Gorgeous George, he remembers that the wrestler was 'free to do and act any way he wanted'. Indeed, my teaching assistant at New York University once commented that wrestling magazines preceded *Playboy* as secret pleasures to be hidden from the displeasure of his parents when he was eleven or twelve.

I do not mean to normalise the transgressive potential of professional wrestling's presentation of the continuum of masculine performance. Quite the contrary. Beyond the freedom to present the self in a wide range of masculine personae are two underlying issues which are expressly at odds with, and I believe, genuinely subversive of the masculine, heterosexual ideal – which may or may not be the same as the masculine real. Both are obvious and yet unaccounted for in most discussions of wrestling. It's not a fair fight, and the men touch and hold each other in ways that are not necessarily violent.

In order to perform a fight, wrestlers cannot fight for 'real'. In order for the audience to see the fight as a fight, the wrestlers must pace their moves, create spaces between and then hold each other for us to look. This simple reality of the performance carries with it a fundamental problem for new wrestlers. How can one prove his machismo when the first thing he must learn to do is to give ground, to take the hits and bumps as performed by the other guy, and to lose the match if and as ordered? He must, that is, learn to co-operate with the man he is positioned against. To be successful – to pull audiences and be offered another contract – they must construct the fight together, pull their punches, hit the floor instead of each other and show pain when none is felt. They must be intimate and opposite at the same time.

As wrestler turned scholar Laurence De Garis comments, professional wrestling's status as a suspect, transgressive sport is rooted in amateur wrestling's exceptionally high level of extended physical contact between men, that is to the idea of 'grappling'itself. De Garis notes 'Wrestlers, both amateur and professional are often questioned about engaging in close physical contact with members of the same sex, especially while barely clothed.' And he recalls that as a high school and collegiate wrestler his own response was: 'It's not gay, it's kicking ass' (*Professional Wrestling* 3). This denial is evident in the ways in which the wrestlers learn to work with each other. In the workouts at Gleason's Gym, lessons in developing and managing a wrestler's body always implicitly include learning how to channel and/or deny sexual as well as violent impulses. Paradoxically, the wrestlers learn to touch without touching, to be touched without being touched, to deny what is there for everyone to see in their physical expression, acts which are loving as well as violent.

Wrestling is poised at what Kenneth Dutton in his discussion of the male body beautiful calls the point of 'hesitation between admiration and attraction' (66). Both the practice and the performance of professional wrestling may be viewed as simultaneously homophobic and homoerotic – what De Garis terms 'homosensual' (E-mail, 23 Dec. 1996). The contract is simple, and yet not so, in De Garis' words: 'If I give you my body, you'd better respect it' (E-mail, 24 Dec. 1996). The lesson in how to be with other men is intimately connected with the lesson on how to be a man. In the wrestling performance sexuality is always co-mingled with violence. The central visual image is the apparently conflictual but actually mutual embrace of two men. What we see repeatedly as the struggle reaches its resolution is one man mounting, or attempting to mount, the prone body of another. Emasculation or love? Sometimes it's hard to know the difference.

There was a woman wrestler – Sky Magic – at Gleason's in New York for most of the last year I was there. She had come to wrestling from competitive bodybuilding, hoping to increase her earnings so that she could quit her day job as a graphic designer. By the time I left New York for Christchurch, New Zealand, she had vanished. When I asked De Garis recently what had happened to Sky, he told me that she'd gone on to kickboxing because 'wrestling wasn't macho enough for her' (E-mail, 24 Dec. 1996). Perhaps she was right.

References

This essay has been adapted from *Professional Wrestling: Sport and Spectacle* (University Press of Mississippi, 1998). It was presented at the annual meeting of the Australasian Drama Studies Association at Waikato University in 1998. Many of the ideas offered here first appeared in 'The Doggie Doggie World of Professional Wrestling', *The Drama Review* 34:4. (Winter 1990), and have been developed in discussions with Richard Schechner, Larry De Garis, Vernon Andrews, Jessica Johnston, Carol Martin, and Peter Falkenberg.

Bakhtin, M. M. *The Dialogic Imagination: Four Essays*. Ed. Michael Holquist, trans. Caryl Emerson & Michael Holquist. Austin: U of Texas P, 1981.

– *Rabelais and His World*. Trans. Hélène Iswolsky. Bloomington: Indiana UP (1984).

Bly, Robert. *Iron John: A Book about Men*. Reading, Mass.: Addison-Wesley, 1990.

Carter, Angela. 'Giants' Playtime'. *New Society* 29 (January 1976): 227-228.

De Garis, Laurence A. A. 'Professional Wrestling's Commercial Exploitation of Homophobia'. Paper presented at the annual NASSS Conference, Birmingham, Ala., 1996.

— E-mail to the author, 23 December 1996.

— E-mail to the author, 24 December 1996.

Dutton, Kenneth R. *The Perfectible Body: The Western Ideal of Physical Development*. London: Cassell, 1995.

Jolley, Clifton. *I Remember Gorgeous George*. PBS Special, prod. & dir. Clifton Jolley. n.d.

Twitchell, James B. *Carnival Culture: The Trashing of Taste in America*. New York: Columbia UP, 1992.

9.
The unclassic body

Adrian Kiernander

Throughout much of the twentieth century in Australia, theatre on the English model, or what was perceived and valued as English in the outposts of Empire, has frequently privileged spoken English over other forms of language, verbal and non-verbal. In theatre reviews of plays by Shakespeare in Sydney into the late 1960s the voice was supreme, even though it was frequently considered deficient in the mouths of Australian actors. The body was almost always invisible, or at least meaningless and outside the bounds of normal theatrical commentary, except in as much as it reinforced or violated the classical (and phallic) ideal.

The actor Leonard Teale was savaged for the unclassical and flaccid use of his voice and body as Macbeth in 1957. Performing in a dramatic role which was perceived as noble, Teale was criticised for 'a "dinkum Aussie" nasality', and an inclination 'to slouch about the stage with the slovenly air of one not prepared to be uppity about the distinctions that might be expected of a general and a king' (Browne 1957, 4). In contrast, the actors playing Banquo and Ross were commended for 'being able to communicate by deportment and diction that *Macbeth* is a play of big men in big events'. Any explicit praise for an actor's physicality is typically expressed in terms of erect deportment, as in Bruce Beeby's 1950 portrayal of Brutus 'with an excellence of bearing throughout' (Browne 9 Oct. 1950, 4).

On some rare occasions a violation of the physical ideal was allowed, indeed seen as appropriate and worthy of favourable comment, especially when it coincided with a deliberate rejection of vocal purity in the depiction of villainy, as in John Alden's 1950 portrayal of a racially marked Shylock

> as warped in body as in mind. The fingers work as undecided between acquisitiveness and strangling. The dark face lights up now and again with a keen or malevolent flash of the eyes. This Shylock so rarely looks at those he addresses; they must measure him by the speech which comes, ungainly and ugly

> with ghetto accent, lunging from his heavy lips. (Browne 3 Mar. 1950, 2)

It is difficult to see anything other than an acceptance of blatant racist stereotyping in this unusual approval of so radical a departure from the physical and vocal ideal.

One of the most significant contributions that the prominent Australian actor and director John Bell has made to the development of theatre in Australia since 1970 has been his success in focusing theatre practice away from its previous dependence on the voice, and towards an awareness of the body that produces and comments on it. In the process, working with both classic and contemporary texts, he has shifted the emphasis away from classical (non)uses of the body, towards a theatre which celebrates those qualities which are explicitly unclassic.

It is possible to see two distinct uses of the term 'classic' here in the phrases 'the classic play' and 'the classic body': I want to argue, however, that they are ultimately the same. The concept 'classic' in both contexts is used as a way of identifying what is regarded within an established, official culture as being of the highest social and cultural value, and occupying the most noble and elevated point of a fixed hierarchical system. The classic play is not just a script that survives the period of its first performance. It is above all an example of the highest art: eternal, unified, abstract, cerebral, pure, as opposed to those performance texts which are merely quotidian, ephemeral, popular, non-literary, and contaminated by too-close contact with their social contexts. Likewise the classic body, as the term is used by Bakhtin, denotes an idealised physical type with the same characteristics as the classic text: the classic body – remote, self-contained, harmonious, eternal – is the opposite of the temporal body: imperfect, messy, communal, porous, penetrable, mutable, mortal. The carnivalesque grotesque body described by Bakhtin is just one form of a temporal body which is defiantly and joyously free from classic constraints.

The classic body and the classic play are not merely similar or parallel. They co-exist, and depend upon each other. The classic play, to retain its classic characteristics, requires performance by classic bodies, at least in the heroic roles – hence the disapproval by critics of many performances by Australian actors compared with their English counterparts until well into the 1960s. Likewise, there are very few places outside the classic play where the classic body can exist in physical form and be put on display. For centuries, theatre and its analogues have been used as an instrument of political power (Orgel); the classic body at home in the classic play is an important part of that instrument. The preservation of the classic, therefore, is not just culturally conservationist but also politically conservative. Both these manifestations of the classic are corpora which are supposedly transcendent, separated from the mundane necessities of the lived world, and both serve as hegemonic tools which are inherently anti-egalitarian, which reinforce the concept of cultural hierarchy and legitimate the concept of a social elite. They are both fair targets for opposition or subversion in the pursuit of more egalitarian social structures.

Bell's project of experiment with the staged body, especially as a director, began in 1970 with his return from (and reaction against) immersion in the classical tradition in England, mainly at the Royal Shakespeare Company. His first success came with two new Australian plays which were written in styles which demanded an interrogation of classical performance. *The Legend of King O'Malley* by Bob Ellis and Michael Boddy dealt with Australian political history, but without the formality that the subject might imply. The historical figure around whom the play was based, while undeniably an influential mainstream Australian politician who drove the first peg into the ground to mark the start of the construction of Canberra, was also socially marginal in terms of the ideals of the Westminster system which were being replicated in the southern hemisphere. A Texas-born real-estate agent, insurance salesman and con man, he was shipwrecked on the Australian coast and made his way on foot from Rockhampton to Adelaide, finally being elected to Federal parliament. The script demanded, and received, an exuberant, irreverent and vaudeville-influenced production where the bodies, if not always actually grotesque in a Bakhtinian sense, certainly lacked self-control. The sitting of Australia's Federal parliament was staged as a gathering of boisterous clowns, chanting childish slogans, shouting each other down and given to making rude noises, in a production which was credited with issuing in 'a new style of vaudevillian Aussie comedy' (*Age* 26 Nov. 1991).

The second production was *Biggles*, by Michael Boddy, Marcus Cooney and Ron Blair, which at the end of 1970 inaugurated the

Nimrod Theatre. This, by contrast, showed a comically hyperbolic example of the classical body in its central figure, the hero of a series of schoolboys' stories by Captain W. E. Johns. Squadron-Leader Biggleswerth is a classical body as only the hero of an early twentieth-century boys' own story can be – necessarily free of any of the unruly or untidy habits that afflict flesh and blood. The first half of the play is set at the prize-giving ceremony at a boys' school, where the heroes re-enact their experiences of a mythical, clean and morally uncomplicated First World War. Biggles and his companions Bertie and Ginger largely conform, parodically, to the idealised stereotype in a world free of any appetites or bodily functions, contrasted in the Nimrod production with the excessive physical bulk of author and actor Michael Boddy playing the roles of their various opponents – ranging from a school bully to the comic German villain, von Stahlein. Nevertheless there are moments where a post-Edwardian awareness begins to creep in, for example a song set to the tune of a well-known Anglican hymn, 'The Church's One Foundation', where the three dutiful heroes warn their presumptively adolescent listeners of 'the ills of masturbation'. The words of this hymn undermine the classical ideals of the sentiments they express, and the double-entendre reveals an awareness of more grotesque bodily functions and effects, especially a line warning the potential young masturbator that 'it is a sticky wicket that you are batting on'. The greatest challenge to the classic body comes in the second half of the play, which brings the main characters forward in time to an Australian Returned Serviceman's League Club in 1970, where they are now portrayed as geriatric Colonel Blimps touring the world (during the period of the Vietnam War) warning of the dangers of Communism and the Yellow Peril. Here the three eternally perfect specimens of British manhood were revealed as decrepit, confused and pathetically sexualised, with bodies that were explicitly foregrounded in their imperfection and inadequacy.

A different, and less parodic, physicality was required in Bell's ground-breaking production the following year of *The Removalists* by the then little-known playwright David Williamson. This production featured a high level of cold-blooded physical violence on the tiny stage at the first Nimrod Theatre, where the spatial constriction powerfully intensified the connections between all participants in the event.

Bell was far from being the only Australian theatre director to be interested in this kind of project. One of his close collaborators at the time, Rex Cramphorn (who acted in *King O'Malley*) was even more explicitly interested in transcending the traditions of restrained European stage classicism, through the exploration of a more populist, less formal and fixed theatre practice. To a greater extent even than Bell's, his actors changed their performances from day to day, so that 'the productions were always in a state of flux and changed according to the changing moods of the group and according to their travels, so an audience could not say it had seen the definite and finished version' (Nowra). Cramphorn also made conscious reference to Asian theatre forms and training regimes as a way of energising the performing body. Cramphorn was quoted in an interview with Katharine Brisbane: 'The motivation behind our research was the problem that the basic equipment of the actor in European theatre is so limited. We wanted to extend the language an actor can have – his face, arms, his whole body. At present we are using only ten per cent of what is made use of by the oriental theatre. If nothing else works out I'd like to take the actors to Bali next year, to study and draw what use we can from what we learn' (Brisbane).

Forging a fluid and more physical performance technique for new Australian plays was an important project, but there was nothing especially radical about it – indeed it could be seen as a quite conservative undertaking, an attempt at preserving and celebrating a long-established approach to theatre in Australia. Australian theatre first came of age in the era of melodrama and vaudeville, both unclassical in their popular unrestrained, exaggerated, indecorous and passionate uses of the body.[1] Where Bell's project can be seen as considerably more daring was in his ongoing and explicitly Australian attempts to declassicise works from the traditional European repertoire.

Goldoni was the first to benefit from this new treatment of the classic. Bell devised and directed a revision of *The Servant of Two Masters* entitled *How Could You Believe Me When I Said I'd Be Your Valet When You Know I've Been a Liar All My Life*. For this production at the end of 1972, Bell deliberately instituted a new training regime for the actors to break them of classic habits and introduce them to alternative, and more popular, less classic uses of the acting body. A classic play was to be performed using techniques derived from Australian popular theatre, and Bell and his actors went back to a living popular tradition to explore how this was to be achieved, with special tuition from Johnny Lockwood and Gloria Dawn, performers who had developed their skills in the Tivoli tradition of vaudeville.

The ultimate goal however was a more physicalised Shakespeare, the holy of holies of the classic tradition. After a number of interesting and partially successful attempts, including *Macbeth* (1971, directed by Bell) played as a ritualistic black mass, *Measure for Measure* (1972, directed by Bell) where the sympathies of the production were slanted towards the unrestrained underworld characters, and *Hamlet* (1973, co-directed by Bell and Richard Wherrett), Bell finally succeeded in thoroughly physicalising Shakespeare in his 1975 *Much Ado About Nothing*. Here Bell used the stereotypical figure of the Italian immigrant to Australia as a rehearsal device explicitly to loosen up the actors' bodies and prevent them merely standing around intoning the words. This device became a feature of the final production, with the words of Shakespeare distorted in strong mock-Italian accents, interlarded with Italian catch phrases ('Mamma mia!'), and upstaged by an exaggerated physicality. This had at least one establishment critic sniffing in disapproval at the abuse of the English language and the dilution of the English qualities of some characters, but it proved enormously popular with audiences (Kippax). Bell subsequently extended this technique, which clearly worked in comedy, into the realm of the more traditionally solemn plays in a production of *Romeo and Juliet* (1979) which again used a polyglot mix of accents and an Italian-style masculine exuberance of physicality; this had the effect of transforming the play from a nobly poetic, doom-laden acknowledgment of the force of destiny into a vital celebration of bawdy energy which gets out of hand and goes horribly wrong.

Since 1990, Bell's artistic direction of his own Bell Shakespeare Company has extended this experiment with anti-classic physicality within the preserve of normally classic drama. Movement training was introduced into the rehearsal process in the company's second year to help the actors extend their technique for an expressionist *Richard III*, which he directed while also playing the lead role. Both the costume design by Sue Field and the production concept encouraged the actors away from stately English regality into distorted and exaggerated postures and movements akin to cartoon characters. While Bell does not subscribe to any clearly identifiable corporeal training system, subsequent productions by the Bell Shakespeare Company have opportunistically explored different physicalities for differing purposes. Guest director Stephen Berkoff's 1996 production of *Coriolanus* emphasised the overblown masculinity in the plot, foregrounding muscular naked torsos in a choreography inspired by martial arts.

Bell's 1998 production of *Henry 4*, a compilation of Shakespeare's two Henry IV plays, used extremely unclassic bodily imagery to portray England, not as the Other Eden of John Dover Wilson's idyllic imagination, but as a nation of lager louts and football hooligans. In this modernised production designed by Justin Kurzel (sets) and Deborah Riley (costumes), Prince Henry (Joel Edgerton) had the movement and gestural patterns of a young London foreign exchange dealer on a drunken night out, and the rival armies performed the immediately recognisable rituals of English football fans in full cry. The battle scene was preceded by the singing of the Liverpool Club theme song, and the fighting was realised as mobs hurling beer cans, and clubbing and kicking each other. There was nothing either ideal or eternal in these bodies. The play which Dover Wilson saw as a celebration and reaffirmation of traditional and classical English values became an unflattering portrait of a modern Britain populated by very unclassic thugs.

The most extreme uses of the body in the company's work to date has been Barrie Kosky's *King Lear* (1998) designed by Peter Corrigan, in which Bell played the lead role. Here the characters were made to inhabit a devastatingly bleak world of grotesque, incongruous bodily contact, and physical abjection. The script was extensively cut, physical imagery taking the place of much of the poetry. Here were bodies at their least classical – old, sick, ravaged, un-English – Cordelia (Deborah Mailman) was Aboriginal, Oswald (Kazuhiro Muroyama) was Japanese and spoke parts of the text in his native language, as did the Russian Kent (Rostislav Orel). Lear's knights were portrayed as lolloping dogs with bare chests and exaggerated genitalia. Edgar (Matthew Whittet) disguising himself as mad Tom smeared his face and mouth with his own shit. Lear's loss of sanity was matched by a progressive physical deterioration; and for much of the second half of the play he shuffled about dressed like a bag lady, mocking the mystique of the phallus by distributing rubbery dildoes which he pulled unceremoniously from a battered carpet bag, in a space which resembled the waiting room of some ominous institution for the unwell, filled with rows of blue plastic chairs occupied by grotesque figures wearing distorted oversized fairground full-head masks. The dead Cordelia at the end of the play was stripped to a shift, limbs exposed, and was portrayed as pregnant. The action was presided over by the Fool (Louise Fox) as an overgrown Shirley Temple, taking the fool's licence to violate all decorum, theatrical as well as in every other way, beginning the second half in front of the curtain wearing the King's robes singing 'What Kind of Fool Am I?' In the most intensely intimate grotesque act of physicality, Goneril and Regan (Melita Jurisic, Di Adams) sucked out the eyes of Gloucester (Russell Kiefel) from their sockets with their mouths; and unlike the Olivier film where Lear appears at the end tidied up and transcendent, there was no physical redemption in this version of the story. In a play that has become a sacred treasure of the European classical tradition, these bodies and their functioning were at an unclassic extreme, obviously penetrable and at the mercy of time, illness, and degradation. It was a brutal and hard-hitting physical transformation of the ugliest images in the script, the audiences sharing in a powerful experience of both personal and social devastation.

Bell's interest in the staged body throughout his career in Australia, at the Nimrod and subsequently at the Bell Shakespeare Company, is clearly evident in his work as a director, and it is one of the qualities that have been associated with his unusual success. He is a rare phenomenon as an actor who has been self employed and in professional control of his own career, in the sense of being the artistic director of the company where he works, during most of the past thirty years. This exploration of the unclassic has clearly received positive responses from audiences in Sydney and around Australia.

Some greater understanding of the significance and impact of Bell's theatre work is provided by exploring Bakhtin's concept of the classic body (*Rabelais* 320-2) in conjunction with Deleuze and Guattari's model of human subjectivity. Deleuze and Guattari (*Anti-Oedipus*) analyse the concept of bodies not as independent and integrated organisms but rather as componentry within desiring-machines. The idea of the individual subject is replaced by a focus on the connections and linkages within and between bodies, so that forces of desire flow seamlessly across what might otherwise be seen as significant boundaries, making the important unit the link between a food source and an ingesting mouth, or a writing hand and a reading eye. In the case of theatre this creates a way of seeing live performance as a complex of intertwined desiring-machines linking, among many other factors, the playwright's hand with the actor's memory, the actor's visible body and sounding voice with the spectator's seeing eye and hearing ear, as well as the complex forces of desire which are articulated reciprocally around scopophilia, empathy and libido, and the need for response in the forms of laughter, applause, silence, and adulation, any of which can influence all the others. Any theatre location or event is thus an intricate aggregation of machine parts characterised by complex feedback loops of desire, further intensified by the uncertain and continuous two-way migrations of nomadic subjectivity between actor-machines and character-machines.

Such an understanding of subjectivity can be linked with Bakhtin's concept of the grotesque body, which is similarly open to flows of desire and other associated forces. Bakhtin's discussions of bodily protuberances and orifices, and the flowing in and out of material fluids and substances, use much more concrete imagery than Deleuze and Guattari's evocation of flows of energy and desire. But the implications are the same – they describe material bodies which are open to the world, which exist within a context which influences them, and which are themselves engaged in a perpetual process of mutation, both within themselves and in their effect on other bodies with which they engage.

According to this model, the classic body is revealed as an attempt to deny the grotesque elements of the desiring-machine, an impulse towards the molar 'singular, organised, self-contained organic body' (Grosz 172). The ideal classic body is eternal, immutable and unreceptive, without points of linkage to the world outside it. It is hermetically sealed off, all orifices and protuberances de-emphasised, a 'totalitarian and fascist' instance of the body without organs (Deleuze & Guattari, *Thousand Plateaus* 163). Because the classic body is by definition inaccessible, impenetrable, beyond reach, it institutionalises and intensifies the concept of desire as lack; disarticulated from the desiring-machines around it, it has no desires of its own, though it may still be the object of an unreciprocated, static and paralysed desire in others. No actor has ever actually achieved this state, but it remains the ideal of the classic body on the illusionistic stage, cut off by the fourth wall from the realm of the onlookers, and encased within the circle of its own concentration. It is the aspiration towards this status as the black hole of desire which so severely proscribes any contact or awareness flowing back from the stage to the auditorium in strictly naturalistic theatre.

Any audience, especially before a performance starts, is a potentially carnivalesque grotesque body as desiring-machine – disparate, collective, (dis)assembled, heteroglossic (or alternatively a body without organs, over the surface of which the energies of performance can play); but under the hierarchical conditions of the bourgeois theatre of the twentieth century – with darkened auditoria, fixed seating, well-behaved, silent and static audience members – this carnivalesque potentiality can be neutralised by the would-be classic body of the performer and the immortalised, sanctified classic play, the spectators reduced to a subjugated group (Deleuze & Guattari, *Anti-Oedipus* 348-49). This theatre with its plinth-stage aspires to the condition of high classic art, cut off from the quotidian and trivial concerns of the world outside; it encourages the fantasy of the art of theatre as a transcendent and eternal 'institutional object' which is self-validating and beyond question.

On the other hand, wherever the actors are open to the grotesque in themselves, and when they relinquish their classic status by an acknowledgement, acceptance and utilisation in performance of the permeable boundaries of their own material bodies, the theatre event can be transformed into what Guattari has referred to as a group-subject, the participants intricately and reciprocally cross-linked internally and across the divide between the acting and audience areas (Bogue 86). It is no coincidence that those theatre spaces in Sydney most closely associated with anti-classic performance, the first two Nimrod venues at the Stables and Belvoir Street, are those without raised stages and where the audiences are wrapped around the acting area, so that they make connections with the actors and each other through, across and around the performers. This was a conscious feature of the design of these spaces on the part of the architect Vivian Fraser, and a major contributing factor towards the success of the informal, unclassic performances which have characterised the Nimrod and its successors in those spaces, Griffin and Company B.

Under these conditions where classic plays are rendered fluid, responsive and unfixed – where the materiality and functionalism of bodies is foregrounded, and where they are seen as linking promiscuously into the worlds and bodies of the audience, the live performance becomes an intensified event located inextricably within a wider social practice, problematising, multiplying and realigning the connections between the participants within larger social and political networks. The audience, transformed into a group-subject, 'calls into question its goals, and attempts to articulate new significations and form new modes of interaction', bringing about 'a structural redefinition of the role of each person and a reorientation of the whole' (Bogue 86). It is under such conditions that theatre is released from its classic glass case, designed to protect the world from contamination by the stage as much as the other way around, and can start to branch out into an unstructured, rhizomatic network of synapses extending outwards, and circulating desire and intensity beyond the time and place of the performance event and the members of the audience who were present. Such a play, in both its references to a world outside and in its fact of grotesque live performance, works not so much as a representation or reproduction of reality but like a map whose 'whole orientation is towards establishing contact with the real experimentally' (Deleuze & Guattari, *On the Line* 25).

The idea of the classic is international, but it has had a particular significance in Australia for much of this century because it is associated with the cultural values of Britain as the colonising power. The project which has engaged Bell and his many co-workers over the past thirty years can be seen as a comprehensive attempt to dismantle the 1950s Australian preoccupation with the classic, in both theatre and social structure. This project extends across many aspects of theatre practice, and includes the architecture of the theatre space as well as the content and style of the plays performed. Above all, it has affected both the repertoire through the appropriation and transformation of classic texts from the European past alongside the development of new Australian plays, and the manner in which the bodies of the actors performing that repertoire present themselves before the public. The effect has been to shatter the glass case separating off performance from its context, and to re-establish it as an important component in the flows of social energy, vitally linked into the world of the performers and spectators, and facilitating an ongoing process of dynamic social redefinition and flux.

References

Boddy, Michael, & Ellis, Bob. *The Legend of King O'Malley; or Never Say Die Until a Dead Horse Kicks You*. Sydney: Currency P, 1987.

Boddy, Michael. Blair, Ron & Cooney, Marcus. *Biggles*. Unpublished ts.

Bakhtin, Mikhail. *Rabelais and His World*. Trans. Hélène Iswolsky. Bloomington: Indiana UP, 1984.

Bogue, Ronald. *Deleuze and Guattari*. London & New York: Routledge, 1989.

— 'Gilles Deleuze: The Aesthetics of Force'. In *Deleuze: A Critical Reader*. Ed. Paul Patton. Oxford & Malden: Blackwell, 1996.

Browne, Lindsey. *Sydney Morning Herald,* 8 Aug. 1957.

— *Sydney Morning Herald,* 3 Mar. 1950.

— *Sydney Morning Herald,* 9 Oct. 1950.

Brisbane, Katharine. *Australian,* 8 Nov. 1971.

Deleuze, Gilles, & Félix Guattari. *Anti-Oedipus: Capitalism and Schizophrenia*. Trans. Robert Hurley, Mark Seem & Helen R. Lane. Minneapolis: U. of Minnesota 1983.

— *On the Line*. Trans. John Johnston. New York: Semiotext(e), 1983.

— *A Thousand Plateaus: Capitalism and Schizophrenia*. Trans. Brian Massumi. Minneapolis: U of Minnesota P, 1987.

Grosz, Elizabeth. *Volatile Bodies: Towards a Corporeal Feminism*. Sydney: Allen & Unwin, 1994.

Kippax H. G. *Sydney Morning Herald,* 25 June 1977.

Nowra, Louis, 25 Nov. 1991.

Orgel, Stephen. *The Illusion of Power: Political Theatre* in *The English Renaissance*. Berkeley: U of California P. [1975].

Wilson, John Dover. *The Fortunes of Falstaff*. Cambridge: Cambridge UP, 1964.

Notes

1 It is interesting that many of Bell's most adventurous productions have premiered at the end of the year, which is the most important Australian carnival season. Christmas and the start of the summer holiday period, as well as being the time when nineteenth-century theatre in both England and Australia, traditionally took leave of absence from high seriousness and indulged in the annual pantomime.

10.
Liminality and corporeality: Tess De Quincey's butoh

Edward Scheer

> *Hans Bellmer: 'The body is like a sentence that invites us to rearrange it.'* (Foster 103)

Lights came up slowly to reveal an indeterminate shape on the floor. Gradually it stirred and assumed at first only vaguely anthropomorphic characteristics. Like a doll by Hans Bellmer, scarcely human, an assemblage of prosthetic limbs. The image formed and reformed for the audience, and began to separate from the floor on which it lay, but the Bellmer resonance persisted in the emptied-out attitude of the body. There seemed to be no discernible personality, no aesthetic, nor was there gesture informing us of a technique, just the hollow shell of a body, an uncanniness suffused with potentials for movements which are largely unmade. The performer seemed to maintain a relation to the impulse, as Grotowski and Artaud would have it, not willing to diminish the potential energy and affectivity of the tensile poised body, resisting the habitual gesture even to the point of apparent stillness.

This was the first time I saw Tess De Quincey at the Performance Space (TPS) in Sydney, 1989. She would later describe this dance, *Movement on the Edge*, as one in which 'the calligraphy of the body shapes a landscape' (De Quincey, *3 Solo Performances*). A body writing was taking place, though the inscriptions were hard to read unless you knew butoh. The glacial pace of the dance, the slow advance on the audience, and then the sudden tumble to the floor repeated ad nauseam. An amalgam of Bausch cruelty and butoh rigour reflecting the training De Quincey had been through with Min Tanaka's Mai-Juku company in Japan. But what landscape was being shaped thus? De Quincey suggests a fragile and extreme place of being, not a purely butoh body nor a 'Japanese' corporeality. It seemed a genuine hybrid to me at the time. De Quincey describes how it came about:

> The reason I went to work with Min was because he was working differently to anyone else within that tradition and

> from the beginning he was working internationally and he was less concerned with Japanese identity and was more interested in human identity. Mai-Juku was always an international company. I didn't find it foreign when I went to Japan in terms of working with Min it seemed to me completely natural. There were elements I had to learn about which were outside of me; about the detail of the space which normally I would have walked over and not seen. My step would have gone over and I wouldn't have realised that there was a world beneath my foot. Then you learn to re-focus and you adjust and its like having a macro camera lens with you and you look at things in a different way. (Interview)

Contemporary Japanese performance genres have come to represent a performance horizon for many of Australia's most innovative physical performers. De Quincey has approached this horizon insistently and vigorously, from her work with Mai-Juku between 1985-1991 and in her own early performances in the butoh tradition in pieces such as *Movement on the Edge* (1998) and *Another Dust* (1990), in her Body Weather workshops and performances such as the Lake Mungo project (1991-94) in far western New South Wales, Australia, to her most recent short piece *Butoh Product #2 – Nerve* .[1] More recently, her performance mode has multiplied in her collaborations with Stuart Lynch, shifting away from a strict butoh influence to a more fluid style which is designed to be more responsive to local 'physical contexts' in pieces like *Compression 100* (1996) and the duration events (six-hour, twelve-hour and twenty-four-hour performances, from 1996). The early pieces are especially emblematic for this study which is concerned with what Victor Turner has named 'liminality', as they were constructed by De Quincey to investigate 'the division between worlds' and the 'field which lies within division' respectively (*Another Dust*). The body's divisions, its cultured organisations and economies are re-distributed in these dances which reflect and reproduce a larger, experimental, cross-cultural oscillation in Australian performance. As well, De Quincey's own movement between cultures mirrors the function of Turner's liminality.

Turner located the concept of liminality in the French folklorist Arnold van Gennep's division of rituals of passage into three stages: separation, liminality and re-aggregation, where liminality refers to a 'betwixt and between condition often involving segregation from the everyday scene' (Turner 101). Turner uses this term to signify a range of experiences from 'suspensions of quotidian reality' (102), to performance in general and particularly to 'performances characteristic of liminal phases and states' which 'often are more about the doffing of masks, the stripping of status, the renunciation of roles, the demolishing of structures, than their putting on and keeping on' (107). He relates this concept to 'life-crisis rituals' for individuals (for example, birth, nuptial or funerary rites) and for entire groups and cultures including 'collective response to hazards such as war, famine, drought, plague, earthquake, volcanic eruption, and other natural or man made disasters' (101).

This connection is especially evident in recent Japanese performance traditions which grew out of the crisis engendered by the devastation of Hiroshima and Nagasaki at the end of World War Two. This destruction was not only physically realised, an image of national identity was shattered also, what Tadashi Uchino among others has described as 'Japan's Japan' and replaced by 'America's Japan' (43). It was in response to this that Tatsumi Hijikata developed the dance practice butoh, as a rejection of both forms of identity. In the process he constructed a life-crisis ritual for himself first of all and for Japan in general. More recently the Japanese performance group, Dumb Type, particularly their work directed by Teiji Furuhashi and their most recent work *OR* (1997) – in some respects a homage to Furuhashi – have constructed a similar life-crisis ritual structure around the threat posed to the human body by AIDS and by technological culture generally. Their approach is antithetical to Hijakata's retreat into the body as organism. Dumb Type's appropriation of technology to manifest an aesthetic of the 'human system interface' embraces an approach to technology as the future for the organism. Butoh does not imagine a future for the organism, but simply reflects the negation of the body in terms of its docility, its functions and capacities.

Meateorology: De Quincey on the Body Weather laboratory

Mai-Juku's Body Weather training, developed in Japan by Mai-Juku's founder Min Tanaka and practiced in Australia by De Quincey, comprises a set of provocations to respond precisely to this question of physical negativity and physical future. It is an attack on the organism's inertia to release its potentials in terms of 'sensorial understanding of space and of body' and to promote the 'observation of the body as an environment within a greater environment' (De Quincey, Brochure). The training is split into three areas: one, MB (muscles/bones), a form of aerobic workout; two, Manipulations, exploring 'parameters of flexibility' with partners; three, Ground Work, exercises designed to encourage awareness of differential speeds in the body, a kind of alertness tuning.

De Quincey describes Body Weather as an 'open investigation' and a 'laboratory', which suggests that approaching Body Weather from Western culture might be productively done through what Grotowski calls the 'total act' defined as 'an extreme solemn gesture' which does not 'hold back before any obstacle set by custom and behaviour' (92-3). It is 'modelled in a living organism, in impulses, a way of breathing, a rhythm of thought and the circulation of blood' and must be 'ordered and brought to consciousness, not dissolving into chaos and formal anarchy'. In this way it is possible to learn to 'respond totally, that is to begin to exist. For each day we only react with half our potential'. Grotowski talked about not giving a technique or a bag of tricks to the performer but taking something away: namely the habits and resistances of the performer's body. Body Weather for De Quincey is a training in precisely this way:

> It's training through resistance – we all have habits whereby we escape, if you throw out the habits or constantly address them you have to find new pathways. But the action in Body Weather is to give resistance to people in the training so that they have to work extra hard. All aspects of the Mai-Juku Body Weather training are tough because you push people to go to their limits and in the breaking of the limits you find new space and new forms. In the basic workout you're pushed to your limit, you're exhausted but you've got to keep going, you've got to find your next wind, to work through the pain. If you can't take that kind of pressure you won't find the necessity to stand on stage ... There are other ways of course. Body Weather is just one way but it does create an intensity and it is an operation through resistance. (Interview)

Body Weather constructs a quality of presence through a technology of pressure and force, to which the body responds out of necessity. The nomencature suggests a kind of choreographic meteorology, denoting atmospheric character, and could be used to describe Body Weather in the sense that it seems to construct atmospheres for the body to exist within. For De Quincey, the idea of seeing the body as weather, as a natural dynamic system, is explained through a liminal framework where the body is always part of a larger eco-system:

> At different times of the year different parts of the body start to buckle under. It's the weather of the body, the temperature, the climate: external climate meets internal climate. This work is about finding where the borderline exists. The concept of the skin being the breaking point is not at all where Body Weather philosophy places the delineation. You can be far outside your skin just as the outside can be received far inside and the interaction between the two is extensive. Hijikata used to speak all the time about walking outside down the stairs of the body, to turn the body inside out. (Interview)

This latter phrase refers to the final section of Artaud's banned radio broadcast *To Have Done with the Judgement of God* (1947/48) made several months before Artaud's death, in which he invokes a dance of negation which will liberate the body. Artaud says 'When you have given (man) a body without organs, then you will have delivered him from all his automatisms and restored him to his true liberty. Then you will teach him again to dance inside out.' René Farabet, the director of the Atelier Création Radiophonique at Radio France, broadcast Artaud's words in 1972. The recording itself had gone underground and was not officially released on a label until Harmonia Mundi's version of 1986. Copies of the speech on tape circulated prior to this, one of which reached Hijikata and became 'one of Hijikata's most treasured possessions' (Holborn 14).

The Paris-based critic and choreographer Sumako Koseki has said that 'from its early stages' butoh has been greatly influenced by Georges Bataille and Artaud, and that one of the first groups called itself La Maison d'Artaud, the House of Artaud (de Bonnerive 57). Koseki adds, again in reference to the above piece, that 'I never saw Artaud, I just heard his voice at the end of his life ... and that, that was truly butoh.' For Koseki, butoh is characterised by its foregrounding of the relations of the actor to the earth and to death; 'when one acts, one has to go through a kind of death, a negation of what is at that precise moment, one's life' (de Bonnerive 55). In 'Le Théâtre de Seraphin', Artaud describes the process of performing as a way of negating the being of the actor but for Artaud, as for Hijikata, this is not a death, since life itself is a negation. 'When I live I don't feel that I'm living. But when I act, it is then that I feel that I exist' (Artaud, *Théâtre* 229). This is not an expression of the actor's ego, it is part of Artaud's vision that 'you have to have the will to live' ('Will'), and that means refusing all derivation and starting again from scratch, creating oneself anew.

For Artaud, life is crisis and necessitates rituals which can transcribe this crisis, embody it and make it liveable. Cruelty is liminality.[2] This is the function of theatrical performance for Artaud. Body Weather's training regime can be seen as a ritual preparation for this kind of cruelty in performance which, separated from the world and divorced from the body as a docile instrument of power, permits the emergence of the new and, as butoh has done for Japan, gives shape to new historical circumstances.

It is a technology that opens onto a liminal space, a space of potential in which new forms can emerge beyond the parameters of individual tastes and codes, into an in-between, indeterminate zone of relations. De Quincey stresses, however, that it is not intended as a therapy or as a healing process and affirms its connection to its origins in Japan:

> Body Weather is a training in relations, in mental and physical states and how they effect each other. Japan is about relationship so you're looking at the gap all the time. It's not about you, it's not about me, it's about the modulation of space between us ... loaded with history, meaning, relation. If I see a modern dancer the arm will cut through space and the identity of the person becomes apparent, like self expression. Whereas in the butoh world it's the opposite: you are being danced by the space, the arm doesn't cut through the space, it's integral with the space so it gives a very different relation ... But one of the things I used to feel very strongly about, seeing Mai-Juku group performances, was again the in between spaces between the

> bodies, because we used to work as a group body, so the common space and the common body was/is at issue all the time. From this follows the softness of delineation which again is about the arm cutting through space or being an integral part of it and so the softness of the contours of the body are really important. It's a different story with most of the other companies I see and I think it's because the group trains as strongly as it does or did [Min disbanded it in 1997]. (Interview)

Movement on the Edge and *Another Dust* also represent the liminal in temporal since, as solo pieces, they represent a separation from Mai-Juku. But De Quincey had yet to develop the new performance identity that followed with the Stuart Lynch collaborations and her recent solo pieces. These early performances were intercultural moments in a precisely liminal sense as they staged an unmasking of the Western body as carrier of the butoh virus. Yet a more personalised, embodied observation of butoh practices emerged, though it had to come from behind a thick mat of hair. Later De Quincey formally marked the transition:

> I cut my hair off after the first couple of performances at TPS. The history of my hair as a performer lay in Mai-Juku, so when I left it was important to cut it off. I mean how do you reconstruct yourself as a performer after that experience? Also you're coming out of Japan, you look Western but the inside of your head is functioning quite differently. One has to change in relation to the West. You can't teach Body Weather the same way here, you can't push people the same way. (Interview)

De Quincey says 'if butoh is to survive as a contemporary performance practice, it has to find a ... relationship to (its own) integral values within the shifts between a local and a globalised identities' (Interview).[3] Acknowledging cultural specificity is one step on a journey which does not end in a closed field but in a liminal space. Think of a beach or a dry lake bed or a desert, which is where De Quincey is currently working on the first of three performance projects, *Triple Alice*.

In her most recent short work *Butoh Product #2 – Nerve* De Quincey continues the body writing experiment begun in *Movement on the Edge*. This is done through performance poet Amanda

Stewart's textual montage and projection. In this, as in other of Stewart's works, the sounds and images of words are collapsed back on themselves and we have the bare material of language on display. De Quincey worked within a similar paradigm to return the performing body to its being on stage; standing squarely, facing off the spectators, holding ground until the impulse to move takes over. While the earlier pieces presented a more inscrutable hybrid performance presence, a mobile Bellmer doll, this piece performs hybridity in its overall structure. The hybrid of fractured linguistic performatives and withheld fragmented gestures, suggests that the Body Weather training is still present, though the sentences of the body have been rewritten. Even without locomotive movement, the pulses of the body's capacities for movement were in evidence. A fragile, shifting landscape of text and body released from the requirement of saying anything – revealing their being – also releases the spectator to see what Artaud described as 'action and creation in a dynamism never characterised, never situated, never defined, where it is perpetual invention which is the law' ('Notes'). This is an invention of the performing self first of all, and also of a hybrid performance trajectory in Australia, a life-crisis ritual for an ever present liminality.

References

Artaud, Antonin. 'Notes pour une "Lettre aux Balinais".' *Tel Quel* 46 (Summer 1971): 10-34 (17). Author's translation.

– *Le Théâtre et son Double*. Paris: Gallimard, 1964.

– 'Le Théâtre de Seraphin.' In *Le Théâtre et son Double*. Paris: Gallimard, 1964.

– 'You have to have a will to live.' *Revue K* 1 (1947).

de Bonnerive, Michele. 'Sumako Koseki: La voix d'Artaud à la fin de sa vie, c'est buto.' *L'Autre Journal* 5 (26 Mar.-2 Apr. 1986): 55-57.

De Quincey, Tess. Alice Springs Body Weather Laboratory Information Brochure, 20 Sept.-10 Oct.1999.

– Interview with the Author, Sept. 1998.

– 3 Solo performances: 'Movement on the Edge', 'Another Dust', 'is'. Catalogue. Denmark: Forlaget Drama, 1994.

– *Another Dust,* Program Notes, 31 Jan.-11 Feb. 1990.

Foster, Hal. *Compulsive Beauty*. Cambridge Mass. MIT Press: 1997.

Grotowski, Jerzy. *Towards a Poor Theatre*. Ed. Eugenio Barba. London: Methuen 1986.

Holborn, Mark. 'Tatsumi Hijikata and the Origins of Butoh.' In *Butoh: Dance of the Dark Soul*. New York: Sadev/Aperture, 1987.

Turner, Victor. *The Anthropology of Performance*. New York: PAJ, 1986.

Uchino, Tadashi. 'Deconstructing "Japaneseness": Towards Articulating Locality and Hybridity in Contemporary Japanese Performance.' *Disorientations Cultural Praxis in Theatre: Asia, Pacific, Australia.* Ed. Rachel Fensham & Peter Eckersall. Melbourne: Centre for Drama and Theatre Studies, Monash University, 1999: 35-53.

Notes

1 Presented in the program *Spur,* TPS, 4 April 1999, as part of the Antistatic events.

2 One can usefully compare Turner's (1986) 'collective response to hazards such as war, famine, drought, plague, earthquake, volcanic eruption, and other natural or man made disasters' with any of the various metonyms for the theatre which Artaud mobilises in *Le Théâtre et son Double.*

3 One should also recognise the liminality in Hijikata's development of a formless form which owed as much to European dance styles as to Japanese traditions and which profoundly rejected them both.

11. What can't be seen can be seen: butoh politics and (body) play

Peter Eckersall

Asobi, a Japanese term that connotes play and amusement, is rarely associated with the physical or cultural dynamics of butoh. Yet as performer Yumi Umiumare, who danced with Maro Akaji's dark-soul (*ankoku*) butoh group *Dairakudakan* for ten years, argues: 'these days their work seems more like pop' (Interview).

Bodies in performance are subject to the interplay of context and culture, and for this reason what was once rare in art and distasteful to society can become commonplace and fashionable. To cite Jameson, a cultural turn of 'postmodern mutations where the apocalyptic suddenly turns into the decorative (or at least diminishes abruptly into "something you have around the home")' (xvii). If attempts to signify butoh have become playful (for example, a trend seen in the increasing emphasis on performing the sensibilities of cuteness [*kawaii*] in Japanese post-butoh dance) and bodies are the decorative agents of the ludic[1] condition, have we in fact reached an endgame for butoh? Alternatively, might artists not intensify the qualities of play in performance, escalate and increase their velocity to reach a point at which they explode and divulge an anti-playful opposite? This is to engage in what Philip Auslander observes as a 'transition from transgressive to resistant political art' in the postmodern era (58), resistance that might be found in this instance in an intense accumulation of signs on and through the body and their reproduction *ad infinitum* to the point of absurdity. However, there are apparent resistances to some bodies as signs; resistance also to Asian bodies opening up new spaces in contemporary Australia. Umiumare and her collaborations with Malay-Australian performer Tony Yap might be productively read in this way.

Umiumare's 1998 production of *Fleeting Moments*[2] and her continuing work with Yap in *How Could You Even Begin to Understand*[3] are the basis of the most sustained examples of butoh-related body performance in Melbourne over the last few years. I say butoh-related (and again reflecting a trend in Japan) because it has become a contested, in some respects orientalist and overused terminology; its genealogy and stability as a modality of body performance has been undermined, especially with respect to radical and transgressive forms of experimentation. Nevertheless, the hyper-presence of *asobi* and the intensities of the ethno-cultural interplay in the collaborative efforts of these artists are grounds for an investigation into the radical cultural politics of body play. The strategic discourse for this is now clear: 'As well as being the site of knowledge-power, the body is ... also a site of resistance, for it exerts a recalcitrance, and always entails the possibility of a counterstrategic reinscription' (Grosz 64, Gilbert 18). Thus I will suggest that disjuncture and partial resolutions are visible in Umiumare and Yap's work; tensions between notions of interior and exterior forms of physical engagement, fractured histories and cultures and a technologicalisation of the body that seems to emerge from an East-West hybridity constitute a moment of extreme playfulness. This draws our attention to questions of culture and counterstrategic notions of identity within the postcolonial space of Australia and experiences of its/our continuing dislocation in the region.

Fleeting Moments, Umiumare's major choreographic work to date, and a continuing series of duo works under the umbrella title of *How Could You Even Begin to Understand* (first performed in 1997) constitute the body of work to be considered here. Both works play with cultural temporality and displacement, and there is an evident concern to contrast deeper notions of selfhood that might be uncovered by re-examining the past (historical narratives and in the sense of coming from somewhere) with the fleeting and superficial nature of contemporary existence.

Relevant here is how Marilyn Ivy has noted the tendency in Japanese culture to imagine and memorialise the past with her notion that such 'Discourses of the Vanishing' (from the title of her book) 'can only be tracked through the poetics of phantasm, through attentiveness to the politics of displacement, deferral, and originary repetition' (20). *Fleeting Moments* was inspired by eleventh-century court poems written by two famous Japanese poets, Lady Sarashina and Izumi Shikibu. A third poem written by Gina Louis in 1998, like the earlier poems, is concerned to capture and express the 'transient nature of all things'. In Ivy's terms not only Japan's past, but the notion of Japan itself in this performance becomes like the poetics of phantasm. Japan is not only displaced by distance but also by the critique of modernity that forms the conceptual framework of this piece. Thus, Umiumare asks: 'Am I lost in the rush of twentieth century modern life, here in Australia, far from Japan? All around me, moments, fleeting. Memory is not perfect, it can only bring back images' (Program).

The performance of *Fleeting Moments* began reflectively and slowly. It utilised the sensibilities of low controlled movements reminiscent of Noh performance, although a pervasive atmosphere of playful sensuality over-coded the more austere rigidity of classical Japanese forms. It enacted a world of pleasures where play between bodies took the form of contemplation and desire. The transliteration of the poems into movement and its sensibilities was oblique and not at all literal, rather the performance was a kind of focused meditation on loss punctured by moments of extreme physicality. One might note the tension between the textual poetic references to the inevitability of change and a melancholy longing for a vanishing and phantasmic past (unchanging) that was inscribed on the dancers' bodies through languid movement and glorious *kimono* costumes. Midway, an escalating sense of crisis developed as formally sensuous bodies were colonised by images of the modern. Performers became constrained by contemporary Japanese fashion, their gestures overcome by ceaseless manic attempts to answer mobile phones. The action spilled into the audience and what was formerly discrete and controlled became chaotic and frenetic. The piece concluded with a imaginary return to another place of contemplation; in the words of the poet Lady Sarashina, 'I yearn for a tranquil moment, to be out upon the sea of harmony' (Umiumare, Program).

The Heian court is typically remembered as an island-like society that saw the development of many ancient contemplative and playful arts (poetry, dance, music, incense appreciation, etc) while surrounded by a tumultuous world that was in reality engaged in constant warfare. There is a sense by which the first movements of the piece depict a nostalgic and idealised picture of court life, an unreal Japan beyond the threshold of social reality. At a second level, the conditions of play suggesting the courtly life of ancient Japan were overrun by excessive corporealities; impressions of the modern dystopian as opposite were imposed upon the bodies of performers, their repetitious and manic actions accumulated to the point of explosion. Modern forms of *asobi* (fashion, gadgets, chattering mobile phone social existence, etc.) were represented in gestural forms that quite literally tipped the body over the edge. Everything had become *asobi*, to the extent that the pleasurable possibilities for *asobi* were negated and the repetitions of playfulness possessed the performers' bodies, turning into images of distress like a computer virus.

Other performances from Umiumare and Yap's *How Could You Even Begin to Understand* series are described by them in simpler terms, in marked contrast to the theatrical complexities of Umiumare's *Fleeting Moments.* Speaking about the conceptual approach of the former, Umiumare says:

> At the extreme edge our work as performers our performing bodies may be exoticised, orientalised and fetishised. *How Could You Even Begin to Understand* sought to undermine these depictions of Asianness and replace them with an exploration of contemporary Asian-Australian and regional points of view. ... We discovered a common association with the philosophical principle of *Yin* and *Yang,* oppositional elements that are found in all manner of Asian experience and daily life. (Interview)

In the *How Could You Even Begin to Understand* series the two artists collaborate, working in a kind of spontaneous counterpoint that seeks to embody the shifting sensibilities of a *yin-yang* formula. Performances are therefore simple in structure and tend to be focused solely on the performers' bodies.

A former actor with the rigorous physical performance group Institute for Research on the Art of the Actor (IRAA),[4] Tony Yap is a strong presence in the work (to the point that Umiumare has commented that she might momentarily disappear) and the central locus of this work is always Yap's high-energy Malay trance dance. As I observe Yap's work, his body assumes the Malay-Indonesian dance form with such strength and concentration that it seems to explode – eyes popping, every tendon visibly pumped – even the act of standing motionless makes his body perspire profusely. There is an impression of something cybernetic about this performance, as if the hybridisation of form and context have uncovered a form of body-technology. To my mind, the body's viscera seems to become visible, organs and mechanisms that usually reside passively inside the body are bought to the surface and their movements made visible. I imagine a Deleuzean body without skin, the musculature an architecture of titanium rods and pistons. Taken out of its notional 'traditional eastern' context and in contrast with Umiumare's physically expressive sense of ludic wonderment, the body's mechanics in this work seem to extract pain and make it visible. So destabilised is the performer from a modern self and so filled with the unknowable identity of a Malay trance master that the body seems to enact a crisis in identity representation. I am left neither watching a moment of play (the work is too cruel) nor am I able to see Yap's performance persona at ease with his search for a ritualised and performative Malay cultural essence.

Working within such heightened states of corporeality and exploring modalities of play, I want to suggest that both artists are motivated to ask questions about selfhood and the essence of being. Yap seeks to be fully exposed in his work, suggesting that the work is most successful when the work 'becomes a way of life and there is nowhere to hide' (Interview). His work with trance is motivated by a need to work in a way that connects with his Malay upbringing: 'for a long time I wanted to work on non-Asian performance, I now want to bring things back' (Interview). Umiumare now sees Japan in relief and tries to join together the cultural contexts of Japan and Australia in her work.

Keeping in mind personal histories and artistic motivations, the fact that Asian-Australian bodies are rarely seen on the Australian stage and even more rarely in control of content situates these works within a rubric of postcolonial discourse. Yap's 'postcolonial' trance dance makes a power-play within Australian identity politics. Like the mobile phone mania that inhabits the bodies of the dancers in the 'modern' section of *Fleeting Moments,* there seems to be an accumulation of signs, gestures and behaviours that enter and invade the body, their rapidity and intensity becomes disturbing, and the autonomy or unity of the body is rendered precarious. Thus, where questions of power can be applied to notions of unified identity, these become intermingled with alternative histories and symbolic representations of the performing body. In the context of Howard-Hanson ethno-nostalgic Anglophilia, and a cultural shift that has exposed racism and a continuing ambiguity about Australia's place in the region, the playful technologies of these bodies are perhaps above all about their Asianness and their countervailing sense of dis-ease with migratory location. They act as sites for cultural interaction and interrogation and while Umiumare and Yap are performers with divergent trajectories, in tandem they seek accommodations, harmony and balance. Perhaps their physicalised demonstration of *yin-yang* philosophy, where the countervailing forces in the space become a question of mutual respect, diversity and reappraisal in performative terms can become a model for reconciliation and negotiation of difference.

The performances discussed here remain deeply concerned with past and otherness. As Ivy argues, modernity accommodates the past through displacement. Ideas of historical cultures that survive or are retrieved do so by drawing attention to what is lost. This constitutes a sensibility of 'vanishing'; a poetics of 'fleeting moments' or trance moments. Denoting something to be original and authentic (the past) is also a sign of absence in the same way that the development of polymorphic experience of culture draws attention to the inevitable loss of rigid cultural binaries. This is also a form of strategic play with symbols and myths, histories and identities.

Such a poetics of displacement might perhaps rejuvenate butoh as an interesting and progressive site of performance, one that remains true to its historical moment but offers new directions for a corporeal politics of transgression. When all is *asobi,* then the only strategy is to work through this fact and emerge somewhere over the edge. The presence of noise and clamour is therefore exposed as covering over something else that cannot be heard. It cannot be seen but it is sensed, our dis-ease is the source of butoh.

References

Auslander, Philip. *From Acting to Performance.* London & New York: Routledge, 1997.

Gilbert, Helen. *Sightlines; Race Gender and Nation in Contemporary Australian Theatre.* Ann Arbor: U of Michigan P, 1998.

Grosz, Elizabeth. 'Inscriptions and Body-Maps: Representations and the Corporeal.' *Feminine Masculine and Representation.* Ed. Terry Threadgold & Anne Cranny-Francis. Sydney: Allen & Unwin, 1990. 62-74.

Ivy, Marilyn. *Discourses of the Vanishing. Modernity, Phantasm, Japan.* Chicago: U of Chicago P, 1995.

Jameson, Fredric. *Postmodernism or the Logic of Late Capitalism.* London & New York: Verso, 1991.

Rolf, Robert T. 'Japanese Theatre from the 1980s: The Ludic Conspiracy'. *Modern Drama* 34.1 (1992): 127-36.

Umiumare, Yumi. *Fleeting Moments.* Theatre program, 1998.

— Interview with author, May-June 1999, Melbourne.

Yap, Tony. Interview with author, May-June 1999.

Notes

1 Ludic: a state of playfulness, cuteness (*kawaii*) and whimsy. My use of the word is inspired by Rolf.

2 *Fleeting Moments* directed by Yumi Umiumare, was performed by Yumi Umiumare, Lynne Santos, Sarah Potter and Tony Yap. Set design by Chris Arnold. Lighting by Shane Grant. Music composed by Anne Norman, Liza Lim, Yuji Takahashi and performed by Satsuki Odamura, Rosanne Hunt, Deborah Kayser.

3 Version One of *How Could You Even Begin to Understand* performed at the 1997 Experimenta, Melbourne, and was produced in collaboration with Chinese artist Lim Tsay Chaun. Second and subsequent versions featuring Yap and Umiumare alone were performed at the 1999 Anti-static Festival, Sydney, and the Horsham Regional Art Gallery, 1999. A concluding full-scale performance work that hopes to reemploy Lim and draw together the threads of each version is planned for 2000.

4 IRAA was established in Melbourne in 1987-88 by Renato Cuocolo and Cira La Gioia. Yap was a foundation member of the company and worked with them until 1995-6. IRAA was influenced by the ideas of Jerzy Grotowski and like Grotowski had an interest in Asian performance practices. Since leaving IRAA, Yap has moved almost completely into dance forms of performance. Besides working with Umiumare, he is a teacher, chorographer and performer who has experimented with the notion of trance-dance as an expression of cultural identity.

Part III

Sitings

12.

Filthy spaces: the investment of non-theatre venues in Melbourne 1990-95

Julian Meyrick

This chapter is an overview of three theatre/performance productions which occurred in Melbourne in the early 1990s. They each involved the use of what are sometimes called 'found spaces', both as venue shells and as part of the experiential impact of the shows themselves. Though the focus is a specific time frame, a certain historical vista underpins the analysis nevertheless. Crudely summarised, it is that Melbourne, as a modern post-industrial city, had, by the late 1980s, a surplus of factory buildings standing empty. At the same time fringe artists, faced with rapidly rising rental costs in established theatres, were on the look out for alternative performance sites. State and local governments, aware of the building surplus and keen to promote an arts-led reclamation of inner city areas, became amenable to the issuing of temporary performance licences.[1] As a result, Melbourne enjoyed a mini-boom in site-specific work, both from hard-line experimental companies and from quasi-established, funded ones.

The shows examined demonstrate how particular buildings were invested with theatrical significance: what values they represented for the companies that used them and for the audiences they attracted. In conclusion, there is an attempt to contextualise this kind of appropriation, for it is clear that these venues were more than just available, they were also desirable. They stood for something. The question to be asked is not only 'what use were these buildings?' but, in Marvin Carlson's phrase, 'how did they mean?' As Carlson argues:

> No longer do we necessarily approach theatre primarily as the physical enactment of a written text with our historical concern anchored in the interplay between that text and its physical realisation. We are now at least equally likely to look at the theatre experience in a more global way, as a sociocultural event whose meanings and interpretations are not to be sought exclusively in the text being performed but in the experience of the audience assembled to share in the

> creation of the total event. Such a change in focus requires also a change in the way we look at the places where theatrical performance occurs, which may or may not be traditional theatre buildings. (*Places* 2)[2]

As his use of Pierce, Barthes and Eco indicates, the approach Carlson favours in deciphering the 'repertory of architectural objects' (6) that makes up the urban landscape is predominantly semiological: choice and utilisation of theatre venues shares similarities with the way cultures and individuals acquire and make sense of their language. Drawing on the pioneering work of the Prague School, Carlson argues that theatre buildings can be explicated using the rubric of structural linguistics. Theatres are 'spoken', not just built; 'read', not just inhabited. Applying his model historically, he attempts to go beyond a catalogue of changing architectural styles to show instead the ways in which power, privilege and display have been inscribed on the 'ludic space' (11) of different theatre buildings.

Semiological explanations represent less a break with text-based views of performance than an expansion of the notion of 'the text' to include features previously considered contiguous. Such approaches evince well-known faults.[3] Carlson's encyclopaedic historical scholarship addresses some but not all of these problems. As a result, while some of his insights are useful, another viewpoint is woven into the account. This is phenomenological, one based on the projective reality of the perceiving subject. Here, theatre is seen less as an intersection of reciprocal structural processes than as a place in which individuals are primarily and sensorily located. Theatre buildings are, after all, not just 'read', they are physically experienced. This is particularly true of found spaces which foreground the meaning-flow of the shows they contain. The filth referred to in the chapter title is not metaphoric, either syntagmatically or paradigmatically; it is 'real' filth. Audiences visiting these spaces directly experienced cold/dirt/discomfort. Clearly, there was a meaning to these conditions. Equally clearly, these conditions were a meaning in themselves. As Stanton Garner summarises:

> The phenomenological approach ... is uniquely able to illuminate the stage's experiential duality. On the one hand, the field of performance is scenic space, given as spectacle to be processed and consumed by the perceiving eye, objectified as field of vision for a spectator who aspires to the detachment inherent in the perceptual act. On the other hand, this field is environmental space, 'subjectified' (and

> intersubjectified) by the physical actors who body forth the space they inhabit. From this perspective, theatrical space is ... governed by the body and its spatial concerns, a non-Cartesian field of habitation which undermines the stance of objectivity and in which the categories of subject and object give way to a relationship of mutual implication. (3-4)

The buildings described below were literally 'in your face'. The raw, unmissable features of their 'near sphere' (their odour, dankness and lack of warmth) threatened the distanced perception of the 'far sphere' modern audiences typically utilise. Any 'reading' must be off-set by the stark conditions of the spaces themselves. Whether the result is a smooth, binocular semio-phenomenological analysis of the kind recommended by Bert States (8) or the application of two contrasting view-points thrashing it out for dominance, is less important than whether between them they capture the reality of these confronting non-theatre venues.

The use of found spaces went against all the trends which had influenced Australian theatre architecture in the post-1945 period.[4] Artists working in them sought to create 'theatres' only loosely, and in one important sense did not seek to create theatres at all: they were not interested in the re-use of spaces but in the unique qualities of certain locations for one-off productions. The result was a particular aesthetic: raw, uncomfortable, unconventional. Venues ranged from the very large to the tiny. Often they were chosen with aspects of a show in mind. Some were out-of-the-way, and part of the challenge for an audience was to find them at all. Many had only crude auxillary facilities; some had none. When such artists did attract funding, it was channelled into the shows, not the venue.

Performers and spectators thus found themselves framed in new and perhaps unforseen ways. The body in these spaces – both the actors' bodies and the 'body' of the audience – was not clean, it was not safe, it was not 'well lit'. Such performances – as a 'body' of work – created a liminal aesthetic which sought to re-invest a lagging alternative theatre with a renewed counter-cultural edge.

Three Examples

(i)

Name of Company:	Gilgul Theatre 1991-3
Name of Show:	*The Exile Trilogy: The Dybbuk, Es Brent, Levad*

Performers:	Louise Fox, Elisa Gray, Michael Kantor, Yoni Prior, Thomas Wright, Rosalie Zycher
Venue(s):	Carlisle Street Machine Engine Shop, St. Kilda; the Beckett Theatre, Playbox; Everleigh St Railway Yards, Belvoir Street Theatre, Sydney.

The (self-consciously) Jewish Gilgul Theatre is a group of artists associated with the *enfant terrible* of contemporary Australian theatre, director Barrie Kosky. The 'Exile Trilogy' was a series of thematically and performatively linked musical theatre pieces devised between 1991-93, which achieved an outstanding level of critical success. Given its deconstructive style, multiple narrative sourcings and extensive use of Yiddish, a potted summary of the *Trilogy's* themes is unlikely to account for its impact. Many critics argued that literal understanding was unnecessary to either its meaning or enjoyment. Instead what they praised was its visceral power and physical expertise, its riotous (but controlled) use of form.

> Kosky entwines the narrative with the prophecies of Ezekiel, Yiddish vaudeville, Judaic mysticism, psychoanalysis, the Kabbalah and the fate of its original performers, the Vilna Troupe, which itself endured a kind of Diaspora. [He] accretes layer after layer of image from which he conjures histrionics ... [But] though it has intertextuality, it tells its story effortlessly. One could enter the theatre knowing *The Dybbuk* only by repute and come out astonished by the pastiche pageantry. If the production was entirely in Yiddish it would still impress with its insistent and nightmarish imagery and its vivid and beguiling music. (Boyd, 'Exactly').

The doings of the Vilna Troupe – the company responsible for the original *Dybbuk* in the 1920s – formed a meta-narrative frame for all three pieces: the story of a Jewish woman possessed on her wedding night by the soul of a dead lover underscored Gilgul's second play, *Es Brent,* in which God is put on trial by the survivors of a sixteenth-century pogrom. *Levad,* the final part of the Trilogy, presented the fragmented memories of actress Eva Askenfield, a founder member of the Vilna Troupe, mixing in references to the Holocaust and the 'Jewish experience' which formed a substratum to the other two plays. Kosky's comment that the pieces sought to give voice to 'the fractured and displaced recollections of dead, wandering theatre souls' (Hoad,

'*Es Brent*') highlights the dialectic between formal estrangement and emotional coherence which gave them their compulsive force and appeal.

The *Trilogy* is particularly interesting for its use of different theatrical sites. *The Dybbuk* and *Es Brent* were originally performed in a disused machine engine shop in St. Kilda, Melbourne. *The Dybbuk* was staged three times, twice in the engine shop, once in Sydney at the Everleigh Railway Yards, Redfern. *Es Brent's* Sydney venue was, by contrast, a purpose-built stage; Belvoir Street Theatre. *Levad* was staged twice, both times in purpose-built theatres (first Playbox, later Belvoir Street), although elements of the engine shop were reflected in its stage design (see below). Production budgets reflected and influenced venue choices. Gilgul's selection of the engine shop for the first production of *The Dybbuk* was partly economic; it came free of charge courtesy of a local Jewish businessman. The Everleigh Railway Yards, where Sydney audiences saw the show, certainly did not; in fact, Belvoir Street's substantial public funding was integral to its outfitting as a performance venue. *Es Brent* was, like *The Dybbuk,* minimally staged. But it attracted public funding and thus could pay its performers award wages and increase its cast size (to six). The solo show *Levad* was commissioned for Playbox Theatre, where a comparatively large design budget was offset by a lacklustre venue (the Beckett) together with restrictions on its access.

Gilgul's choice of an engine shop as its original performance site was integral not only to the *Exile Trilogy's* staging, but to the evolution of the shows themselves. *The Dybbuk* and *Es Brent* were both developed in the venue, and according to Michael Kantor, a founder member of Gilgul, its configuration, atmosphere and incidental features became an essential dimension of their final performance presence:

> It was covered in a good two inches of pigeon shit. You had to squelch your way through the place. But it instantly evoked some old mysterious space. And it also had this very long carriage way that ran all the way through it. It wasn't a railway line ... but everyone who walked in there said 'my God, that looks like you're looking down a railway line' – which straight away formed the set design. (Kantor)

As well as the layers of accumulated dirt, the engine shop bore many traces of past non-theatre use: work benches, tool shelves and assorted bric-a-brac. Gilgul's designer, architect Peter Corrigan, was in the fortunate position of being able to exploit an environment that had in effect been scenographically established – and just as well, for *The Dybbuk*'s budget was minimal.[5] Although funding was forthcoming for the company's second year of operation it made no attempt to turn the engine shop into a theatre, to clean it up permanently, put in a lighting rig or fix audience seating. In fact, it was with some reluctance that Gilgul returned to the space at all, having originally intended to stage each new show in a different venue. *Es Brent*'s larger budget allowed at most for a few purpose-built design items and another industrial cleaning of the space (the pigeons had returned en masse). However, the company could count on its first show being 'read' into its second in much the same way that the miscellany of the engine shop had formed a connotative backdrop to *The Dybbuk*.

> The residue of the last piece formed the starting blocks for the next piece. The fact that there were still candles sitting around; the fact that there were still these bits of wood hanging around the space; and the meat hooks were still hanging in the air; got us very quickly back into the mould of what we were meant to be thinking about. (Kantor)

But if the engine shop brought with it a dramatic atmosphere, it also imposed less user-friendly parameters. The floor was poured concrete. The Gilgul cast, largely untrained in the methods of physical performance, found themselves bruised and battered from the raw, athletic acting the shows demanded. The space never remained clean for long. At the end of rehearsals clothes and bodies would be covered in dirt and oily residue. There was a serious accident in which a company helper fell through the roof and had her hand almost severed. During the return season of *The Dybbuk* in the winter of 1993, the space was so cold one performer contracted pneumonia. Yet these difficulties seemed to be part of the engine shop's appeal. They did not need to be ameliorated because they were an essential dimension of its embodied dramatic value.[6]

The Dybbuk and *Es Brent* proved more popular than Gilgul could have hoped. After *Es Brent*, the Australia Council solicited an application from the company for annual funding (it declined to submit one), while Kosky found himself feted as a director of unique talent and ability. Such success attracted the attention of mainstream theatres, and Gilgul was invited to stage the last part of the *Trilogy* in conjunction with Playbox's 1993 subscription season. With this offer came the production resources an established company could provide, but it meant severing the relationship with the engine shop. *Levad* was to be presented in the Beckett Theatre, a 170-seat studio space located at the Malthouse, Playbox's inner city venue. The environment was thus quite different from the found space. The Beckett's function is to provide a muted atmosphere suitable for the different shows passing through it. Any physical features beyond the standard decor must be supplied by the artists coming in. What the engine shop provided naturally now had to be designed:

> I always felt this incredible divide [with *Levad*]. Because here was me in my shabby costume and stinking old salt ... and a couple of feet away people were sitting on very nicely padded seats in ordered rows with those little lights up the side of the stairs. And I'm meant to be down on the sixth level of hell! It was like they were watching me through a window from another world. (Prior, Interview)

Not only was a layer of meaning stripped away but an important performance condition was also voided. *Levad* was not developed in its performance space. It was rehearsed over five weeks in a room dedicated to that function alone. The series of creative conversations gridding the evolution of the *Trilogy*, which had once centred on the engine shop, were reshaped to conform with Playbox's lines of command. Set drawings had to be ready in advance to meet the deadlines of the workshop and the Beckett was available only at certain times. Thus the design was agreed before the show, and developed while the performer, Yoni Prior, was unable to work with it until the production week itself. The company was also stuck with the fact that the Beckett as a theatre could only be 'read' differently by an act of extreme expropriation:

> In the end they had to literally wrap the theatre in plastic they hated it so much. They wrapped the floor, they wrapped the ceiling, they wrapped all the bannisters in black plastic because it stank ... And instantly it became a design. And so ugly a design! Suddenly there was this corrugated wall, and the corrugated wall, speaking candidly, was Peter [Corrigan] attempting to get the resonances of Carlisle Street into a theatre. It [didn't] work ... It was just design upon design upon design ... The problem is that you go into the Beckett and it's not offering you anything, it's only sucking. You have to offer, offer, offer lots to fill it up because it's not helping you in any way. (Kantor)

The focus of the company's efforts had shifted. Its first two shows had been propelled more by enthusiasm and artistic inspiration than resources and remuneration. In the best sense, Gilgul had been outside the frame of reference of the established industry. Its grunge look and unpolished skills, mirrored so perfectly by the grimy environment of the engine shop, were not so much a design aesthetic as an attribute of its theatrical persona. Two years later the situation was different.[7] After *Levad* closed the *Trilogy* was transported to Sydney and sold as part of Belvoir Street Theatre's 1993 season. Restaged outside the found space, *The Dybbuk* and *Es Brent* lost their original impact, although *The Dybbuk* was at least performed in a disused railway yard. *Levad*, now in a theatre more conducive to its needs, arguably improved. But the shows were not 'read' in the same way. Gilgul (the 'Jew Crew' as Kosky quipped at the 1993 Sydney Critics' Awards) was now an acknowledged success. For the company, some reviewers and maybe the audience as well, its meteroic rise from lowly fringe endeavour to lauded theatrical front-runner collapsed its shows together in an inter-quotational ribbon of ambivalent meaning. What had been a set of parameters intrinsic to the engine shop itself was now a 'look' in a mainstream process laboriously recreating the felt circumstances in which the Trilogy was first evolved.

Along with mainstream money came mainstream meaning. Though one can over-romanticise its cash-strapped origins, Gilgul's choice of the engine shop for its first shows exemplifies not only a relation between artists and space but between artwork and audience: a cultural exchange of meaning, not just the utilisation of an architectural configuration. When the found space was abandoned, the company was vulnerable to a recuperation of its cultural challenge and it is possible to see in Gilgul's work since an attempt to find once more the creative inspiration the engine shop provided.

(ii)

Deviser/Director:	Lyndal Jones
Name of Show:	*Spitfire 123 (From the Darwin Translations)* 1996
Performers:	Milijana Cancar, Simon Duncan, Deanne Flatley, Helen Hopkins, Nadja Kostich, Shelley Lassica, Rees Muldune, Boris Rotar, Michael Sheridan, Bryan Smith.
Venue(s):	Lonsdale Street Electricity Power Station, Melbourne CBD

If the *Exile Trilogy* was a beginning for Gilgul, *Spitfire 123* formed part of a well-established body of achievement for installation and performance artist Lyndal Jones. With a background in dance, theatre, the visual and video arts, Jones' work, stretching back to the 1970s, is marked by an interplay of different media and the deployment of cross-disciplinary exegesis. This discourse forms a backdrop to the art works themselves and occasionally plays an active role (as program notes) in helping the audience/viewer interpret the piece on offer. These are arranged in self-consciously sequential patterns, as 'series'. To date Jones has produced three: *At Home,* a five-piece series over a three-year period (1978-80); *The Prediction Pieces,* a ten-piece series over a ten-year period (1981-92); and *From the Darwin Translations,* a six-piece series over a six-year period (1992-98), of which *Spitfire 123* is the fourth part. The series themselves range from pure installation pieces in recognised gallery spaces to pure performance pieces in purpose-built theatres, and a wide variety of hybrids in between.

Spitfire 123 stands out from the rest of Jones' *oeuvre* in the style and deployment of its diverse media: it sought to combine elements of video installation, music presentation and theatre performance in a single work which nevertheless presented its sections differently by utilising four contiguous spaces. As *Spitfire 123*'s audience moved from room to room the type of art work on offer and its style varied. But the thematic preoccupations, chosen imagery and selected formal devices remained constant. The effect was to arrest narrative expectations and replace them with a cooler, more reflective viewing strategy – 'observational' as a number of critics described it. Again, this was deliberate, springing from the creative strategy Jones brings to all her works, a strategy laid out in point form at the time of *The Prediction Pieces.*[8]

Though necessarily limited in capturing its experiential impact, segments of *Spitfire 123* exist in published script form (Jones, *Spitfire*). Appended to the performance text is a statement of artists' intentions and a description of the show's literal action and master images. In the first section, 'Studio', the audience was confronted by an installation of ten TV sets on which, after a short exchange between two actors, images of red poppies in a field appear. In the second section, 'Stage', a woman with long red hair sang on a sound stage to guitar accompaniment, while a man got dressed as a Spitfire pilot and images were projected onto a monitor. In 'Bunker', the site of the longest, performance-oriented section, four men and four women danced, moved about and spoke into microphones about their sexual fantasies, while liminal meanings in the action hinted at the complicated gender relations between them. And in the final section, 'Alley', the audience, moved outside the venue, witnessed a scene in which the cast, its numbers increased, walked up a darkened lane to a wire barrier, froze on hearing a plane fly overhead, and then ran past into the night.

As its title suggests, *Spitfire 123* was dominated the sounds and imagery of the World War II fighter plane (though other meanings of the word 'spitfire' were alluded to). Jones made a special trip to England to obtain film shot from a pilot's aerial point of view, having an actual Spitfire fitted with a cockpit camera for the purpose (the footage was screened in the 'Stage' section). The sound of a plane flying overhead was a recurrent device, as were the Remembrance Day poppies and the figure of a kitted-out Spitfire pilot. Jones' concern with evolutionary theory intersected with the iconic image of the pilot as 'hero' – sexually alluring, courageous, 'the fittest' – and extracts from Darwin's *The Descent of Man and Selection in Relation to Sex* were used in the 'Bunker' section of the show and quoted in the program. But if *Spitfire 123* relied on an intricate aesthetic legacy drawn from Jones' earlier work, it also drew on the immediate conditions of its found environment. Jones' aims as an artist are site-specific, to 'find the place in a space' as she puts it (Jones, Interview). All her pieces are developed for particular buildings. *Spitfire 123* was staged in a disused electricity power station. Its atmosphere, architecture and incidental features fundamentally conditioned many of the artistic choices Jones made:

> I heard that there was this old reclaimed building Melbourne City Council were going to give some people access to; so I went and had a look through it ... The electricity supply workers had just left the week before – it had bits and pieces of old furniture in it ... [It] was big and tough, and *filthy* – [but] I said, all right there are four areas here that look fantastic. We are going to make a rule: the set has to come out of the furniture that's in the space. The only thing we can bring in is technology and performers ... We even found the chairs in there which [the audience] sat on. The very first space had a beautiful wall [and] a big bench along the wall and beautiful windows. I wrestled with that space a lot but [finally] made it a place the audience could walk around in. I was giving the audience roles in different events, hoping that they would experience not only the event, but themselves and

> *know where they were.* (Jones, Interview [Original emphasis])

The power station's four big spaces and brutal, Soviet-style facade provided *Spitfire 123*'s sections with separate but phenomenally-linked connotative niches. Over eight weeks the production was developed in the found space. By night Jones wrote up her performance text; by day she rehearsed that text with the performers or observed their contributions which, in turn, were conditioned by an exploration of the power station's features and the personal associations these held for them:

> For the third piece the only set were lockers and old electric lights that came out on angles ... simply the lighting that was there ... We made the piece in there. One of the dancers [saw] that there was this old concrete block ... and one of the women was talking about sex with a horse (or something!) and he actually lay down and lay back on it and said 'and what do you think of this, uh?' And I said, keep it, it's fantastic! People were making those kind of offers all the time. The whole spatial development of the piece was wrestled out of the place. The fact of those levels, and the industrial sense of it. And it was written for a deserted building. That was the whole sense of it. (Jones, Interview)

When *Spitfire 123* opened it was received by critics with mixed responses. The twelve-page program was felt by some reviewers to be staking a claim to significance the show itself did not fulfil. '*Spitfire 123* is a performance of impressions where meaning is elusive, suggested, imagined but not stated,' noted Helen Thomson. Yet what is also evident is that those seeing the production made particular connections with the different media employed in each location and were divided over which sections worked:

> I wanted to see what happened with an act of translation; what [an audience] would do with that. And what I found was that they did very little with it. By and large, people who were visual artists ... loved the first [section] and the [fourth] one outside. The music people enjoyed the second [section]; some of them, the more theatrical of them, liked the third one too. The theatre people hated the first [section], were mixed about the second one, liked the third one and got terribly bored in the fourth one ... People were pissed off with me ... that I didn't make a coherent work. They could see that meaning was accumulating, in some kind of a way. In fact it was the same piece done in four different ways, really: it was about a group of people and then there is the sound of the

> plane overhead, then there is their reaction. (Jones, Interview)

Audience members 'read' *Spitfire 123* vagariously – younger audiences more enthusiastically – which might be expected given the multiple perspectives of the show's concerns. Of interest to this discussion, however, is not resistances to postmodern experimentation among those with an investment in a particular form, but the identification of the power station as a problem venue. It was critically denounced as an aggravation to the 'observational' feel of the show. For some reviewers the power station was not exciting and adventurous but cold and cavernous, attributes which seem to adversely affect their experiences of the art produced within its walls. [9]

If *Spitfire 123* had been developed in a different building would it have had a different effect on such reviewers? Essentially a series of compounding disappearances – neither theatre, nor musical piece, nor performance art, nor video installation – clearly the form, like its content sources, referenced genres in passing rather than reproducing any one of them. *Spitfire 123* created a complex cross-media sign system within the atmospheric recesses of a dark and forbidding building. The show remains a key event in recent Australian experimental performance, and its Ian Potter gallery performances and tour to the United Kingdom Germany and Holland in the following year were highly successful.

(iii)

Name of Company:	ACTA (Going Through Stages)
Deviser/Director:	Peter King
Name of Show:	*Dazzle of Shadow* 1993
Performers:	Michael. Collins, Trevor Patrick, Damian Richardson, David Wicks.
Venue(s):	15th Floor, Tivoli Building, Melbourne CBD

The work of Peter King also marks a nodal point in Melbourne theatre. As director of a group of experimentally-minded collaborators, Going Through Stages,[10] his numerous productions – over fifty to date – influenced a wide circle of artists not immediately associated with the company. These shows span a broad stylistic spectrum from orthodox stage presentation to abstract, site-specific performances. *Dazzle of Shadow* falls firmly in the latter category but even so it is hard to pick out one show from King's *oeuvre* and treat it in isolation. Instead, the form and force of the production is firmly inscribed on the company's total body of work, which is both a reference map for its numerous citations and an authorising stamp for the validity of its stage world. To 'read' *Dazzle of Shadow* is to 'read' Peter King, his preoccupations, methods of work and ultimate artistic aims.

King's work can be seen as a series of endlessly recessing footnotes. His shows consist less of images or actions with specific meanings than iterated and proleptic structures of overlapping performance moments. These link an elusive, cerebral discourse and a visually splendid and corporeally precise *mise en scène*, one using dance, music, physical performance and spoken text in a various combinations. Yet though the intellectual under-pinnings of productions are dense rarely are they quoted directly. While it is too much to say that one could enjoy a Peter King show without knowing its informing sources, as can be the case with postmodern work, it utilises a double language whose terms find no exact equivalence in one another. 'Tenor' and 'vehicle' do not cohere. Instead they spiral away from each other producing gaps, moments of hard, crystalline un-meaning, intentionally difficult for a spectator to reconcile with what a particular show is purportedly 'about'. The effect is to splice narrative into competing ribbons. An audience has a choice: whether to pick through the thematic fragments of a given show's structural ellipses, or to simply enjoy the sumptuous stage visuals.[11]

Like a number of Going Through Stage's past productions, *Dazzle of Shadow* was developed for a particular locale, in this instance the fifteenth floor of what used to be the Tivoli theatre site but is now a blandly typical city office building. So why this particular found space?

> I wanted height. And the true answer is pragmatic: the building had just been purchased by RMIT. So even though it was the largest single project grant ever given by the Australia Council [$90,000], the building came for nothing apart from maintenance. So that's why that building was chosen. But its siting was perfect ... Outside one window you saw illumined the Capitol Theatre (by the Griffins) ... I wanted 360 degree fenestration .. I would have preferred if the windows had been double-glazed because the building is actually contravening building regulations ... Some nights you could hear the Chinese gentleman playing 'Bolero' on the

> flute [on street level] right up on the fifteenth floor. But I needed that standard, Western panorama of the city ... I did not want to take over or bring in the narrative of the Aboriginal 'ground'. (King, Interview)

Dazzle of Shadow brought together two of King's on-going concerns: architecture as practical system and as metaphor; and the effects of dominant discourse, in this case the writings of white Australian anthropologists on the different racial and language groups bracketed by the term 'Aboriginal people'. At the heart of the show lay three citations: the possibly apocryphal tale of 'sky-trees' falling down and creating the hole that is the sky; C. P. Mountford's description of watching Albert Namatjira paint (particularly the statement 'darkness had enveloped us by the time we had reached the main gorge'); and Strehlow's report of a Maryvale dance ceremony as the last of its kind, given the policies of Aboriginal assimilation then in force ('a silence that knows no end is about to close in upon this peaceful site'). Bracketing these fragments and giving them a further twist was the Jacobean poem 'The Night' by Henry Vaughan, sung towards the end of the show.[12] What the show did not do was deal with issues of 'Aboriginality', either in a constructed or an ethnic sense. Instead, it fed into the anabolic mechanism of its chosen stage style the rhetorical trope of classic anthropological writing, thus chipping away at its assumptions. Mountford's and Strehlow's statements were seen to constitute a large-scale, officially-endorsed cultural projection, one crushing the life out of the people they believed they were neutrally observing.[13]

Since it was so much 'not about the land', an urban location for *Dazzle of Shadow* was essential. In this respect, the Tivoli building provided a 360° panorama of the city outside. This could be factored into the show's reference system and stage style, the light from the illuminated buildings around providing a sensory context for Ian De Gruchy's spectacular use of projection (eleven projectors were used, all at different angles, covering the entire room). There were some practical problems. Vertical access was difficult, since everybody had to ascend to the space via a single cramped lift. The point-load on the floor was also a concern given the weight of the percussion instruments the composer had specially designed for the production. But basically the venue was a flat, featureless box: broad, deep and low-ceilinged. Nothing remained of its previous use and its aseptic decor suggested no immediate function either. It was an ideal screen for the un-rooted anthropological project the company wanted to problematise, a found space whose acquired meaning would lacquer over its residual nature.

The show itself was divided into three sections: the first a live group performance, the second a dance solo and the third a combination of performance, dance and music. A choreographic vocabulary was drawn partly from the movements of 'hysterical' patients as notated by Charcot and collaborators at the Salpêtrière asylum and partly from the phonetic acting system of Michael Chekhov:

> The ideas were to do with synaesthesia. Chekhov published a list of sounds and appropriate gestures, and the appropriate emotion for each sound and gesture. And [*Dazzle of Shadow*'s] performers were to have those, and they were diminishing ... Chekhov's list of phonemes is not exhaustive. There are certain sounds you can't make. So the performers were in a state of potentiality at the start, not making ... any sounds or any particular movements. But as those strong systems were rehearsed, [this potentiality] diminished. So you finally got stuck with the shrunken number of phonemes provided by Chekhov and [his] shrunken number of movements ... And that was a parallel to the anthropologists' or linguists' inability to transcribe the phonetics of so many Aboriginal language groups. (King, Interview)

As with the *Exile Trilogy* and *Spitfire 123*, the show was evolved in the space itself. An eight-week period was broken into two halves: during the first month the four performers and King rehearsed the diminishing chains of sound and movement in which the narrative fragments were to be 'told'; in the second, these were spliced with scenographic and musical ideas which had until then been developed separately. King's schemata of the performance – looking something like a John Cage's score – combined all performance details into a single spatio-temporal 'week'. But his plan hit a snag when the chains of sound and movement did not 'take' with the performers. Abstruse and difficult, they seemed impossible for their bodies to physicalise. At the one-month mark when new elements were being introduced, what should have been a layering turned into a salvage operation. Rehearsals with the performers soaked up more and more time: two, three, four hours each day spent going over routines which had vanished by the following day. The show – already centrifugal in its internal relations – seemed unable to provide a unifying structure to compensate (indeed, how could it when even the *idea* of a central point of view was under challenge). The performance dimension of the show threatened to topple into incoherence.

But while the show's live aspect suffered, its scenographic side thrived. Perhaps the found space itself had something to do with both outcomes. In its lack of atmosphere, history and incidental feature there was nothing for the cast's physical sign system to anchor to. Their work slid off the walls much as it did off their bodies. As a corporate building whose views were more valuable than its intrinsic environment, the 'inside' of the venue was wholly determined by its 'outside' position. Yet what for the performers was a spiritual hole became for the disembodied slide-world created by De Gruchy a succession of amenable folds on which to project endlessly suggestive motifs: words, whirls, bars, stars and, at one point, even the city-scape panorama – the metropolitan Melbourne outside the venue 'read' back onto the parameters of the show itself.

Owing to past disagreements with a number of Melbourne critics *Dazzle of Shadow* attracted only one (mixed) review from an established newspaper. But even if more had been written, it would be hard to gauge its impact. Inextricably bound up with themes and images of the company's previous work – and seen that way by its loyal core audiences – tending towards arbitrariness in its gestural system but less so in its use of slides, lighting and music; and designed to subvert any easy summation of its underlying 'message'; its final effect is perhaps immeasurable: staged in a found environment as inscrutable as the piece itself, which faithfully framed it at times and at others provided no supporting echo at all.

Conclusion

The found spaces discussed in this chapter highlight the dangers, difficulties and potential benefits of siting live performance outside purpose-built theatres. The relationship between a given production and its building is likely to be complex, more so if developed in a venue, as well as for it. To say that a show is conditioned by the space it choses is an understatement. There is no artistic choice which is not fundamentally transformed by the physical environment in which it must be realised. Venues do not house theatre productions; they create them. This is truer still if we factor in the coding around found spaces, which enforces an established pecking order of cultural worth. Carlson comments:

> The physical surroundings of performance never act as a totally neutral filter or frame. They are themselves always

> culturally encoded, and have always, sometimes blatantly, sometimes subtly, contributed to the reception of the performance. The student of theatre work seeking to understand the presentation of a play without some knowledge of this performance matrix will inevitably be dealing with a partial perspective and in many cases with a seriously flawed one. (*Places* 206)

The most important aspect of the 'performance matrix' of the venues described above was a negative one: they were not theatres. More than being simply architecturally different, they were read as a challenge to the values of conventional theatre, the outline of this 'absent other' forming part of their investment. This provided those artists utilising found spaces in the 1990s with a clear historical pedigree: that of the alternative theatre movement of the 1960s and 1970s. Although far from homogenous, one important characteristic underwrote this movement: the disavowal of established notions of 'theatre' and an attempt to create radically new production styles and performer-audience relations. In Australia it quickly became associated with a coterie of domestic writers and the discovery of a 'national voice'. But there was always more to the New Wave than the production of playtexts. Another important strand was the conversion of select industrial buildings into new theatres. The companies cohering around these venues found their house style conditioned by (literally) concrete parameters. The publication of many New Wave playtexts has made an important section of its work accessible but also has skewed historical perceptions, privileging the written component. In reality, no part of the movement's achievement was separable from any other.

The fragmentation of alternative theatre during the 1980s is a complex phenomenon. Decreasing public funding, declining audiences and the collapse of key companies fuelled what was already a predisposition to fissuration, given the range of artists represented. But core values were not entirely lost. Two of the artists discussed in this chapter had their roots in 1970s alternative theatre: King, an active member of the Australian Performing Group, and Jones, a founder member of the UK company Cunning Stunts. It is possible to see in the use of found spaces generally an attempt to rally counter-cultural forces, to continue the New Wave's exploration, not only of different styles of theatre, but of different ideas of it.

To some extent this rallying was successful. A review of all Melbourne Fringe Festival productions from 1988 to 1995 situated outside purpose-built theatres (some forty-seven works) shows the increasing use of such venues: from two in 1987 to ten in 1995. The range of venues changes qualitatively also. 1988-89 lists found spaces which are vaguely theatre-like: halls, galleries, café stages. After 1990 the selection is more varied: a fabric warehouse, a textile factory, a deserted brewery, the Luna Park funfair and even a shopping mall. Some of these productions clearly touched a nerve: *Nobody*, a show about homelessness performed in a city back street, was closed down in its first week after the then state Premier, Jeff Kennett, pressured Melbourne City Council to revoke its performance licence (Thomson, Review).

A selection of Melbourne shows produced outside the Fringe Festival in the same period (forty-three works) again reveals an extensive range of found spaces. But the status of most projects is different. There is a greater proportion of commercial, funded and festival work. The investment of an old stables for *Titus Andronicus*, for example, was a logistical exercise of some magnitude. It involved expensive tiers of seating, a full lighting rig, a large design and a cast of fifteen. Produced for the 1991 Melbourne International Festival of the Arts by an alternative company, Theatreworks, its budget was a comparatively large one of $180,000. Whatever challenge was intrinsic to the show, its cultural setting recuperated it: the production came across as another large-scale show, marketed and priced accordingly. This sounds a warning bell as to the value of found spaces. Their use is not only a culturally-coded exercise, it is a contested one. It is a rare international festival now which does not have its quota of site-specific work, but the values lying behind the investment of such venues are more conventional. The shows are heavily capitalised and commercially sold. There is often a surreptitious attempt to re-introduce the features of the mainstream theatre experience: greater warmth, refreshments, better audience seating. Not that such conditions are in themselves undesirable, but they affect the framing of productions just as these are determined by the buildings chosen. The venues are 'read' as theatres, even when they do not resemble them.

It is likely that with the introduction of medium-density housing into inner-city suburbs the investment of found spaces for theatrical purposes will decline. Gentrification and re-zoning in the late 1990s have seen a drop in the absolute number of appropriate buildings available. With their demographic targets now reached, there is less incentive for state and local authorities to look favourably on the issuing of temporary performance licences. In recent years the emphasis has been on creating 'arts precincts' by recycling old town halls which, as listed buildings, have a limited functional use anyway. All of which herds artists towards the use of existing theatres. Increasingly, the choice is not between purpose-built venues and found spaces, but between purpose-built venues and no venue at all.

References

Allen, Richard & Karen Pearlman. *Performing the Unnameable: An Anthology of Australian Performance Texts.* Sydney: Currency/RealTime,1999.

Boyd, Chris. 'In Exactly the Right Spirit.' Rev. of *The Dybbuk.* by Gilgul Theatre, Town Hall Motors, Melbourne. *Financial Review,* 29 Nov. 1991.

Carlson, Marvin. *Places of Performance: The Semiotics of Theatre Architecture.* New York: Cornell UP, 1989.

— 'Four Approaches: Historical Survey of Theatrical Forms.' *Approaching Theatre.* Andre Helbo et al.. Bloomington: Indiana UP, 1991. 48-56.

Crimeen, Bob. Rev. of *Spitfire 123* by Lyndal Jones at the Lonsdale Street Electricity Power Station. *Sunday Herald-Sun* 14 April 1996.

D'Arcy, Eamon. 'Stop Building Studio Spaces.' Spinks. 107-109.

Elam, Keir. *The Semiotics of Theatre and Drama.* London: Methuen, 1980.

Fraser, Vivian. 'Designing for 'Found' Spaces.' Spinks. 97-102.

Garner, Stanton. *Bodied Spaces: Phenomenology in Contemporary Drama.* New York: Cornell UP, 1994.

Hoad, Brian. Rev. of *Es Brent.* Belvoir Street Theatre, Sydney. *Bulletin,* 14 Dec. 1993.

Jones, Lyndal. *The Prediction Pieces 1981-1991: Writings and Images from the Archive.* Sydney: Contemporary Art Archive, 1992.

— '*Spitfire 123*: First Performance.' *Performing the Unnameable: An Anthology of Australian Performance Texts.* Ed. Richard Allen & Karen Pearlman. Sydney: Currency Press/RealTime, 1999. 74-86.

— Interview with author. 29 March 1999.

Kantor, Michael. Interview with author. 23 Feb. 1999.

King, Peter. 'Dazzle of Shadow: Lines for the Desert', Royal Melbourne Institute of Technology , 1993. 203-217.

— Interview with author. 22 April 1999.

Mackintosh, Iain. *Architecture, Actor and Audience.* London: Routledge, 1993.

Melbourne Fringe Festival Programs. 1988-1995.

Morphett, John. 'Theatres – The Commercial Realities.' Spinks. 111-116.

Nicholson, Derek. 'The Views of a Horizontalist: Design in Performance.' *Aspect* 32/33 (1985): 63-80.

Pavis, Patrice. *Languages of the Stage: Essays in the Semiology of Theatre.* New York: Performing Arts Journal, 1982.

— 'Production and Reception in the Theatre.' *New Directions in the Theatre.* Ed. Julian Hilton. Houndsmill: Macmillan, 1993. 25-71.

Prior, Yoni. Interview with author. 19 Feb. 1999.

Schechner, Richard. *Environmental Theatre.* New York: Hawthorn, 1973.

Spinks, Kim, ed. *Australian Theatre Design*. NSW: Australian Production Designers Association, 1992.

States, Bert O. *Great Reckonings in Little Rooms: On the Phenomenology of the Theatre*. Los Angeles: U of California P, 1985.

Thomas, Martin (with James Waites). 'Our Living Arts Centres: Or Notes on the Breeding of White Elephants.' *New Theatre Australia* (July-Aug. 1989): 6-9.

Thomson, Helen. Rev. of *Nobody* by Wendy Dent. *Australian* 7 Oct. 1994.

Thomson, Helen. *The Age*, 17 Apr. 1996.

Thorne, Ross. 'Performing Arts Centres: The Phenomenon and What Has Influenced Their Being.' Spinks. 3-67.

Welchman, John. *Modernism Relocated: Towards a Cultural Studies of Visual Modernity*. St Leonards, NSW: Allen & Unwin, 1995.

Notes

1 Strategies the government used to attract people back into the city included the 'Postcode 3000' campaign – the conversion of city office blocks for residential use; and the Swanston Street Walk Project – the re-zoning of Melbourne's most central road as a pedestrian precinct. The increase in cultural expenditure by local authorities in the early 1990s (especially the Melbourne City Council) should thus be viewed in light of wider social and political goals.

2 For a shorter version of his analysis of historical trends in theatre architecture, see Carlson, 'Four Approaches'.

3 For an outline of the semiological approach to live performance see Pavis, *Languages of the Stage* and Elam. For a response to the criticisms of formalism and the undervaluing of social context, see Pavis 'Production and Reception'.

4 Three trends in Australian theatre architecture set the pattern for – and account for the violent rejection of – contemporary purpose-built theatres. The first laid the emphasis on facades, foyers and auditoria, and was predominantly concerned with seating capacity and venue flexibility. From the 1950s onwards it resulted in the so-called 'edifice complex', the rapid proliferation of multi-purpose arts centres around the country. Some have argued that this marked a return to the 'theatre experience', that audiences are attracted to venues providing a broad range of amenities, seating comfort and technically slick productions (Morphett). Others point out the drawbacks many of their stages present: inflexibility, poor acoustics, bad sight-lines and exorbitant hire costs: (Nicholson, Thomas, especially Mackintosh 110). Alongside the cultural centre movement was a more artist-centred trend, one concerned with the search for what Ross Thorne dubs 'the ideal theatre' (Thorne 57). This focused on audience–stage relations and on venue adaptability. Theatres were to become 'spaces', endlessly reconstituted according to the changing needs of particular projects. But the results were not much better than the larger theatres and these venues too have been the target of censure (D'Arcy 107-108). The practical failure of both the cultural centres and studio spaces resulted in a *third* trend, the conversion of pre-existing spaces, usually disused factory buildings. So well-known is this approach that a list of companies springing up in the wake of Whitlam's 1973 doubling of the federal arts budget is virtually a list of the buildings they inhabited (see Thorne 52). These alternative buildings served well the alternative drama they housed, and not just in a functional sense. The

conversion of industrial spaces was accompanied by an aggressive rejection of traditional theatre structures and the cultural *habitus* they inculcated. Instead, the venues were allied with the creation of a more 'honest' and 'truthful' dramatic confrontation between actors and audience. Some substance was given this by the fact that the new venues were frequently much smaller than existing purpose-built theatres and their stages located closer to the (usually makeshift) tiers of audience seating. Spectators could not escape, even if they wanted to, the connotations of buildings which so stridently proclaimed their non-theatrical origins. The result was a perceptual dissonance of a culturally productive kind. The buildings were 'read' into the work, which in turn was informed and constrained by the buildings. Fruitful though the conversions trend was, it had its limits and by the 1980s these had to some extent been reached. A number of venues were bought by developers and either re-converted to non-theatre use or knocked-down. New conversions taking place were noticeably more capitalised than earlier efforts. In Melbourne, the Malthouse (1990) and the Gasworks (1992), were venues laying claim to a functional explicitness but which recreated a 'theatre experience' ambience within a non-theatre shell. Yet at the same time as the allotment of theatres was diminishing, demand for them at certain times of the year was increasing. The 'festivalisation of the arts' during the 1980s saw a marked increase in the number and size of festivals all over Australia. These brought in their wake new marketing and production pressures and new demands on venue hire.

5 This did not mean that important design choices could not be made. One that had a profound effect was the decision to play *The Dybbuk* across the space – to access the width, rather than the depth of the potential stage area: 'What was great about the space [was] that it had the three caverns. But we began actually facing the back cavern ... [But] what we eventually did was have [the audience] sitting along the middle one, facing the side of that, rather than facing either end of the space – which is where we started ... The idea was that people would walk towards the audience from this endless [room] ... At the very least it gave you a greater sense of "the road". Most simply it gave you more of a sense of sitting on the side of a road watching this journey pass you ... the [show] was directed towards ... the outside, where the audience had come from.' (Prior, Interview).

6 This was true not only for the performers but for Gilgul's audience as well: 'The thing about that space was that it really gave [the audience] someone to be ... [it] endowed them with roles ... You'd stand about in the foyer and there wasn't a seat in sight... and then [you would] [have] to go in one by one through that little door and sit there and endure the same sort of discomfort and cold and wind the actors were enduring, and hear all of the real sounds of the pigeons on the roof and the trams going outdoors and really be part of the fantasy that was being set up on stage. And particularly with *The Dybbuk* you had to *work*, you had to move your head, [otherwise] you couldn't *see* what was [happening]... [But] it was a hoot. It was an adventure. It was involving. It was an event.' (Prior, Interview).

7 The increase in Gilgul's ticket prices reflect the change: the price of seeing *Levad* at Playbox was $27, a 60% increase on either *The Dybbuk* or *Es Brent,* both priced at $18.

8 *Towards a Manifesto for an Art that Crosses Disciplines*:

(1) A space is a place – it holds a history, it forms a context.

(2) An artist is a person (not an object, not a body). She/he has a history, forms a context.

(3) An artist is engendered and thus so are the projects she/he produces.

(4) What we do is what we say. (A form has a content. A content has a form).

(5) An artist is engaged at all levels of production (in thinking as well as privately creating/publicly performing) in a physical act.

(6) Many works are made, in producing one. Not only does process determine product – every thought and act we call process is also product.

(7) The relationship of the viewer/audience is with the art work, not the artist. (Jones, *Prediction Pieces* 9)

9 Bob Crimeen was typically severe: 'On a night when winter invaded Melbourne early, chill air inside – and for the mindless (and wordless finale) outside – the cavernous power station numbed just about everything beneath the cerebral cavity, too. To add to patron discomfort, the audience must stand for three of the four parts of *Spitfire 123,* played out in three separate spaces within the building, then in an external under-the-stars lane. With an audience the size of that on opening night, the single-level playing spaces are uncomfortably squeesy and, one imagines, a sight-lines nightmare for patrons less that AFL ruckman height.'

10 Most particularly Ian De Grucy (visual effects designer), Michael Scot-Mitchell (production designer,) Jonathon Mills (composer) and David Wicks (performer).

11 Commenting on *Axes Edge,* for example, Welchman notes the effect of this kind of aesthetic schizophrenia: 'As always in King's theatre, the governing *motif* of [a] production ... is present as both a locus and a metaphor. These motifs are literally and symbolically present at all moments in the development of the pieces. And one can claim that it is the play of consumption and transference between the material expectations of *place* and the symbolic codings through which places are socially and psychically articulated that is the crux ... of [his] work' (204).

12 The final stanza, which reflects the show's overall themes, is quoted by King in an unpublished paper:

> There is in God (some say)
> A deep, but dazzling darkness; As men here
> Say it is late and dusky, because they
> See not all clear;
> O for that night! Where I in him
> Might live invisible and dim.

13 King writes: '*Dazzle of Shadow* is a disfiguring, a defacing, of some affective parts of the anthropologists who made the Aboriginal Other their own Same. Their project, however unthinkingly, was one of spatial, social and spiritual destruction ... From the cities which conferred degrees, anthropologists set off into the interior to find, and to inherit, perhaps usurp, social, spatial and secret truths indited and performed there, and returned to the coastal cities and publish texts that showed what they had discovered and overmastered within ... They made the interior a mirror ... They projected on it their own reflections, "darkness visible". Anthropologists became graveside orators,

necrologues, burying what may have been dazzle and darkness about the shades' (King, 'Dazzle of Shadow' 2).

13.
Obsolescent bodies and prosthetic gods

Anne Marsh

> *Miniaturized and biocompatible, technology lands on the body. Although unheralded, it is one of the most important events in human history – focussing physical change on each individual. Technology is not only attached, but is also implanted. ONCE A CONTAINER, TECHNOLOGY NOW BECOMES A COMPONENT OF THE BODY.* (Stelarc, 'Enhanced Gesture')

Throughout his career Stelarc has been probed, pierced and plugged-in. His body, consistently referred to as 'the body', has been used as a kind of experimental laboratory: a physical space on which, and within which, certain ideas have become manifest. The psychological ramifications of this activity have not been of interest to the artist, nor has he been concerned about how these ideas and images, in performance and photo/video documentation, might represent for the spectator, certain psycho-social dilemmas.

In the 1970s and 1980s Stelarc's spectacular body suspensions were meant to illustrate the obsolescence of the body. The action of piercing the skin with hooks and suspending it in space was supposed to demonstrate that by stretching the skin it would be possible to hollow out the body: to get rid of the soft, decaying internal organs and fill it with technological components, better able to adapt to a more demanding environment. Most specifically, this redesigning of the body would enable it to live in extraterrestrial space; in the 1990s Stelarc began to relocate his body in cyberspace.

Stelarc has consistently presented a discourse which appears dualistic and at times polarised in its representation. The suspension events conjured images of ancient rites and shamanism. Experiencing almost intolerable levels of pain, the artist endured physical suffering to create his art. Lying on sharpened stakes like an Indian Fakir and soaring through the air above a cathedral in Copenhagen, the artist transcended the ordinary world for the average spectator. To these images, the artist added lectures and papers outlining his theories of the obsolete body. Concurrently he had created the Third Hand and begun to externalise his internal probings by wiring the biological and physiological body for sound. The body amplifications performed with the Third Hand and/or laser eyes mapped the surface of the body, amplifying heart beat, blood flow, muscle movement. In recent events, Stelarc is wired to a muscle stimulator programmed by a computer and operated by touch screens at remote sites so that audience members can activate 'the body'. Technology invades the body in these performances as the artist is choreographed by the machine.

The early suspension events present a masochistic image of the body, which becomes entangled with sexual rites, catharsis, shamanism and ritual. Stelarc's work at the end of the twentieth century and in the twenty-first century might be said to be 'double-dipping' in terms of cult value. On one hand it falls under the fashionable umbrella term 'modern primitivism', where it can be found on the Internet along with other body art rituals. On the other hand, Stelarc presents events and creates dialogues about biological-technological interfaces and the techno-invasion of the body (Marsh, *Body and Self*). Here he is projecting a profoundly anti-humanist position where the psycho-social subject as we know it disappears. In this dualistic way, the work hovers on an ontological axis between 'primitive' ritual and bio-technological spectacle.

The double exposure of Stelarc's work as modern primitivism and cyborg theatre presents a polarity of Being that is underwritten by Western metaphysics. The male body has shamanistic powers in the brave new world where the project of modernity comes to fruition through a synthesis of mind, body and technology. Throughout the techno-debate one witnesses a binary language steeped in gender. On one hand woman is nature, on the other technology (culture) is described as the 'dark continent'; a phrase originally used by Sigmund Freud to describe female sexuality. It was also the name given to Africa to denote a primitive and unknown power. Whether nature or technology, woman is to be dominated and controlled, but there is always the fear that she will get out of control (the hysterical machine that wreaks havoc on mankind). Woman's bestial sexuality (the sexual vamp) and her terrifying phallic power (the mother-monster) are aligned with the unknown force of technology. The 'dark continent' must be colonised and controlled, the abject body arrested to resist the 'return of the repressed'.

The dualistic structure of nature/culture is dominant throughout visions of the techno-future. In mainstream representations the warrior myth is prevalent. In the headquarters of the military and on the big screen physical strength, heroism and patriotism are dominant tropes. Films such as *Robocop* and *Close Encounters* feature conventional narratives concerned with good and evil. Cyborg cowboys are sent to do battle in futuristic societies (dark continents) where the Other is out of control, representing a threat to a white, civilised world. In this way the techno-body is aligned with masculine virtues: heroism, patriotism and conventional myths recur as 'he' conquers hysteric eruptions where culture and nature collide. The 'feminine' capacity of the machine to go wild or mad is thus quelled by a hyper-rationalised subject enhanced by technology.

Everywhere the techno-discourse collides with the body, inscribing itself upon it like a psychological tattoo, a register of ideology. Postmodern, post-industrial, global capitalist society has generated a psychological crisis which is of more immediate concern than the obsolescence of the body. Most people, new world pending, will continue to exist in their (quasi) biological bodies, even if they are enhanced technologically. Furthermore, the techno-enhancement of the body and its increasing interface with electronic circuitry and computer chips may cause more psychological and social breakdown than the physical and material advancement warrants. The project of modernity resonates throughout techno-territories and it is not surprising to find a collective consciousness projecting conventional imaginary fears, as the psycho-social returns in the tradition of the repressed.

The construction of sci-fi futures and cyborg identities are predicated on modernity's internal hysteria. The philosophical and critical discourse which surrounds many of these enterprises is likewise fractured. The capacity of advanced capitalism to subsume difference through a process of cultural osmosis has been the subject of critical inquiry since Adorno and Horkheimer analysed the culture industry in the 1940s. This is no where more apparent than in the current colonisation of cyberspace.

Computer games, such as *Doom* and a host of other war games, animate their genesis in military technology, recreating scenarios of destruction as virtual warfare becomes entertainment. But these leisure-time simulations, geared to stimulate the mind, are not as worrying ethically as the interfaces between biology and technology which are played-out in Stelarc's work and the bio-technic/genetic laboratories of the first world. There is a technological colonisation of the body which manifests in the concept of the cyborg. This entity is among us and inside us. The miniaturisation of medical technology has been able to perform miracles, enabling the blind to see, the deaf to hear, the lame to walk and the barren to reproduce. There is a liberationist subtext in many of these narratives, as human beings doomed by their own mortality grapple for bio-technological solutions that will preserve the body and allow it to mutate. Donna Haraway's feminist manifesto for cyborgs in the 1980s also embraced the notion of liberation through technology by celebrating a post-gender society where enhanced feminists could transform their bodies and leave the oppressions of the past behind. In Haraway's thesis the cyborg represents a new being, an ontology and politics that transforms previous socialist models (Haraway, 'Manifesto' 67).

Stelarc argues that 'evolution ends when technology invades the body. It is no longer of any advantage to either remain human or to evolve as a species. Only the hum of the hybrid is heard' (Stelarc, 'Strategies' 7). According to the artist, the biological body has become obsolete because technology mediates more successfully between the body and the world: 'DISTRAUGHT AND DISCONNECTED, THE BODY CAN ONLY RESORT TO INTERFACE AND SYMBIOSIS' (Stelarc,'Enhanced Gesture'). In Stelarc's view it is the body-species split which should concern us, not the mind-body distinction. He says:

> The body must burst from its biological, cultural and planetary containment. The significance of technology may be that it culminates in an alien awareness – one that is POST-HISTORIC, TRANS-HUMAN and even EXTRATERRESTRIAL.

Many of Stelarc's pronouncements echo the words of Marshall McLuhan, Jean Baudrillard and Paul Virilio. But where the critics analyse the problems associated with this new alienation, Stelarc embraces the promise of a new evolutionary future mapped by mankind.

This world has been developing since at least the middle of the nineteenth century (Crary & Kwinter, Foreward, 15). Its postmodern variant manifests as a seductive mix of rationalism, a culture of systems and programmes, and a new medievalism steeped in the iconology of dungeons and dragons. This paranoid and sometimes hysterical projection represents, and is represented in, a technological imaginary which sees it(self) in terms of apocalypse, damnation, restitution, reincarnation. There is a strong mythical and perhaps even mystical energy projected inside the new black boxes and fibre optic tubes which now sustain and entertain life on this planet.

The techno-body model represented in Stelarc's work in the 1980s and 1990s is still a kind of Western shamanism, even though it no longer participates in the masochistic rituals of the suspension events. The use of bio-technological interface in performance creates a spectacle of the body plugged into the machine. Some of the sounds are 'controlled', produced by deliberate contractions of the body, others are involuntary or stimulated electronically. The subject is enhanced but simultaneously gives up his position of control over his own body. The body is invaded by an alien technology and the subject/individual disappears.

In his projection of the future for mankind there is much talk of loss: the end of history and sexuality, the death of the subject as we know it, the resolution of the Oedipal conflict. In the performances the male nude's loin cloth has been replaced by a belt of technological devices, the artist's sexual identity is concealed by a cluster of tiny mechanisms which turn the body into a monumental soundscape. The noise is the body erupting below the surface of the skin: the heart beat, reassuring the spectator with its rhythmic thud, is intercepted by the hysterical sounds of the muscles and blood flow as they pulsate through the organism. Amplified and exteriorised the internal body sounds scream through the auditorium, enveloping the public spectator in the abject interior.

In this new world the body is an objectified body, it is 'the body'. Subjectivity is annexed/deferred. The eye/I of the future is disembodied by the changing surface and interior of the bio-techno cyborg. According to Stelarc 'It is time to transcend human history ... to achieve post-human status ... IT IS TIME TO VANISH. To be forgotten in the immensity of extraterrestrial space' (Stelarc, 'Post-Evolutionary'). The speaking subject, the subject of history, is lost in this prediction: it is the end of history. Stelarc rejoices in the end, plotting alternate trajectories through the bio-technological universe. There is a sense of Baudrillardian apocalypse in Stelarc's futuristic pronouncements for humankind. Baudrillard argues that the subject has been reduced to a position of 'uninterrupted interface' ('Ecstacy' 127) between machine and communication network. The subject's death represents the endgame of a modernity perfected where 'man' is merely the interface between mechanical means of communication. It is this vacant position which causes him to announce that 'the body, landscape, time all progressively disappear ... the theatre of the social and theatre of politics are both reduced more and more to a large soft body with many heads' (129). The subject 'is now only a pure screen, a switching center for all the networks of influence' (133).

Stelarc's concept of a biological/technological interface is exactly the type of 'schizophrenic state' which causes Baudrillard to dissolve into hysterical textual tears. The idea that the body as a pure object is capable of becoming a 'post evolutionary projectile accelerated to attain planetary escape velocity' ('An Interview' 133) appears to inscribe the ultimate state of schizophrenia where mind and body are permanently separated. In Baudrillard's prognosis all 'meaning' is eclipsed; truth is dead, murdered by the implosion of simulacra as technology accelerates beyond reality on the giddy plane of the hyperreal. 'Beyond this gravitational effect which maintains bodies in an orbit of signification ... all atoms of meaning are lost in space' (Baudrillard, 'The Year 2000' 18). Baudrillard vacillates between a remorse for a lost presence, the surety of the humanist subject, and an intoxicating pleasure in the death of the real.

Stelarc's experiments appear to fulfil Baudrillard's predictions; however, the performances also highlight the problem of the body. Baudrillard's theory operates on the clean surface of the video monitor, the television screen. His vision of the subject as interface is one in which the mind is bombarded with commodified visual flux: there is no corporeal body. Baudrillard's concept of the body is Stelarc's empty vessel: a capsule which has already been hollowed out, a skin which operates as an exoskeleton through which images are processed by osmosis. Despite the artist's futuristic vision, his body is in the here and now; it bleeds and pulsates, experiencing the real as pain. During the amplification events the audience is saturated by the sounds of the inside of the body, which create a spectacle by projecting the softness and wetness of the inside onto the world around it.

Stelarc does not lament the disappearance of the human subject. The study of the psyche is no longer meaningful, it is time to redefine what is human (Interview). The artist claims that technology has become part of human hardware: an appendage of the body and an expression of humanity. The fantasy of becoming Other is echoed throughout this discourse as 'man' seeks to take control of evolution, to transcend nature. Stelarc argues that:

> Technology, symbiotically attached and implanted into the body creates a new evolutionary synthesis, creates a new hybrid human – the organic and synthetic coming together to create a sort of new evolutionary energy. Technology is an evolutionary energizer. It's not just simply instruments to collect more and more information. The role of information is really not what's important any longer, it's actually

> physically modifying, physically changing the form of the human body – redesigning the human body is what we should be striving to do. The human body is obsolete. It realises its own obsolescence. It's probably the highest of human realizations. I don't think it's the folly of a technological mind. The body realizing its limitations can now proceed in redesigning itself to adapt to its new expanded cosmic environment ('An Interview' 17).

The ideas expressed here are not new, the epistemology is steeped in familiar relations of power and control. The sense of the omnipotence and authority of 'man' is stamped across the surface of the text. The marriage of the body and technology is presented as the next stage in the evolutionary chain, one which will allow man an existence in the galaxy as compared to a less glamorous life on earth. This desire to conquer creation has a long history throughout patriarchy and the modern era. It is at this juncture where techno-bodies are more powerful, more resilient and more capable of fulfilling man's desire that the cyborg represents a kind of urban shamanism. Writing about the technological enhancement of 'man' in 1930, Freud said:

> Long ago he formed an ideal conception of omnipotence and omniscience which he embodied in his gods. To these gods he attributed everything that seemed unattainable to his wishes, or that was forbidden to him. One may say, therefore, that these gods were cultural ideals. To-day he has come very close to the attainment of this ideal, he has almost become a god himself ... Man has, as it were, become a kind of prosthetic God. When he puts on all his auxiliary organs he is truly magnificent; but those organs have not grown on him and they still give him much trouble at times ... Future ages will bring with them new and probably unimaginably great advances ... and will increase man's likeness to God still more. But ... we will not forget that present-day man does not feel happy in his Godlike character. (38-39)

Freud's idea of a kind of techno-man-god helps explain the vestiges of shamanism in Stelarc's amplification events. However, it is a postmodern shamanism without ritual significance. The work seduces a postmodern audience hungry for the future and longing for the past, it is a kind of techno-cowboy culture with ambiguous memory traces etched into its surface. People are intrigued by the work because it has a kind of magic: a mix of death and life but its promise of the future still resonates with a psycho-social imaginary, a collective unconscious which casts the future. As one recent commentator has remarked: 'We look good to ourselves in machines:

they are the natural extensions of our narcissistic selves ... There is no escaping our romance with the machines we have created in order to recreate ourselves' (O'Neill 264).

Artificial intelligence and bio-genetic engineering volunteer for battle in the war waged by the species against its 'nature'. There are serious issues at stake, not the least of which impacts on psycho-social theory itself. Ever since Freud put the spotlight on the unconscious, 'man' has been acutely aware of the fragility of 'self'. In the intermediate years the anti-humanist position has been bolstered by decades of theory which has insisted that 'nature' itself is a social construct. This debate has been most earnestly presented within feminist criticism which has tackled the problem of sexual difference. In more recent years the debate has escalated in response to the pressing claims of racial and, particularly, indigenous difference.

The colonisation of the body is not a new phenomena despite the liberationist claims of the 'new' worlds (Benedikt). In cyberspace the issues collide. On one hand we witness a convincing community experiment which proves the case for social construction: an anti-humanist liberation where masquerade does business with identity. On the other, sex and violence is alive and well on the Net, as robotic futures and virtual worlds reinscribe conventional myths and stereotypes. The body's obsolescence is predicated on the belief that machines enhance or aid human endeavour and/or they are, or will be in the future, a superior intelligence. There are extremes of positions presented in the literature. Programmers at MIT talk about the mind as a machine, predicated upon an anti-humanist position that argues that there is no 'I' of consciousness, that primarily the subject is a decentred entity. Conversely, philosopher John Searle, in critical dialogue with the MIT commentators, argues that 'no matter what feats of intellect computers perform, the machines will never be thinking, they will only be simulating thought' (Turkle 263). Searle's position presupposes a humanist 'I' who thinks. When artificial intelligence is plugged into the body, when the biological body is transformed through the miniaturisation of technology implanted within it, the biological body and the humanist subject are eclipsed, at least in their material form. However, they do not disappear as constructs, they return to haunt the imaginary in various ways and they are written into the script of cyberculture. Kathleen Biddick argues convincingly that 'humanist history relocates itself in cyberspace' (50).

The current colonisation of the body by technology which seeks to out-do the body in terms of performance and efficiency seems to replay modernity's finest hours of exploitation. As Allucquere Rosanne Stone points out: '[f]orgetting about the body is an old Cartesian trick, one that has unpleasant consequences for those bodies whose speech is silenced by the act of our forgetting' (113). Like his colleagues at MIT, Stelarc is quick to acclaim the obsolescence of the body. A hybrid bio-techno future is embraced in his vision of the subject-as-cyborg, he says '[t]he first signs of alien intelligence may well come from this planet' ('Enhanced Gesture'). By this he means that an alien nature will be born, not of the biological [female] body, but of an unconsummated marriage between man, mind and machine. Woman disappears in this brave new world. Stelarc's vision is one seduced by modernity, a progressive programme which brings with it a cultural and political heritage which has traditionally denied difference and/or actively silenced the Other. The prosthetic gods of our would-be 'new' worlds may turn out to wear the same clothes as their imperialist masters.

References

Baudrillard, Jean. 'The Ecstasy of Communication.' *The Anti-Aesthetic: Essays in Postmodern Culture*. Ed Hal Foster. Seattle: Bay Press, 1983, pp. 126-134.

— 'The Year 2000 Will Not Take Place.' *Futur*Fall: Excursions into Post-Modernity*. Ed. Elizabeth Grosz et al. Sydney: Power Institute of Arts, University of Sydney, 1986, pp. 18-28.

Benedikt, Michael, ed. *Cyberspace: First Steps*. Cambridge, Mass.: MIT Press, 1992.

Biddick, K. 'Humanist History and the Haunting of Virtual Worlds: Problems of Memory and Rememoration.' *Genders* 18 (Winter 1993): 47-65.

Crary, Jonathan & Sanford Kwinter. 'Foreward.' *Incorporations*. Ed. Jonathan Crary & Sanford Kwinter. New York: Zone. 1992, pp. 12-15.

Freud, Sigmund. *Civilization and Its Discontents*. Trans. James Strachey. New York & London: Norton, 1961.

Haraway, Donna. 'A Manifesto for Cyborgs: Science, Technology and Socialist Feminism in the 1980s.' *Socialist Review* 80/15 (1985): 65-107.

— *Simians, Cyborgs, and Women: The Reinvention of Nature*. New York: Routledge, 1991.

Horkheimer, Max & Theodore Adorno. *Dialectic of Enlightenment*. Trans. John Cumming. New York: Allen Lane, 1972.

Marsh, Anne. *Body and Self: Performance Art in Australia 1969-1992*. Melbourne: Oxford UP, 1993.

— 'Bad Futures: Performing the Obsolete Body.' *Continuum* 8/1 (August 1994): 280-291.

O'Neill, John. 'Horror Autoxicus: Critical Moments in the Modernist Prosthetic.' In Crary & Kwinter pp. 264-267

Stelarc. 'Enhanced Gesture/Obsolete Desire Post Evolutionary Strategies.' *Remote Stelarc*. Exh. cat. Ballarat, 1990. N. pag.

– 'Strategies in Redesigning the Body.' *Lot's Wife* (Melbourne: Monash University Student Association), 22 June 1988; p. 7.

– 'Post-Evolutionary Desires: Attaining Planetary Escape Velocity.' Unpublished paper, 1987.

– Interview with the author, 19 Aug. 1987.

– 'An Interview with Stelarc'. *Obsolete Bodies: Suspensions.* Ed. James D. Paffrath & Stelarc. Davis, Calif.: JP Publications, 1984, pp. 16-17. (date correct)

Stone, Allucquere Rosanne. 'Will the Real Body Please Stand Up? Boundary Stories about Virtual Cultures.' In Benedikt, pp. 81-118.

Turkle, Sherry. *The Second Self: Computers and the Human Spirit.* New York: Simon & Schuster, 1984.

Wajcman, Judy. *Feminism Confronts Technology.* Cambridge: Polity Press/Basil Blackwell. 1991.

14. Animated suspension: dance parties and the choreography of community

Jonathan Bollen

> *The Mardi Gras Parade is our public celebration of gay and lesbian pride, the time to claim our space, break down barriers of invisibility and hatred, and make a statement to the broader community. ...*
>
> *The Parties – Sleaze Ball and Mardi Gras – are private celebrations for our community. A safe place. A space where we shed our inhibitions. Free from harassment.*
> (Sydney Gay & Lesbian Mardi Gras)

In October 1994, in an advertisement printed in one of the community's newspapers, Sydney Gay and Lesbian Mardi Gras (SGLMG) turned to the public-private distinction to articulate definitions of its events: the parade is public; the parties are private. This is perhaps a perplexing turn given the foundational status and ongoing use of the public-private distinction – in or out of the closet – in regulating the manifestation of homosexuality. Certainly, it is an audacious turn given that 'private' refers to events that were attracting at the time in excess of 16,000 participants. But the distinction has a practical salience for the organisation: the parade takes place on the streets of the city, out in the public domain; whilst the parties take place inside the enclosed, access-controlled site of what was once Sydney's Royal Agricultural Society Showground, now Fox Movie Studios.

The advertisement records one moment in an ongoing problematic: the attendance of heterosexuals at Mardi Gras Party and Sleaze Ball. Whilst there are no hard figures on the numbers attending, the straights-at-the-parties problem is enacted as post-party anecdotes of unpleasant experiences, as letters of complaint published in the community press, as public meetings and consultative discussions between SGLMG and its members, and as reportage in the community press and mainstream media. In response, SGLMG has developed an increasingly elaborate set of policies aimed at reducing the number of heterosexuals attending the parties. Negotiating a fine line between reverse discrimination and cultural respect, these policies have been highly controversial. They have also been more or less successful. In this regard, defining the parties as private events has been a strategic, salient, and sustainable move.

Whilst the straights-at-the-parties problem raises important questions about the process of 'imagineering' a gay and lesbian community in Sydney, it is the salience of defining the dance parties as private that I wish to consider here.[1] There can be little doubt that the Mardi Gras Parade constitutes a public display, both as a communal demonstration of political solidarity and as a presentational spectacle celebrating sexual diversity. In both orthodox and derogatory senses, the Mardi Gras Parade is an ostentatious event: it is both a show and a showing off, a body show of bodies showing off. And like all ostentatious events, it incorporates a structural distinction between those doing the showing and those witnessing the show. Indeed, the history of the parade may be measured, in part, by the increasing significance of the distinction between 'us' in the parade and 'them' in the crowd.[2]

In contrast, there are many ways in which the parties simply do not show, at least not to those outside the event. As I have mentioned, Mardi Gras Party and Sleaze Ball are staged as all-night parties in an enclosed, access-controlled site comprising three or more permanent pavilions and numerous temporary structures, bounded by high walls and temporary fencing. In order to see the event from the inside, you must buy a ticket before they sell out, and to do that you must be a member of SGLMG or know a member who has a ticket to spare. Failing that you might pick up a ticket at exorbitant expense from a scalper outside on the night, or you could try scaling the fence at an inconspicuous location and dodging security staff. But with scalpers there is always the risk that the ticket is counterfeit, and if inside illegitimately there is the risk of being bounced from the party, back outside where you belong.

From the outside, you can see who is going in to the party, and if you wait around long enough or return in the morning, you can see what they look like coming out at the end. Looking through the turnstiles or a section of see-through fencing, you may catch a glimpse of what is going on, outside the pavilions inside the party. But what happens inside the pavilions and on the dance floors therein remains permanently hidden from view. Even on the inside, where watching parts of the event is one of the things you can do, there is never any one place from which you can see it all. Some party-goers may spend much of the night participating in spectator mode, and there are places built-in to the party which facilitate spectatorial practice: raked seating overlooking dance floors, a VIP lounge overlooking a stage, chill-out areas with tables and chairs. But more often than not, and even when spectating, you are in and amongst it, part of the spectacle rather than looking on from outside, entangled in the 'murky intertwining' of practices, 'below the thresholds at which visibility begins' (de Certeau 93).

But there are also ways in which the potential of the parties to show in various residual forms has been actively resisted and rigorously regulated. After presenting a ticket and passing through the turnstiles, and if you are carrying a bag, you will be directed to submit to a bag search designed to prevent party-goers from taking into the event, among other things, photographic cameras, video cameras, and mobile phones. Cameras are prohibited to prevent 'bootleg' documentation of guest star performers, but also to protect the anonymity of party-goers in general. Mobile phones are prohibited because they interfere with radio equipment used to stage-manage the event, but they also present the possibility of a real-time communication link with the outside world: the possibility, for example, of a live on-location radio interview recounting what is going on inside.

SGLMG does issue a limited number of press passes to photographers who work for gay and lesbian media. However, these are issued on the condition that photographs taken only appear in the publication the photographer represents. Where photographers have failed to comply with this condition, they have been refused access at subsequent parties. Photographers are also given instructions as to where and what kind of photographs may be taken: not in the toilets, not on the dance floor, with minimal intrusion and party-goers' consent. Following these instructions and working under difficult conditions – crowdedness, darkness, flashing lights, incessant movement – photographers take photos within a limited array of genres: party-goers posing outside the pavilions, performers performing on stage in shows, hazy dance floor vistas taken from on high, scenic installations and deserted dance floors shot before the party and after.[3]

These are the images that appear alongside post-party reportage in gay and lesbian newspapers and magazines, and some have been published as photographic essays or displayed in art exhibitions. Whilst performers sign release forms and posing party-goers indicate their consent, it has been photographs of the dance floor that have been most problematic. For example, included in William Yang's retrospective exhibition for the Mardi Gras Festival in 1998 was a photographic diptych of party-goers on the dance floor at Sleaze Ball 1995. Alongside the diptych, Yang exhibited a letter from SGLMG detailing the organisation's concern to protect the anonymity of the party-goers and requesting that the photographs not be included in the exhibition. In response, Yang masked the faces of the party-goers with black strips and titled the work *Invisibility #2*.[4]

As a member of SGLMG and as a party-goer I have learnt to negotiate the ticketing policies, and I have enjoyed the restrictions on access and the regulation of documentation pursued by the organisation. Yet as a performance analyst researching the parties, I have encountered numerous dilemmas. Devising on-location documentation strategies and gaining permission from SGLMG to implement them was a difficult and frustrating task, until I resolved that the concerns of the organisation were probably more interesting than the video documentation I was unable to produce.[5] But even the documentation procedures I undertook with permission – recording observations and accounts of what happened on an audio-recorder and scribbling brief fieldnotes in a notebook – were hardly up to the task. On many occasions, particularly towards the end of a party, after struggling to retain an analytical frame of mind, struggling to remain distinctly apart from it when everyone around me was either getting right into it or completely out of it, I have asked myself 'Just what can I say about all of this?', 'How can I describe what is going on?', and most distressing of all, 'What does it all mean?' Of course, even for regular party-goers, dance parties can defy comprehension and may on occasions provoke an almost existential sense of crisis. Indeed, knowing this can happen and knowing what to do about it – go for a wander, head in for a dance, look out for some friends – is, I have learnt, an important dance party skill. But I raise these questions here, because they represent some of the demands encountered in documenting and analysing dance parties as performance, and because they resonate with shifting concerns that have emerged within performance studies.

Prior to researching dance parties, I had been accustomed to a relatively stable and speculatively ideal position from which to witness, document and analyse a performance. In the semiotic approach, performance is analysed as a *mise en scène*, 'an object of knowledge' comprising 'a network of associations or relationships uniting the different stage materials into signifying systems' (Pavis 25). Analysing performance as *mise en scène* means investigating the productive aspect of making a performance, but more so the aspect of making sense of a performance. It takes up a spatialised relation to performance, a relation transacted from a point of view which, as Mark Minchinton argues, has enabled analysts to comprehend the performance as 'a single, coherent text, a known and knowable place', composed of 'completed artefacts, placed in a field of coherence' (16). However, a dance party is an unwieldy event, densely convoluted and excessively diffuse. It affords no stable spectatorial position and does not show as a whole. Rather, it involves party-goers in an oscillation of performer-spectator relations and engages their participation at close quarters. For performance anthropologists, this involving engagement may entail a blurring of boundaries (liminality) and a coming together (communitas). It may also entail a fragmentation in which the performance itself cannot be abstracted from the diverse experiences of participants (Drewall 24-25). This is the dimension of performance that Minchinton emphasises in orienting an analysis towards 'the actors' explorations of space-in-time, their here-and-nowness in the material world' (17-18).

Drawing on the work of Michel de Certeau, Minchinton characterises a relation between the 'tactics' of performers' practices and the 'strategies' of textual abstractions. He recognises performers as tacticians, working with and within, alternately disrupting and displaced from, the 'coherent places' of strategically enforced orders: the text, the writer-director-choreographer, the popular press, and a particular kind of objectifying, textualising, coherence-enforcing performance research (16-18). Similarly, I approach an analysis of dance parties oriented towards both what I shall term the strategic dimension of *making* a production and the tactial dimension of *doing* a process. The strategic dimension would encompass the practices of making a dance party: the establishment and design of a venue; the scheduling and management of an event; the harnessing of an array of cultural materials and resources, technologies and knowledges; and their structural assemblage as a material production. On the other hand, the tactical dimension would encompass the practices of doing a dance party: getting ready and going out; getting in and moving around; dancing and getting into it; socialising and getting out of it; camping it up, being glamorous, and having a good time; losing the plot, getting over it and finding your way home.

But 'what we do need to recognise', Susan Melrose has argued, 'is that the strategic can readily be talked and written about, whereas the tactical resists this and, in so resisting, seems to establish itself 'beyond' conventions of knowledge' (85). Or to draw a metaphor from Raymond Williams, the strategic aspects of making a dance party 'precipitate' artefacts that show, and these are relatively easy to observe, document, and analyse; whereas the tactical aspects of doing a dance party are experiences lived 'in solution', inseparable from temporal process and the mobility of practice (63). Making and doing, product and process, artefact and experience – these aspects may be irreducible, but they are not unarticulated. In what follows, I trace some moments of transition, occasions of predication where the tactics of doing engage the strategies of making, and where the articulation of dance party experiences invite shifts in conventional questions asked of performance. In short, I want to ask: Not what does it show, but how does it feel? Not what does it mean, but how does it happen?

In promoting a dance party, SGLMG and the community newspapers have often used two representational strategies: a map and a schedule. Since Mardi Gras Party 1994, these have been incorporated into small party-guide pamphlets, prepared by the organisation and distributed to party-goers when they buy tickets. Inside the first of these guides, entitled *Everything You Ever Wanted To Know About The Party But Were Too Mardi Gras-Frenzied To Ask*, is a map of the party site, depicting and identifying the main spatial structures: Royal Hall of Industries, Hordern, Dome, Dag Bar, Drag Bar, Dyke Bar, Operations/Medical, One-Stop Dispensary, and Cloakroom. Alongside the map is a schedule headed 'What's happening' where, for each of the dance venues at the party, the names of the DJs and the times of their shifts are listed along with the names of lighting designers and other information about the venue and what will happen there. Information about when shows are happening and who is performing is never officially publicised, but circulates as rumour and speculation which readily slot into the schedule. Taken together, the map and the schedule outline a skeletal structure of the dance party as produced by SGLMG: a bounded space-time schema installed across a site-landscape, mobilised within an event-schedule, and internally regionalised through a differentiation of places and a scheduling of happenings. This skeletal structure sketches the parameters within which the practices of doing dance party are undertaken, but it can tell us nothing of the practices themselves, of the mobile trajectories of doing dance party.

Party-goers' preparation for an upcoming dance party is undertaken within a context of mobilisation initiated by the organisation and elaborated as party promotion in the weeks leading up to the party. In the poster and party-guide, in advertising and party-previews sent out to members and published in the community press, SGLMG provides information on when and where the party will be held, where to buy tickets and how much they will cost. Also disseminated are the thematics of party design, giving a sense of what the party will look like and offering a stylistic for party fashion. Deciding to go to a party entails becoming part of this mobilisation. It means embarking on a trajectory of party preparation that will coincide with the trajectory of party production at the event itself. But importantly, the process of getting ready is undertaken, not only in relation to information and imagery about the event, but also in relation to other party-goers' preparations. The context of mobilisation initiated by party-producers is collectivised as party-goers negotiate the upcoming event and participate in each other's preparations. In the weeks before the party, the representations of the event that generate its context are taken up at the level of social practice as a stock set of questions come to dominate conversations: Are you going to the party? Have you got your ticket yet? What are you wearing? Have you organised your drugs? Who are you going with? What are you doing beforehand?

For many party-goers, once they have purchased a ticket the process of getting ready is dominated by an attention to 'look'. Working out what to wear may entail reading the imagery used to promote the event and interpreting the thematics of party design. From the production side, SGLMG encourages the uptake of party design as party fashion, particularly at Sleaze Ball which has traditionally been billed as a 'costume ball'. In the past, SGLMG has included fashion suggestions in party publicity and even briefed local fashion houses to ensure they have appropriate items in stock. In turn, fashion houses and outlets have put together ranges of party-wear from existing or specially designed stock, and they have created shop-window displays, staged party fashion parades in the weeks before the party and advertised in fashion supplements published by the community press. From the perspective of party-goers this mini-fashion system operates at the level of invitation and suggestion. It may lead to the creation of fully-fledged costumes, or the purchase of a new outfit, or it may just inflect the fashion choices of party-goers through a theme-related accessorising. Yet for the party-goers I spoke to, an engagement with the thematics of party design was often less important than a desire to simply 'look good'.[6] Here the process of working out what to wear is predicated not so much on the party design, but on an array of party fashions comprising an assortment of styles and materials: lycra sports-wear, glamorous evening wear, kinky fetish wear, second-hand retro-wear, fashionable streetwear and fashion-house underwear. Putting together an outfit means drawing upon this array of fashion styles, mixing and matching what you have got, making or purchasing something new, and 'getting a look happening' for the party.

Drawing on a know-how of party style enables party-goers to anticipate their appearance within the party environment – how their 'look' will show at the party – but more so it enables party-goers to anticipate their experience of the party itself: how their 'look' will affect how they party. This is where fashion choices anticipate the demands of the event and respond to the opportunities of party-practice. It is also where a range of practical considerations come into effect, like one party-goer who 'wore shorts and tights because I knew it would be cold' and who said she only got dressed up 'if it's a really big night ... [and] if I've paid more for my ticket' or another party-goer who went shopping for 'something that's really showy but not very much there' because he wanted 'freedom of movement' and 'one had to consider the heat of the place'. Here, too, a distinction between going in costume and going in more regular party-wear can anticipate quite different party-experiences. In a discussion after Sleaze Ball 1995 I was told that costume is more 'social' and you have a 'chattier' time; whereas wearing regular party-wear was described as more 'sexual' and you have a 'cruisier' time. In this way, an attention to 'look' may entail an engagement with the thematics of party design, a negotiation of the stylistics of party fashion, but readily translates into a way of investing in the event and of crafting particular kinds of dance party experience.

Undertaken within a context of mobilisation, the process of getting ready generates a collective sense of movement towards the upcoming event. This movement towards is literalised as party-goers travel together to the party site and mingle outside the entrance with other party-goers. At the point of arrival, a mass of 'getting ready' trajectories coincide when, within a few hours, thousands of party-goers are funnelled through the turnstiles and enter the party site. However once inside the party, the collective directionality of a movement towards dissipates as party-goers spread throughout the site, tracing diverse trajectories for the duration of the event. In my experience, this transition registers as a distinct shift in movement quality. Inside the party, people are no longer moving in one direction, their paths intersect and interact in unpredictable ways: I adjust my pace to move without bumping into people; I find a way of moving less focussed on a target (getting there then) and more focussed on negotiating the crowd (moving amongst others). There is also a temporal shift, a kind of relaxation after the stressed attention of getting there on time, towards a recognition, as one party-goer put it, 'Now, you've got this whole evening ahead of you'.

In analytical terms, this shift in movement quality is important in understanding how dance parties do not show as a whole, how the coherence of the upcoming event as a making that shows dissipates across diverse experiences of doing dance party. Of course, individual party-goers readily offer narrative accounts of their own party-experience, yet like reports on what happened written by party-goer journalists, or photographs of what showed taken by party-goer photographers, these are fragmentary accounts. In recounting their experiences, party-goers skip across the party site, linking disparate locales within discontinuous trajectories ('How did we end up there?') and recounting an uneven flow of time relative to the pointillism of scheduled event ('And then it's just one big blur'). Indeed, these markers of memory loss may stand as metonyms for tactics of doing dance party that cannot be recalled according to the determinants of site-map and event-schedule.

Rather, reading across a set of fragmentary accounts, I have begun to conceptualise the party as a complex, interwoven choreography of trajectories, converging and dispersing, passing and intersecting. The trajectories sketch out party-goers' spatial engagement with the party-site and their temporal articulation to the event-schedule. Trajectories are subject to a certain degree of management – going to meet someone, to catch a DJ or a show – but also to the vagaries of chance: exploring, wandering, going with the flow. The intersections are sometimes 'points' – fleeting encounters, crossings of paths, bumping into someone – but more often they are durational 'bundles', an ongoing coincidence of trajectories, as party-goers meet-up, do things with each other, to each other, together. These 'bundles' of collective party-practice, these actional and interactional 'activities', are bound together not merely by a durational and spatial co-presence, but by an application to particular party practices that oscillate between a socialising orientation towards others and a practice-sustaining attention to self: on the one hand, dancing, chatting, and socialising with others, posing, promenading, and being seen, 'perving', cruising and having sex; and on the other, sitting down, resting, or 'chilling out', getting a drink, something to eat, or taking some drugs, going to the toilet, checking your makeup or changing your outfit.

Of course, at whatever point in a dance party trajectory, you are always some where at some time. In this sense, a spatial engagement with the site and a temporal articulation to the event are obligatory relations. However, the insistence of these relations on how you experience the party is variable, registered more in moments of transition when your attention is drawn from who you are with and what you are doing, to where you are and what is going on. For example, Mardi Gras Party and Sleaze Ball have often been framed by opening and closing shows. These are staged on a spectacular scale in the Royal Hall of Industries, the largest of the pavilions and until recently the only pavilion still open at the end of the party. Usually, the shows are performed by international disco divas or local drag queens, flanked by wave after wave of volunteer dancers, until the stage is overflowing, the pyrotechnics fire, and the crowd on the dance floor goes wild. Often these are called 'community shows', in contrast with those performed during the course of the party by guest stars and a small cast of professional dancers. Certainly, they are moments of climax, attracting an intensely directional focus as occasions of coming together and communal address. But they are also moments of transition when the crowd on the dance floor becomes an audience for a show, when party-goers attend to the spectacle of what is happening on stage before turning back to the dance floor and, after all but the closing show, to their dancing with others.

The production of dance parties, their promotion and reportage, generate artefactual evidence of a making that shows. In controlling access to the dance parties, in regulating who gets to go and how dance parties show, SGLMG addresses this making as content, as what dance parties contain and where their content is shown. In one sense, the organisation's interest in protecting the privacy of the parties is an exercise in image control, in restricting the circulation of dance party content. In another sense, SGLMG is involved in constituting that content for those who attend as an image of gay and lesbian community. Yet whatever content is manifest, and however that content is regulated, the making of dance parties provides only a structural predicate for the process of doing dance party, and the doing of dance parties may not be equated with the residual content of artefacts.

Rather, doing dance party entails a collective mobilisation, predicated upon the material production of site and event, yet generating choreographic effects that are not readily shown. Nor are these effects readily precipitated but to give them some form, I would characterise the spatiality of doing dance party in terms of accommodation, an animated negotiation of the spaces between; its temporality in terms of suspension, an ongoing sustainment of temporal potential; and its sociality in terms of exposure, the relational oscillations of an involving engagement. Beyond that, if dance parties do generate communitising effects, these would arise not in the material production of a making that shows, nor in the labelling of content or the 'look' of who goes, but in the choreography of doing dance party as it is done, in an animated suspension of intersecting trajectories and in the socialising exposure of turning towards others.

References

Anderson, Benedict. *Imagined Communities: Reflections on the Origin and Spread of Nationalism.* New York: Verso, 1991.

Carbery, Graham. *A History of the Sydney Gay and Lesbian Mardi Gras.* Parkville, Vic.: Australian Lesbian and Gay Archives, 1995.

de Certeau, Michel. *The Practice of Everyday Life.* Trans. Steven Rendall. Berkeley: U of California P, 1984.

Drewall, Margaret Thompson. *Yoruba Ritual: Performers, Play, Agency.* Bloomington: Indiana UP, 1992.

Fuller, Gillian. 'The Perils of Performance: A Note from Behind the Barricade at the Sydney Gay and Lesbian Mardi Gras.' *Xtext* 1 (1996): 42-47.

Harris, Gavin. 'Perving on Perversity: A Nice Night in Front of the Tele.' *Media International Australia* 78 (1995): 20-32.

Melrose, Susan. *A Semiotics of the Dramatic Text.* London: Macmillan, 1994.

Michaels, Eric. 'Carnivale In Oxford St.' *New Theatre Australia* 5 (1988): 4-8.

Minchinton, Mark. 'Saboteur, Guerrilla, Pedestrian.' *Writings on Dance* 10 (1994): 13-21.

Pavis, Patrice. *Theatre At The Crossroads of Culture.* London & New York: Routledge, 1992.

Sydney Gay & Lesbian Mardi Gras. 'Too Many Straights?' *Sydney Star Observer* 20 Oct. 1994, 10.

Williams, Raymond. *The Long Revolution*. London: Penguin, 1961.

Notes

1 Drawn from the name Walt Disney gave to his research and development staff, I use 'imagineer' as a verb to emphasise the material, processual, and experiential aspects in the production of a gay and lesbian community in Sydney, along the lines of Benedict Anderson's 'imagined communities'.

2 The first Mardi Gras Parade, held in the evening of 24 June 1978, did not simply address itself as a 'statement to the broader community'. That was the function of a banner and slogan rally held earlier that day. Rather, it extended an invitation to 'scene-queens' along Oxford Street to come 'Out of the bars, and into the street!' (Carbery 7-17). Ten years later the size and composition of the audience had changed: 'the boundaries were drawn: street/walkway; revellers/audience; us/them' so as to 'permit Mr and Mrs Suburbia to be spectators at a gay event comfortably' (Michaels 7). More recently, the 'semiotics of the barricade' have been axiomatic within analyses of the parade, its on-location audience and, since 1994, its televisual audience (Fuller 46; Harris).

3 In the past, SGLMG has also granted access to the parties for a few documentary film-makers – the last, to my knowledge, in 1992 – and many other film proposals have been declined. In recent years, the organisation has hired a video production company to document the shows at a party, but they have never publicly released this material as intellectual property rights and negotiating release agreements make clearance for dissemination difficult.

4 William Yang kindly clarified the details of his exchange with SGLMG over the exhibition in personal communication with the author during July 1999.

5 I was never game, but my friends used to joke about me going to a dance party in drag and smuggling a video camera hidden beneath a very large and otherwise glamorous wig, with the lens just peeping through.

6 The quotation, and those that follow, are drawn from conversations, interviews, and observations recorded during ethnographic research at and around Mardi Gras Party, Sleaze Ball, and other gay and lesbian dance parties in Sydney from 1994 to 1998.

15.

Death Defying Theatre and community: organisational body transformed[1]

Cynthia Barnes

Between 1981 and 1988 Sydney's Death Defying Theatre (DDT) reclaimed an Australian tradition of theatre rooted in the popular; acrobatics based on circus body skills and outdoor physical theatre. During this period the company's exploration of Australian identity reflected the Anglo-Celt background of its members. DDT survived into the early 1990s, however, by aligning with and influencing government policy, which encouraged an emphasis on multiculturalism in Australia's diverse society. The company responded by creating indoor shows staging culturally diverse bodies and stories.[2]

Paul Brown, Christine Sammers and Kim Spinks, who had worked together with Tim Fitzpatrick[3] as mentor since 1975, founded DDT in 1981. These three were dissatisfied with what they perceived as the lack of 'politicised' community theatre groups and the 'elitism' of the mainstream (Brown & Sammers, Interview). They linked the company's philosophy firmly to Brecht's ideas that art is never without consequences and that 'theatre's broadest function is to give pleasure' (Brecht 180). Their manifesto stressed their intention to focus on 'performance over literary text' and 'appeal to a representative cross section of society' Through theatre they intended to 'provide a critical examination of Australian identity, social institutions and cultural tradition' ('Death Defying Polemic'). DDT's performance mode was to be based on a fusion of popular styles linked, like their name, to the Australian traditions of the music hall, the melodrama and the circus.

The three founders initially found work at shopping centres and the Sydney Festival and, with growing confidence, they decided to expand the company by recruiting five new members. They were determined from the start to set up a collective as a formal organisation. DDT evolved two kinds of shows, entertainments and issue-based works which they performed concurrently.[4] When they finally received their first direct grant from the Australia Council in

1984, this distinction was retained because the funding was for one new project rather than a whole year. They continued to fund other activities with the usual one-off payments from various sources such as schools. On the negative side, however, DDT felt this system prevented full artistic development. More positively, because DDT's outdoor entertainments became such a core element, they were an attractive proposition for neighbourhood celebrations and festivals in Adelaide, Melbourne and Canberra.

After an early attempt at an issue-based show called *Crime and Punishment* that was staged indoors, DDT decided to concentrate on outdoor theatre which attracted a wide audience. By 1984 the founders had worked on a number of different issues shows including *Living Newspaper*, 'a comic critique of the press and media monopolies in Australia', and *Riff Raffle* which exposed the dangers of gambling (DDT, *Living Newspaper*). At end of 1984 the founders of DDT were experiencing 'burn out' and they decided to leave the company (Spinks). Their original pact to stay together for three years had not wavered but they had begun to resent the constraints of the formula they had developed for outdoor theatre, which included simplicity in concepts, striking costumes, loud volume and delivery on a grand scale. They were still very committed to the collective devising model, but were conscious that without an artistic director they were not developing.

Subsequently the founders transferred to the board of DDT so that they could maintain an active relationship with the group. In that capacity they were co-opted, along with other ex-members, to act as an 'outside eye' which was seen at that time as a better alternative to appointing and giving control to an artistic director. This meant attending rehearsals and performances, and giving the performers the benefit of past experience. Apart from providing a historical framework for DDT, the three founders continued to have a direct influence on the group. Because DDT were always under pressure to produce results quickly, an inherited formula was advantageous since it could be passed on easily to new members.

In 1985 DDT's ninety-minute Art and Working Life project, *Coal Town*, was devised, rehearsed and premiered during a six week residency in Collinsville, a coal-mining town in Queensland. Brown was engaged as writer and researcher and he also liaised with officials from the Miners' Federation months before the residency. His research on the coal industry, coupled with anecdotes from local people, formed the backbone of the material DDT devised together, first through discussion, and then through workshops during the residency. *Coal Town* dealt with life in the Australian coalfields from the 1960s through to the 1980s, a period of expansion and technological change. In the 1980s the unions were under attack and, in Collinsville DDT discovered that relations between workers and management were based on old-fashioned class divisions. DDT absorbed the rationale of the existing oppositional politics in Collinsville and produced an explicitly didactic show. *Coal Town* used an amalgam of borrowed styles and forms which included, as well as vaudeville, elements of socialist realism and agitprop theatre. As in those early plays the conclusion to *Coal Town* provided a socialist solution with its idealised image of a united group of miners. *Coal Town* also borrowed elements from the British working-class pageants of the 1930s. These included traditional folk songs, tableaux, and an episodic structure, which inevitably linked past events to the present and 'mass-declamations with agit-prop intent' (Wallis 132). While *Coal Town* was not on the same huge scale as the pageants, DDT aspired to a grand-scale outdoor spectacle which moved from local stories to a sense of internationalism. *Coal Town*, which became a successful milestone for DDT, was taken on tour to other coal-mining communities. In 1987 the show was revived for a tour of Western Australia, which included the remote area of the Pilbara.

By 1987 Brown and Sammers had left the board, although they still acted as occasional 'outside eyes', but Spinks, after a year's absence, had returned. Spinks believed the present company's ideology and working practices were sustained by what she described as a 'sense of awe' for the original DDT. She was keen to persuade the 1987 company to adopt a more radical political outlook that acknowledged the formative influence of Australia's New Theatre Movement of the 1930s, which she had only become aware of in 1984.

Although 1988 appeared to be a typical year for DDT, the changes to come had already been presaged by a million-dollar cut to the Australia Council's administration budget. In the next few years, as the Labour Government cut public spending, challenged the power of the unions and supported big business, the strategies for funding arts provision were transformed. As in England during the Thatcher era, the erosion of union power signalled the demise of many of the theatre groups whose opposition to the status quo was class-based.

By 1990, in order to survive, DDT were forced to respond to the current financial climate by making drastic alterations to their ideology, working practices and structure. The changes also coincided with the perception that artistic development was no longer possible within the old format. Brown was asked to draw up a feasibility study which would assist them in applying for funding from the Community Cultural Development Unit (CCDU) which had replaced an assortment of boards at the Australia Council. Paul suggested:

> The company would work on a project basis on theatre that is specifically designed for particular communities. It would no longer work to a formula, and it would assume that each project will throw up its own method of working. The company would need to be aware of a range of possible work methods, and be prepared to adapt these or invent new ones in each project. (Brown)

As a result of the study, DDT decided to reinvent themselves by abandoning their previous focus on outdoor theatre and touring and, instead, target specific communities. Acrobatics derived from circus skills were no longer to be a hall-mark of their performances and workshops, nor would their shows be classified as 'entertainments' or 'issue'-based.

DDT's first action was to relocate their company from a central position to the unfashionable western suburbs which were home to many people whose first language was not English. From there they could respond to the new arts policy which encouraged the provision of cultural outlets for people from diverse backgrounds. In the early 1990s, DDT transformed from a permanent ensemble to a company with an artistic director at its helm and hired personnel for specific projects; CCDU's funding strategy encouraged the setting up of such administrative structures. Given the long history of DDT and the emotional attachment that the ex-members of the group still felt for DDT, an unfortunate consequence of the new regime was its lack of interest in its organising processes of the past. The founders and other ex-members had been sympathetic to the need to change the old performance mode but they were disillusioned with the lack of commitment to a collective, which had previously made DDT an ideal model for other companies. DDT retained the name even though its old associations were incompatible with the foci of the 1990s group. Perhaps trading under a new name would have been a more honest and accurate, if less secure, exercise.

The main body of DDT's work from 1990 to 1993 was tied to multiculturalism, supporting and supported by the Australia Council policy of directing a substantial amount of arts resources to the numerous Australian migrant communities. DDT embarked on a number of major projects which were in the tradition of documentary drama and which, through a performance style of cabaret and collage, aimed to examine and celebrate cultural differences. The involvement of the people whose stories were told by the show was central to these projects, reiterating DDT's definition of community. DDT also experimented with the inclusion of a variety of migrant languages.

Along with this decisive break from the group's old Anglo-Celt identity, and with Fiona Winning at the helm as Artistic Director, the work of the 1990s DDT became increasingly informed by feminist politics. The show *Blood Orange*,[5] for example, explored identity by focusing on the 'health and body' concerns of young women from diverse cultural backgrounds (Winning 74). Certainly, by 1996 the composition of DDT's production team for the show *Noroc!* was dominated by female arts workers and performers from a multicultural background.[6] The show, which explored the fluid meanings of culture and language, used a more experimental approach to performance in its movement and staging, and indicates yet another significant change in DDT's artistic direction.

The longevity of DDT as a community theatre 'body' can be attributed to a willingness to adapt to changing external circumstances and new ideas, which an earlier generation might construe as a cynical submission to practice rather than ideology. However, the evidence suggests that DDT's realignments, and consequent survival through harsher times, provided opportunities for a reaffirmation of political commitment to expanded ideas of communities and, significantly, a reviewer of *Noroc!* enthused about the performers' 'sense of missionary zeal' (Sykes).

References

Brecht, Bertolt. *Brecht on Theatre, 1898-1956: The Development of an Aesthetic.* Ed. & trans. John Willet. London: Methuen, 1974.

Brown, Paul & Sammers, Christine. Interview with author. Melbourne, 2 April, 1987.

Brown, Paul. 'Report to Death Defying Theatre Board'. Jan. 1990. DDT archives, Sydney.

Death Defying Theatre. 'Death Defying Polemic or a Discourse in Three Acts.' July 1981. DDT Archives, Sydney.

— *Living Newspaper* Publicity leaflet. 1983. DDT Archives, Sydney.

Januczewska, Noelle. *Blood Orange* [Schools Touring Show]. *Australasian Drama Studies* 22 (April 1993): 79-108.

Spinks, Kim. Interview with author. Sydney, 10 October 1986.

Sykes, Jill. 'Cultural Differences Explored with Zeal'. Rev. of *Noroc!* by DDT, Performance Space, Sydney. *Sydney Morning Herald*, 8 Apr. 1996: np. On line, Internet, 6 June, 1997.

Wallis, Mick. Introduction, 'Pageantry and the Popular Front: Ideological Production in the "Thirties"'. *New Theatre Quarterly* 38 (May 1994): 132-156.

Winning, Fiona. 'Cultural Policy and Community Theatre'. *Australasian Drama Studies* 22 (Apr. 1993): 73-78.

Notes

1 An extended version of this paper was first presented at the 'Playing Australia' Conference convened by Elizabeth Schafer and Susan Pfisterer, University of London, 5-7 November 1999.

2 In the mid-1980s I was in Australia learning about DDT's ideology, working practices and performance style. As a researcher from Britain I had no preconceptions about the applicability, or otherwise, of Northern hemisphere models. DDT was an inspirational group because of the commitment and integrity of its members. My full study of the history of DDT is 'Death Defying Theatre and Australian Community Performance', MPhil, Goldsmiths College, University of London, 1998.

3 Tim Fitzpatrick, then a lecturer at the University of New South Wales, assembled a group of twelve undergraduates, including the original founders of DDT, to workshop a show called *The Ancient Mariner's Travelling Circus*.

4 *The Really Interesting Gypsies*, first performed in 1980, was devised to appeal to children but also include political material aimed at adults. By 1983 the show, stripped of most of the political material, was labelled as an entertainment. They performed it in conjunction with *Dr Floyd's Fly by Night Medicine Show*, which satirised health care in Australia. It had been devised because DDT had become preoccupied with the notion of uniting their outdoor performance structure with a theatre of ideas.

5 *Blood Orange* was first produced as a community show in 1992 (Janaczewska). Approximately thirty women from non-English speaking backgrounds were involved in performing, designing and the technical aspects. Noelle Janaczewska, who had worked with the group as the writer, was commissioned to produce a revised version for performance by three actors in schools and community venues. This new show opened on 5 March 1993 at the Pact Youth Theatre in Erskinville, NSW with the following cast: Phuong Tuy Tran, Eliza Chidiac and Maria de Marco. It was designed by Martha Jabour and directed by Fiona Winning.

6 *Noroc!* was first produced at the Performance Space, Sydney, 3 April 1996, with the following performers: Aida Amirkhanian, Terese Casu, Deborah Leiser, Michelle St Anne and Liberty Kerr who was also the sound designer. Tanya Gerstle was the director.

16.
The impossibilities of the dance body: the work of Meryl Tankard

Adrian Kiernander

Many of the theatrical visionaries of the twentieth century have dreamed, in theory and on the stage, about creating another kind of world from the one we live in. To create a complex, convincing and comprehensive alternative to the mundane is one of the major challenges for theatre practitioners. This vision, implying an image of somewhere else – something altered, utopias, purgatories, dreams or nightmares – sets theatre practitioners one of the most challenging tasks possible, a task which constantly runs up against the limits of what theatre can do: how to transform the basic raw material of theatre performance, the human body. Film is increasingly making use of technical possibilities in the form of special effects and animation which can help create strange worlds, but there remains the question of how to make it happen live on stage, where the unchanging dimensions and morphology of the body repeatedly bring fictitious worlds back to the familiar.

Many theatrical techniques have been proposed or developed in an attempt to transcend these limitations. Costume and make-up can effect at least minor alterations, and the ancient Greek theatre used built-up footwear and huge masks in an effort to amplify the bulk of actors to the scale of gods and heroes. In more recent times Charles Dullin famously lamented the inability of the twentieth-century stage to depict gods, as theatre of previous centuries had done. The visionary Edward Gordon Craig tried the opposite approach, designing vast, looming structures for the stage which had the effect of diminishing the size of the actors to tiny components within a much larger cosmic pattern; here it was the more easily manipulable built environment which created the altered space.

Some theatre practitioners have extended the possibilities of normal human morphology by using puppets or other manipulated objects. An extensive study of puppetry in Australia by Maeve Vella and Helen Rickards is appropriately entitled *Theatre of the Impossible*. The trained actor's body is itself capable of certain kinds of transformation; recent experiments have developed specific pedagogies, such as those of Grotowski and Barba, which give the performer better balance and greater physical flexibility, allowing for relatively unusual movements and postures to be sustained, and these have been extended by the use of techniques deriving from Asian theatre traditions, such as the development in Japan of butoh and its subsequent influence on and wide dissemination throughout Western theatre traditions.

Meryl Tankard's work for the theatre repeatedly confronts this problem. Her search to create apparently impossible bodies has led her in many directions, using bodies which are unconventional (too short, too tall, too muscular, too fat) as in *The Deep End*, choreographed for the Australian Ballet in 1996,[1] or with un-dancerly movement habits such as the limping gardeners in *Aurora* (1994 and 1996), or putting them into elaborate sculptural costumes which again disguise the shape of the body beneath (in 'The Court of Flora' [1990-3] and 'Seulle' [1997]), or turning her performers into moving projection screens. In *Nuti* (1990-94) they were painted white and moved through a space filled with brilliant projected light against a black background, so that the contours of their bodies were blurred and obliterated. There are two techniques which are recurrent in her work: flying the dancers on ropes so that they can approximate the quality of flight, and putting the dancers behind screens so that only their back-projected shadows are visible.

An early and relatively simple version of flying was used in *Aurora*, Tankard's reworking of the *Sleeping Beauty* story, for both the malevolent fairy Carabosse and the two Bluebirds. Mia Mason as Carabosse was attached by a harness to two fly-lines hung from positions near the wings; this allowed her to be moved in complex patterns, soaring and swooping both horizontally and vertically at high speed while she twisted and contorted her body which no longer needed to support itself on the ground. If Carabosse was to some extent passively manipulated by flymen, later in the same work Tankard re-choreographed the dance of the Bluebirds with two of the dancers, Mia Mason and Sean Parker, in harnesses, this time attached to single lines. Pushing off from the back wall high above the stage, they were in much greater control of their own trajectories as they moved in expansive symmetrical circles, holding hands briefly when they met as their circuits coincided mid-stage.

These techniques are taken much further in *Furioso* (1993-99) and *Possessed* (1998-99), which have become Tankard's signature pieces. The physical environment of *Furioso* was partly inspired by the Cité metro station in Paris, a deep underground chamber lined with plates of cast iron held together with huge rivets. This led to an image of the dancers as abjected figures trapped at the bottom of some kind of well or cistern, illuminated by shafts of light coming directly down on them as if through a grating high overhead, and aspiring to be able to fly or climb out of it. Within this world of frustration and entrapment, bodies were pushed to their limits in an attempt to transcend the forces which were holding them in place. In some images the bodies abased themselves to gravity, as in a section where the dancers repeatedly and obsessively run, leap, fall and skid along the stage on their chests. Others defied it, as when the female dancers were suspended on ropes in an exploration of images of emotional and sexual coupling, which provided some, albeit temporary, respite from the earthbound state. In this substantial section of the work the women's bodies, supported by ropes attached to harnesses around their waists, were able to perform movements which would be unthinkable using more conventional dance techniques. Their bodies held in open, concave curves, they drifted in tight slow circles around their partners; they leaped, arching backward, high into the air off their partners' thighs, falling towards the earth and then up away from it again; they flailed and thrashed uncontrollably, swinging wildly on the end of their ropes, flipping instantaneously from upright to upside-down and back again; they floated above their partners, their hair and arms brushing lightly across the men's bodies in an evocation of enraptured ecstasy.

Even though the effect of weightlessness in this work was to some extent undercut by the visible presence of the ropes, there remained nevertheless a compelling and persistent image of bodies performing the impossible – floating or flying through the air for minutes on end, performing tight and precisely controlled aerobatics. It is a common human fantasy which on one level is realised on the stage. Freud suggests that the dream of flying is generated by memories of infantile games where the dreamer as a child was carried aloft by an adult, often an uncle. According to this scenario, the dreamer's mind obliterates the memory of the adult's supporting hands to give the impression of flight in the dream (Freud 375). Similarly, in the case of the dreams staged with living bodies by Tankard, the spectator witnesses, and on one level of perception, can empathise with an image of a human being flying through the air, the supporting ropes obliterated.

The final image of *Furioso* however, used ropes which are, as far as is technically possible on stage, hidden. Placed far upstage in semi-darkness, these invisible ropes allowed the female dancers to perform the unthinkable; at the end of an hour of fully or partly gravity-bound performance, the women escaped from their confined state at the base of the wall by simply walking up it, bodies parallel with the stage, their heads towards the audience, and the elongated shadows of their legs streaking across the back wall. After the desperate energy of their previous struggles with gravity this looked so easy and effortless – the idea of the impossible as a walk towards utopia. Like all utopias, it was fantasy, and the work left open the question of what the women were walking into, but it offered the playfully exuberant hope of a new start.

Tankard's later work, *Possessed,* explored a wider range of flying techniques using hand and ankle loops attached to the ropes, providing the dancers with the possibility of more speed together with a much greater degree of control, and a more extensive and articulate vocabulary of movement possibilities. At the same time the universe of the rope sections of *Possessed* was a more complex and conflicted heterotopia, the creation and exploration of a world where human beings really can sustain flight. *Possessed,* as the title indicates, dealt with a wide range of aspects of the physicality of possession, a recurrent theme in theatre since at least Euripides' *The Bakkhai* in the fifth century BC. In this work possession was figured in many ways, ranging from the bond between lovers or mother and child, through charismatic political mass movements, to inspired madness. Its representation implied uses of the body which extend it beyond the natural/istic. Tankard's idea of possession in this context is, like the play, ambivalent. On the one hand it has a strongly positive and liberatory aspect, with the possessed experiencing an etymologically literal 'enthusiasm' – or 'enthousiasmos' – a sense of being infused with the spirit of the god. But it also implies loss of (self) control, being owned or colonised by a more powerful force which can be destructive, as Dionysos is for the mortals in *The Bakkhai.* There were images in *Possessed* which suggested both of these ways of understanding the word; both the sense that the dancers were moving far beyond the limits of normal human endurance, and the sense that they were being colonised by obsessive desires and forced into destructive and joyless states.

An initial impulse for the piece was sport, specifically the Winter Olympics in Nagano. Tankard wanted to explore with her dancers the images of top athletes caught in mid-flight. But whereas the best Olympic skier or gymnast can stay airborne for only seconds at a time, Tankard's dancers using ropes sustained the illusion of flight for minutes on end – hence their evident pleasure in performing, even when that pleasure was contrasted with darker elements in the choreography and staging.

The first section of *Possessed,* 'No Time Before Time', was a relatively straightforward exploration of the vocabulary and the possible pleasures of dance with ropes. First one, then three, pairs of male dancers partnered each other in exuberant, circling leaps, one member of each pair attached to the rope with a wrist loop, his partner providing the energy and impulse to fling him off the ground. One of the compelling aspects of this kind of dance was that we saw the dancers' bodies flying at high speed through the air, attached apparently tenuously to the rope; the energy that propelled this movement was a centrifugal force rather than a direct, and doomed, vertical thrust against gravity. The centrifugal force allowed the dancers to fly with an effortless lift-off, curving flight, a moment of suspension at the peak of the rise, another curved flight down and a weightless landing. In this first section the use of the impossible was entirely positive and straightforward, an exploration and celebration of a new manifestation of human power and adequacy. It was the realisation of a recurrent and perhaps generic human dream and fantasy, where people are both freed from constraint and returned to a childhood state of innocence and simplicity.

In 'Lost Tribe', the second section of *Possessed,* the exuberance and the simple optimism of this impossible dance was followed by a more complex critique of the implications of the cult of the body which the first section has opened out. The adulation of athletic physicality has its dark side as well, and the history of the twentieth century provided plenty of examples of how athleticism and muscularity have come to be associated with totalitarian ideologies, nationalistic war mongering, colonisation and myths of racial superiority. Perhaps the 1936 Berlin Olympics, precisely because they were documented by Leni Riefenstahl according to a Nazi aesthetic, are the quintessential Games of the twentieth century. Tankard confronted the darker aspects of the adulation of an ideal physical type, and the choreography in this section alluded to the theories of the impossibly perfect Aryan body celebrated in the authenticating rhetoric of the Third Reich, and its basis in a simplistic version of the Nietzschean superman.

The dancers, wearing large black identification numbers on their shoulders and thighs, were gradually pushed by their obsession (or possession) into progressively dehumanised mechanical callisthenic repetitions, where individual difference was swallowed up in an inexorable and hypnotically slow push towards mass conformity, marked out by the insistent pulse of the drum. The piece was structurally close to classical ballet, and had an almost fugal quality. One female dancer began the piece with a sequence of movements based on images of athletes, which she repeated several times. Then she stopped and a second dancer appeared, performing his own sequence of movements. Gradually the piece built with all the dancers in the company joining in one after another, performing their own and other people's sequences, until they were dancing in unison in subgroups. These subgroups then coalesced first into two distinct groups, men and women, and finally just one. The movements remained fairly constant throughout the piece, and sustaining the high pitch of energy for fifteen minutes required a perceptible effort and created a sense of desperation and pain. This complex series of images presented a real time embodiment of supreme physical achievement and endurance, and simultaneously it alluded to the dehumanising, mechanising effect which that ideal requires for its fulfilment in the offstage world.

Side and back light emphasised the outlines and muscular texture of the bodies. The dancers worked relentlessly in front of the stainless steel tanks at the rear of the stage like manic machine operators in a Fritz Lang nightmare, or as if Riefenstahl's *Olympia* was slipping directly into *Triumph of the Will*. With a unified arm movement reminiscent of the Nazi straight-arm salute built in to the choreography towards the end, and with two of the female dancers wearing their long hair in plaits wound around their heads, the echoes of Berlin 1936 were clear. It was harsh and frightening, like Alexander Balanescu's music which was commissioned specifically for this piece, but at the same time dangerously impressive and seductive – Riefenstahl's films demonstrate the grip that regimentation, precision and mass action have on our minds, and Tankard's work acknowledged this power. But at the end of the piece, the colour in the lights leached out to black and white, and finally all front light disappeared. The dancers became silhouettes against the shiny steel, like memories from a now distant past which will never quite fade away.

'Mother', the third section, featured a woman over three metres tall wearing an impossibly long black skirt who emerged from the darkness at the back of the stage. Even though it was obvious that her height must be the effect of being placed on the shoulders of another dancer, the image was memorable and the gigantic female figure, even standing still, acquired a mythic superhuman quality, like the distant memory of a mother figure as perceived by a small child. Again she was attached to a rope by her waist and as she was whirled about on a line at high speed by the male dancer who eventually emerged from beneath her skirts, the nature of the link between them is unclear – by holding on to the base of her skirt was he merely providing the energy which moved her through the air above him, or was he restraining her flight in an attempt to maintain his full possession of her? To what extent were the wild and dangerous-looking parabolas an image of freedom, and how much were they indicative of an emotional gravitational pull which she could not escape? Her movement could be read ambiguously, as a desire to escape the bond of maternal responsibility and fly off to another (part of her) life, and as a fight against the separation of death to which she finally succumbed. Is there a suggestion that every mother is constructed partly as an ambivalent black witch to her children, usually beneficent, but with one powerful and hurtful trick at her disposal, the ability to stage her own disappearance, flying off for ever?

Much of the second half of *Possessed* played games which were impossible only to the extent that they were forbidden by gender conventions. This was most evident in 'Model' where the men performed conventions of the feminine body which are normally not permitted them. Throughout much of this part of *Possessed* there was a sense of uninhibited freedom which is discouraged in normal, adult patterns of behaviour and identity. *Possessed* ended with a final gesture in celebration of the image of flight, with the most extended rope sequence in the whole piece. The rope work here appeared to find a synthesis between the idea of simple, unstructured freedom and complex repetitive uniformity as five pairs of dancers performed in an intricate series of movements which played games with total and partial unison (sometimes all five pairs moved together, sometimes three or four couples were in unison while the others did something else), with symmetry around different axes, and with individual difference. These moments which were apparently random suggested unstructured and uninhibited freedom but without any change in the quality of the movement, and with none of the desperate effort of 'Lost Tribe'; the patterns would suddenly, again impossibly coalesce. The reduplication of the image achieved its maximum power under these conditions, demonstrating the precision and control of the dancers and the choreography while losing none of the liberating pleasure of an image of free flight.

Shadow bodies

Tankard's other major technical contribution to the theatrical search for the impossible body is her use of back projection. The first hint of this came in a tiny moment in *Furioso* where the women were at the extreme edge of the stage, and where the visual impact was created not by their physical bodies but by huge shadows projected onto the back wall from a light in the wings. The dancers were positioned so that there was the largest possible range in the sizes of their shadows. Those nearest the light source made shadows too big to be seen in full, and they totally dominated the diminutive, life-size shadows of the women closest to the wall. By simply moving her dancers nearer or further, in the hidden light source, Tankard could change their scale.

This technique was fully realised using back-projection in a sequence at the start of the second half of *Aurora*. The Sleeping Beauty narrative had reached the point where the prince was searching for the princess and all she represents. This quest was danced initially by the men alone behind a white screen which filled the entire stage. It was lit by three sets of projectors, each set covering one third of the area. This allowed a variety of shadow techniques to become an integral part of the dance. When a dancer moved upstage towards the projector, his shadow would rapidly increase in size – this created a disorienting paradox for the audience: the 'bigger' dancers were actually those whose bodies were furthest away. Similarly a movement close to the projector would cast a moving shadow which travelled faster than the same movement close to the screen. In a rapid and complex sequence of actions Tankard created a convincing and overwhelming sense of characters completely lost and disoriented in an unfamiliar environment. This was full of strange dislocations as the choreography took advantage of the new physical properties of this world of light and shadow, dancers appeared and vanished in an instant, materialising out of nowhere, or were suddenly overwhelmed by other figures several times their own size. The quest took on the sense of a disruption to the mental state, a feeling of having lost touch with any objective, normal physical reality, and instead being subjected to an anxious and desperately panic-stricken crisis.

A similar technique was used to quite different effect in 'O Let Me Weep', a short piece created for the Barossa Festival at about the same time as *Aurora*. Here there was little sense of crisis. Dancers in period costume moved in silhouette through a light which took the form of projected images of lush details of old-master paintings, to Baroque music performed by the ensemble Fontana Musica. In a later short work for the Barossa Festival, 'Seulle', the idea was taken further. Again the light source was back-projected slides of oil paintings, including the bizarre compositions of Arcimboldo – another impossible use of the body. But a refinement of the three-projector technique was developed, which involved the use of two dancers, each half-in and half-out of beams of light. The two dancers worked together to create the shadow of a single human figure which was composed of the left part of one dancer and the right part of the other. At times one dancer would lean forward and have all but her head in the light, casting a shadow whose head was provided by the partner's shadow. Thus the head could detach and float upwards or drift down, independently of the rest of the body.

The technique was taken to an extreme in Ravel's *Bolero*, which Tankard choreographed for the Lyon Opéra Ballet at the end of 1998. Again the entire work was performed behind a screen, making use of the opportunities for transformations of scale and speed. A further refinement was added with the use of multiple light sources illuminating the same area of the screen from different places, allowing the shadows to move independently of the dancers' bodies, and permitting the shadows themselves to be filled with colour rather than being just black against the light. Finally the use of projectors set low to the stage and angled upwards allowed the dancers, by dropping their heads forward, to create images of headless bodies on the screen, arguably the ideal *soma* to accompany what was described by its composer as a 'piece for orchestra without music', noted for its non-rational and visceral rhythmic insistence.

These forms of the impossible body are tied in with the representation of extreme states of passion, abjection or exhilaration, and Tankard is one of the few current theatre practitioners to have found ways of pushing physical representation to this point. But underlying this representational transformation of the body *in extremis* is a further, and arguably more important impossible body – the fully integrated body in late twentieth-century dance.

Integration has been a problematic concept in theatre dance (Bryson 72). The most stereotypical pose of classical ballet, the arabesque, is an attempt at a fully integrated body as it forms itself into a single elegant arc from toe to fingertip, but even here the supporting leg remains outside the formal aesthetic, a mere strut which has to be ignored in a reading of the curve of spine and limbs. As dance moved into the twentieth century the difficulties multiplied.[2] Subsequently, some modernist dance abandoned the search for integration altogether, concentrating instead on technical explorations of the articulation of joints and the movement potential of individual body parts. At the other extreme, dance theatre in the Pina Bausch tradition has appeared at times to be moving further and further away from any concern at all with the body as integrated sculptural form. For Tankard, neither of these approaches is sufficient. Her project is underpinned by a celebration of the body and its potential, as an emblem of adequacy. Her bodies are not necessarily self-sufficient – they often rely for their effects on a close partnering where two or more bodies work as one, and at times multiple bodies fuse into an apparently single unit, but they are not, except playfully and parodically, fragmented. Part of her achievement has been in the struggle for the re-integration of bodies. Even on the floor in the more conventional moments, the dancers abandon the use of limbs as extraneous supporting structures so that they can become integral parts of the overall structure; the dancers hurling themselves out of control, flipping and arching into shapes which cannot be maintained for more than a few seconds, then falling to the ground. In the screen works, the body as shadow is paradoxically integrated by the denial of anything but the graphic outline; there is no possibility of individual features such as the engaging eyes, or the mischievous/ serene/tragic/sublime facial expressions which were such a feature of, for example, Nijinsky's allure; whole bodies are distilled down to mere outline. This is supremely the case with the rope work where the supports – midriff, wrist or ankle – are fully integrated into the line of the body which is released from gravity by centrifugal force, and where the curve of the spine can extend in an enfolding embrace or a triumphant hyper-arabesque to the extremities of every limb.

Tankard's choreographic work in Australia has ranged across many widely differing styles and forms, but one of the unifying features of the pieces has been an ongoing experiment in the creation of extreme other worlds. She has succeeded, working together with her dancers and other collaborators, in discovering new performance possibilities where bodies can fly, change size, move at superhuman speed, gain and lose parts, and disappear. These techniques permit the creation and exploration of theatrical fictions where the normal laws of physics of the world of the audience are no longer a limiting factor; where audiences can rethink aspects of their own world by contrast with images of impossible worlds of the imagination – a technique normally restricted to writing and denied to the stage.

References

Balanescu Quartet. *Possessed* (Compact Disc). London: Mute Records, 1992.

Bryson, Norman. 'Cultural Studies and Dance History.' *Meaning and Motion: New Cultural Studies of Dance*. Ed. Jane C. Desmond. Durham & London: Duke UP, 1997. 55-77.

Freud, Sigmund. *The Interpretation of Dreams*. Harmondsworth: Penguin, 1991.

Kopelson, Kevin. *The Queer Afterlife of Vaslav Nijinsky*. Stanford: Stanford UP, 1997.

Vella, Maeve & Rickards, Helen. *Theatre of the Impossible: Puppet Theatre in Australia*. Sydney: Craftsman House, 1989.

Notes

1 Information about performers in Tankard's work is complicated because many of the works have been repeatedly reworked and performed with different casts on tour around the world over the course of several years. For example, *Possessed* exists in several very different versions. A short version was performed at the Barossa Festival in 1995. A much longer version, adding new

material, was created for the 1998 Adelaide Festival. This was performed in a pavilion at the Wayville Showgrounds on a raised a stage resembling an enlarged boxing ring with ropes around the performance space and the audience on three sides – an important factor linking with the sporting imagery of the work. It was revised again for a very different space and an end-stage audience configuration with cast changes for performances outdoors at the 1999 Sydney Festival. The work was then taken on tour to Europe in the same year, with further cast changes and modifications dependent on different venues.

2 Commentators on the most dazzling moments in Nijinsky's performances tended to focus on either his legs or his arms, or occasionally and with difficulty both, but not so much on the body as a whole. Photographs show his body at its most harmoniously sculptural when it is crouched lengthwise on the floor, as for the *Dance Siamoise* where the integration is achieved by a process of weaving the parts of the body together, and where the function of support is distributed evenly, or in *L'Après Midi d'un Faune,* where dance, as in some of Tankard's work, adopted a new movement vocabulary which is specifically sexual in its reference, and not aspiring towards the effect of weightless integration.

17.
Learning to read the physical mind

Karen Pearlman

My inquiry is into methods of reading dance and the possibility of recognising the dancer's body as a thinking, linguistically articulate entity. Parts of this chapter will take the form of a dialogue between a reader and a dancer.

DANCER: Are you reading what I'm writing? Am I writing what you're reading?

READER: The reading of a dance can be as inflected or uninflected as the reading of any text. One can say 'they danced in straight lines' or 'they wafted through perfect formations like militaristic lilies'. But does either read the dancer's mind?

DANCER: Neither describes my kinetic experience nor my kinetically originated and articulated creative impulse.

READER: And if I cannot feel your sensation?

DANCER: Then get your theory off my body.

READER: OK, so the reader's experience is not the writer's experience, but isn't there somewhere they can meet?

The Dancer snaps into a foetal position, eyes clenched, fists squeezed, head buried.

READER: Is the dancer dumb?

DANCER: I can't read.

What is reading dance? Of the numerous possible methods of 'reading' dance, only three will be discussed herein: a basic one which I used during the years that I was dancing (drawn from a hodge-podge of allusions to various theories that I managed, surreptitiously, to glean bits of), which I will now call an elemental method. The second, a thorough and very cogent method proposed by Susan Leigh Foster which will be discussed only cursorily. Finally, a method proposed by Randy Martin. Martin's particular essay is being considered because it offers a valuable conjunction of experiences for examining the dancer's relationship to theory. I was a dancer in the company Martin writes about, and am now a reader of his writing about reading my writing.

My concern with reading dancing is ultimately a concern about the ways in which dancers might be perceived to be intellectually illiterate, and, more importantly, the way in which the culture's general physical illiteracy reinforces that old Cartesian notion of the mind-body split. I will be proposing that, in order to create cultural space to get past the complacent acceptance of this divide, dancers and theorists each have to come halfway across the split in an activity which is potentially liberating for both of them.

Learning to read

An elemental reading of dance proposes that dance is made up of time, space, energy and the human body. This is an elemental view of dance in the way that H2O is an elemental view of water. Gestures, impulses, phrases, dynamics, musicality, choreography etc., are combinations of time, space, energy and the body in the way that oceans, rivers, swimming pools and Evian are all affects of H2O – they change in appearance and function but not in elemental composition.

'Reading' the 'elements' of dance can be a conscious process. One can consciously observe the manipulation of time, space, energy and the human body made by the choreographer, executed by a dancer. Even a deliberately uninflected description of these elements is a reading of dance. For example, one can observe a scene and say: the two women (bodies) stood close to each other (space) for a minute (time). Adding a description of the quality of energy expended begins to inflect the reading immediately. In other words, any word describing the use of energy which is inserted into that sentence begins to describe an intended narrative. The two women stood rigidly and close to each other for a minute. Or, the two women stood tiredly and close to each other for a minute. In this way, the reading of a dance by description is already a reading of meaning. While I have since learned that this way of thinking owes a lot to the work of Rudolf von Laban,[1] I was able to use this method of reading as a dancer without ever having read Laban because it is elemental. It was not a big leap from what I was learning to do in dance class, to thinking in this way about what other dancers were doing in performance.

In her *Corporealities*, Foster, a pre-eminent dance theorist, has taken this interest much further when she discusses in depth Frames, Modes of Representation, Styles, Vocabularies, Syntaxes, and the Performance, each as a separate element interacting with and impacting on each other, but each analysable for the meanings in their uses of codes and conventions. I will do no more than highly recommend these ideas to anyone interested in pursuing this topic further because my primary interest here is not so much in what she says, but in why this information remains so obscure, hidden from a dancer's view, like a shameful secret or an enemy of their art. The temptation at this juncture is to argue that perhaps it is not necessary to translate a reading of a dance into verbal language. Knowing what is being written in terms either of codes and conventions, or of time, space, energy and the body, may not be necessary on a verbally conscious level. It could be said that dance can be intelligibly written, and read, through kinetic responses. Dances can be, and very frequently are, made based on how the movement feels. Perhaps what is meant by 'talent' in dance is the capacity to write (choreograph or perform) intelligibly from a kinaesthetic response, without consciousness of or attention to a verbally articulated theory of what one is doing.

Just as a dancer and choreographer can write kinaesthetically, audience members can read kinaesthetically. They can sit in their chairs and, by observing, absorb and participate in the duration of movements, and their proximity to each other. They can understand the communication of energy as effectively as the difference between laughing and shouting. The bodies, well, the bodies are read and read and read. Faster than you can say 'cultural assumption' their sizes, shapes, genders, and looks are observed, made into stories and judged. If the spectator and the dancer are both sufficiently conscious of their kinaesthetic dialogue, this can be a satisfying exchange. Problems begin to make themselves apparent when a choreographer and dancer do not know at what level – verbally or kinaesthetically – they are writing or how to read what they are writing. Dance can only really be legible if it is legibly written. A lack of coherence spatially, dynamically or energetically becomes illegible. A choreographer who denies or is ignorant of artistic tools and ignores their implications is therefore difficult or impossible to read.

If dancers can only read kinaesthetically, they tend to understand only what their own bodies and other similarly trained bodies are saying. There becomes a right and wrong way to dance, and what 'we' are doing is invariably right while what 'they' are doing is invariably wrong. Other forms of dancer or dance become inconsequential, or worse, enemies. In the end, my biggest concern is the way in which the unspoken, the avoidance of what is referred to as an 'over-intellectualising' of dance, actually reinforces the magnificently useless and destructive notion of the mind-body split which continues to govern so much human interaction.

Before looking at the question of 'mind' and 'body', I would like to take up one more method of reading dance called 'overreading', which is practised by Randy Martin. My interest in this method is in the way in which it might alienate a dancer, choreographer or audience member from engaging in a theoretical discussion of dance, and also in the way in which it could enlighten and enliven the debates about dance. I am starting with an almost randomly selected quote, describing a moment in the dance. 'The ending suggests a dialectic between narrative and its other as what is constitutive of the historicity shared by dance and other social activities' (Martin, 'Overreading' 186).

DANCER: What the fuck is that?

READER: It would not be unusual for a dancer to dismiss this analysis entirely as having no direct correlation to anything he or she is dancing.

However, to take the dancer's question seriously for a moment, Randy Martin calls it 'overreading' and it is what starts to happen, to a greater or lesser extent, as soon as your reading becomes inflected in any way. An example based on my experience might be the following: in the context of a lecture/demonstration, a choreographer speaks privately to two dancers. The two dancers are given an instruction: 'Start side by side. Walk back and forth along a straight line. Look at each other occasionally. Don't vary your tempo too much.' They execute their instruction and readings are collected from the audience of students who are asked: 'What is happening here?' Responses, or readings, range from simple narratives – 'One is following the other' – to more decorative narratives – 'It's a wedding rehearsal and they are not sure what to do' – to an expressionistic interpretation – 'They are in love but angry at each other'.

In each case the reader fills in, adds to the observation of time, space, energy and the body, with an interpretation of the meaning of this particular conjunction of these elements. No one ventures: 'They are walking near to each other and occasionally looking at each other without varying their tempo much'. So, in fact, at the core of overreading is a deeply conditioned response of creating narratives, which seems to come more easily than actually just reading or seeing the action and reporting it. Possibly this is because we are trained more to read stories than time, space and energy, so when we see composed interactions of time, space etc., we read them as a story. Possibly it is because the body as cultural signifier is too deeply entangled in narratives to be perceived without them.

Martin's sense of overreading is larger still than this. It is more than just interpreting, it is expanding, mythologising, looking at the world through the prism of the dance.

> Overreading rests on the assumption that the subtext displayed in the dancing accounts for more than that particular aesthetic activity and points instead to the very contours through which a given horizon for social activity is possible. Hence, overreading has a double significance, to read more in the dance than its dancing can bear. (178)

Overreading, or reading more into it 'than the dancing can bear', can be an uplifting activity. It can vindicate the dancer who struggles to make meaning from her over-inscribed body. It can create a relevance, a context and field for expansive thinking for the viewer. It can provide kudos and reputation to the choreographer who is credited with an incredible historical and cultural intelligence. However, to some extent, it undermines the language of a given dance, by measuring, describing, and contextualising it within another language.

Martin's overreading is considered, expansive, full of possibility and excess just like the dance, and, more importantly, as a result of the dance. Yet grounding it in a more elemental reading could possibly increase its validity, and may even help to extend the practice of dance to meet its lofty theoretical ideals. For example, when he discusses a particular solo by Heidi Latsky he talks about the words she says, the way she says them, and the way they are amplified by another performer following her around with a microphone. He does not talk much about Latsky's movement: her increasingly frenzied jabbing and stabbing gestures and her whiplash spins, which seem to be motivated by an external push and which repeatedly hurl her headlong towards, but not to the floor; her emphatic stamping, her catch of her weight and recovery to verticality.

READER: It seems to me that these have as much to say as do the words she speaks, especially when they are conjoined, and that it is the movements which must be read for us to understand what it is the dancer[2] is writing.

DANCER: If Martin would read our negotiated relationships to each other and to the shapes and energies of our own bodies as well as he reads our costumes, props, and speeches, and drew his thesis from our kinetic language, then perhaps a dancer would have a chance of reading his essay because he would actually be reading the dancer's essay and not just the essay of the whole spectacle. I am intrigued by overreading, but filled with anxiety, because it is so difficult for me to read. This is not because I am dumb, but because I speak a different language. I am a kinetic bloody genius, wandering, like a lost soul, in a verbal world.

READER: The advantage of a closer combination of elemental reading and overreading might be a closer connection of actual practice to theory – what we're dancing to what we're theorising.

DANCER: The elemental method of dance reading bears a direct relationship to what I am doing when I'm dancing. It describes my thinking. A conventional definition of 'thinking' would probably describe what I'm doing when I'm dancing not as thinking, but as feeling. I am not thinking 'thoughts', I am thinking action through time, space and energy.

The physical mind

Having established some methods of reading dance, I would like to turn now to consideration of the mind-body split, and the ways in which a dancer, by thinking in time, space, energy and the body, does and does not get round it. These two different issues are, in the end, linked by questions to do with language, and forms of intelligence. A dancer may be considered dumb if she has trouble with verbally articulated concepts, but how much cultural credibility is given to her kinetic intelligence? How much more would be given if the mind were commonly understood to be the body? On the other side of the question, how damaging to, or fulfilling of, her mind's potential is her training as a dancer? If the body is indeed the mind, what happens when you give it saturated access to a limited way of thinking or deprive it of access to a range of ways of thinking? Thinking in time, space and energy may not be thinking in a verbal language, but it is still thinking within a learned language system. Like a verbal language, a body has no choice but to think in the language it has learned.

My body thinks; it makes judgments about the world and its place in it constantly. Further, it articulates its thoughts, onstage or not. My body judges its position in space and articulates its way across a crowded room. There is no question that my body feels, as in sense perceives, but it also feels emotion: anxiety in its stomach, love in its heart, excitement in the back of the neck. If there is any question about the co-dependence of one's physical being with one's thought processes, consider the way in which thinking is impaired when the body is unwell or in pain: 'I can't think, my tooth is killing me.' Or, 'This cold is making my thinking fuzzy.' Or, 'Don't ask me to make a decision until I've had dinner and a good night's sleep.'

Susan Buck-Morss argues that the brain is not the mind, not because the brain is too physical and mundane a location for such a lofty entity as the mind, but because to isolate the brain from the world and call it the mind is incompatible with the way in which the mind functions.

> The nervous system is not contained within the body's limits. The circuit from sense perception to motor response begins and ends in the world. The brain is thus not an isolable anatomical body, but part of system that passes through a person and her or his (culturally specific, historically transient) environment. As the source of stimuli and the arena for motor response the external world must be included to complete the sensory circuit ... In order to differentiate our description from the more limited traditional conception of the human nervous system which artificially isolates human biology from its environment, we will call this aesthetic system of sense consciousness decentered from the classical subject, wherein sense perceptions come together with the internal images of memory and anticipation, the synaesthetic system. (129)

If Buck-Morss is arguing that the brain is not the location of the mind because it is the interaction of the brain with the world which is the mind, then I would like to add to that argument that the brain is not the location of the mind because the whole body is the location of the mind. It is the interaction of the body (including the brain) with the world which is the mind.

Simon Penny argues from a physiological point of view saying that physical thinking 'is not the kind of thinking valorised in the Western Intellectual tradition' possibly because 'it is a kind of intelligence inseparable from the body' (38). He believes, as I do, that '[a]ny attempt to separate the mind from the body is flawed, the presumed location of the mind in the brain is inaccurate'. Penny further adds that

> dance, sculpture, painting, and the variety of other fine and performing arts are premised on bodily training, bodily knowledge that implicitly contradicts the mind/body duality. It has been observed that in certain manual activities of high skill, such as playing the violin, the action is so fast that the nerve signals could not travel up the arm, into the spine and brain, and back again. Motor 'decisions' have been shown, not to pass through the brain, but to remain in the limb. A neural closed circuit, the hand is thinking by itself. (38)

But Penny does not take the leap Buck-Morss ventures by including the body of the whole world in the locating of an individual's mind. For a dancer, a combination of Buck-Morss' and Penny's conceptions of the mind is necessary to describe our thinking bodies, in part because Buck-Morss persists in locating all of the thinking up near the area of the brain. Her description of physical expression stays centered on the face:

> The expressive face is indeed a wonder of synthesis, as individual as a finger print, yet collectively legible by common sense. On it the three aspects of the synaesthetic system – physical sensation, motor reaction, and physical meaning – converge in signs and gestures comprising a mimetic language ... What this language speaks is anything but the concept. Written on the body's surface as a convergence between the impress of the external world and the express of subjective feeling, the language of this system threatens to betray the language of reason, undermining its philosophical sovereignty. (129)

We can extend Buck-Morss' conception of the face as the expressive centre of a whole synaesthetic system to say that the whole body functions in the same way, without stretching too far. While it is true that there are more proprioceptive nerve endings in the hands and the face than in other parts of the body, it is, nonetheless also true that proprioception (self-reception) is taking place through the co-operation of nerves throughout the body. Further, these nerves are co-operating with each other, making judgments based on shared information. 'The processing of movement sensation in the central nervous system relies on population input from muscle spindle endings' (Gandevia et al. 62). Democracy prevails, the nerves collectively process information and come up with a majority decision on what it means.

This conflagration of ideas becomes even stronger with the addition of Roland Barthes who, to quote John Sturrock, 'has chosen the word "body" to describe the source of [these] vital and characteristic determinants of a writer's language where others might have used "the subconscious"' (68). While it seems unlikely that Barthes is referring to the joints, muscles and nerves when he says 'body', it may still be possible to pirate his sense of the word 'body' and apply it to the physical-certainty of a dancer; the physical body is literally the storage system for the 'psychic case-history' (69). The muscles remember what one might consciously forget. This 'psychic case-history' may indeed be seen as an amalgamation of Buck-Morss' synasthetic system – 'the impress of the external world and the express of subjective feeling' (129) – with Penny's neural closed circuit (the body remembering, making motor decisions), with the neurologist's co-operative self-receptors (the body analysing, processing), which gives us a rich picture of a physical consciousness: a thinking body, a dancing mind.

When looking at the functioning of a dancer within the frame of this idea, however, we see something different: a contrived manipulation and limitation of a 'mind'. The trained dancer is a deliberately constructed synaesthetic system, her abilities and limitations carefully designed to conform to a particular aesthetic. If she is an accomplished dancer, she has mastered a particular technique. This in turn becomes her body's only language, the structure of her subconscious. If we accept that the body in relation to the world is actually the mind, and we understand that the dancer is a synaesthetic system or physical mind which is hyper-circumscribed and attenuated in relation to the world, then it is possible to say that a dancer does not just express a theory, she embodies one. The argument would unfold as follows: the trained dancer is either a perversion or an extension of Buck-Morss' 'synaesthetic system'. By training her face (body), she controls it so that a minimum of undesigned expression may slip out.

This control necessarily prescribes limits of expression, in part because nothing can slip out, and in part because mastery of control demands a focus on specific areas of accomplishment and thereby eradicating the possibility of other areas. Obviously this would appear quite differently in different dance languages. One can watch the Australian Ballet in action in a fully-staged performance by the main company and see that a traditional ballet dancer is trained so that nothing accidental, floppy, or not fully extended and directed slips out. Or one can spend time observing, for example, Ion Pearce, Rosalind Crisp, Alice Cummins and Helen Clarke-Lapin dancing together[3] and see that contact improvisers (although this is not the only form in which these four work), might be training so that only the inadvertent slips out, the unadorned physicalised neurological impulse, the immediate response to the present. This immediacy, by design, excludes the language of the directed, extended and specifically pre-determined or intentioned, and either dancer will be chastised (in different ways) for transgressing the rules of their form.

These rules become the dancer's truths in an aesthetic sense. A technique, absorbed by a dancer becomes not only all she can say but all she wants to say. It holds all of her 'habits, pieties, sentiments and affections' (Eagleton 20). This is a key to understanding what the limits are of what can be written or said in dance, as well as the limitations placed on a dancer's thinking. Mastery of a given dance form, since it means amputation of other forms, ultimately means that expression is limited to what can and cannot be said in that form. The dancer's physical mind is structured by her physical language. The limitations of a given technique eventually become its domain and its aesthetics. Rather than expanding the technique to include other things, what can or cannot be said in that technique becomes what is or is not said in that form.

In a parallel manner the technique curtails a dancer's thinking. If we accept the notions of a synaesthetic system and bodily knowledge, then the arduous inscription of the body is also, necessarily, an inscription of the mind. Even if viewed from within the convention of the mind-body split, we see that both mind and body are being inscribed by the commitment dancers have to make to their dancing. Is the unquestioning faith in a dance technique which is required of dancers actually a requisite for learning that technique? Or is it simply a pleasing aesthetic attribute, a piety and devotion which simultaneously props up the technical system and determines the dancer's place in it – place from which she is unseated if she grows up and thinks for herself?

A dancer is a theory because 'she' – by which I mean her language, her identity, her aesthetic, and her synaesthetic system – is her dancing. Her dancing is the dancing of a particular, culturally-specific, historically transient theory of what dancing is.

> DANCER: So what happens if a dancer becomes self-conscious? If I am an aesthetic, and aesthetics are habits, pieties, sentiments and affections, are these not all threatened by this exposure?

READER: Yes, the aesthetic is threatened. Maybe that is why dancers are not taught to read theory.

DANCER: But if I were accidentally to learn ...

Conclusion

Obviously there is a long-standing denial by society that the mind is the body, but why the compliance by dance artists? Why the denial that the body is the mind? Why not teach the dancing bodies to read themselves? Reading dancing, if more widely practiced, could potentially create the pathway to expanded, infinitely more expressive dance languages. Imagine: the Australian Ballet responding to the moment; the contact improvisers extending their limbs fully; the dancers in Russell Dumas' Sydney-based company, Dance Exchange, whose job it is to focus on the task at hand, considering how their task impacts on the spectator; or the dancers in *Chicago*[4] taking on a sensitised focus on 'the task at hand' along with their extroverted display of the execution of the task. These expansions (or perversions as they would probably be called by the unwilling subjects of these experiments) would develop the dancer's sense of theory within dance theory. What if Barthes were mentioned in a dance class and dancers began to consider the body as the sub-conscious and the information absorbed there as the frame through which they view and live in the world? That question cannot reasonably be considered without asking, what would happen if Barthes had learned to dance?

References

Buck-Morss, Susan. 'Aesthetics and Anaesthetics: Walter Benjamin's Artwork Essay Reconsidered'. *New Formations* 20 (Summer 1993). 123-43,

Eagleton, Terry. *Free Particulars*. Oxford: Blackwell, 1994.

Foster, Susan Leigh, ed. *Corporealities*. London: Routledge, 1996.

Gandevia, S.C., McCloskey, D. I. & Burke, D. 'Kinaesthetic Signals and Muscle Contraction'. *Trends in Neuroscience* 15 (1992): 62-5.

Martin, Randy. 'Overreading The Promised Land: Towards a Narrative of Context in Dance'. In Foster. 177-98.

Pearlman, Karen & Richard James Allen. 'Reading Dance'. *New Life on the 2nd Floor*. Launceston: Tasdance, 1996. 31-34.

Penny, Simon. 'The Visualisation of Art Practice'. Art Journal 56. 3 (Fall 1997). 30-39.

Sturrock, John. 'Roland Barthes.'. *Structuralism and Since: From Levi-Strauss to Derrida*. Oxford: Oxford UP, 1979.

Notes

1 Creator of the Laban system of dance notation and a movement theorist who comprehensively systematised qualities of movement.

2 In this case the dancer is also the choreographer of these particular movements, in collaboration with Bill T. Jones. She is 'writing' both through the creation of movement and through its performance.

3 *Orbit* involved Helen Clarke-Lapin, with Rosalind Crisp, Alice Cummins, and Ion Pearce, 'antistatic 99' (The Performance Space, Sydney, March/April 1999).

4 *Chicago*, choreographed by Ann Reinking after the original choreography by Bob Fosse, performed by an all-Australian cast in capital cities in Australia, 1998-99.

18. Mediating the body: dance and technology

Rachel Fensham

> *Mediators are fundamental. Creation is all about mediators. Without them, nothing happens.* (Deleuze 285)

Debates about technologically mediated bodies in relation to dance have been dominated by the fear of disembodiment. When choreographers speak of their fascination with electronic technologies – video, film, television, computers, internet – for making new work, audiences are often divided between technophiles and technophobes.[1] Those opposed see the spectre of technological discourse swallowing up the presumed autonomy and materiality of the dancing body.[2] Mary Ann Doane writes, 'theoretical speculation about electronic and digital technologies, in particular computerisation, is haunted by the possibility of a technology – that is, artificial intelligence – that would eliminate altogether the status of the body as discursive ground and limit' (2-3). The potential elimination of the body, disturbing nightmare that it is for contemporary culture, thus destroys for dance two foundational precepts: the primacy of the dancer's lived experience of the body; and the recognition of embodiment, and indeed dancing, as having social agency within culture. These principles are espoused most clearly by Ann Cooper-Albright when she asserts that the body is 'the place where sensation, representation, physical experience are interpreted both symbolically and somatically' and that dance is a way of investigating 'the process through which bodies make and are made by cultures' (32).

The materiality of the 'felt and lived' body – the 'more meat-and-bones approach' (Foster 41) – has therefore been presented as dance's special contribution to contemporary discourse. So it is significant that many dancers, indeed many more dancers than actors, are using technology in performance: making dance videos, constructing dance experiments with computers, and projecting dance through teleconferencing around the world. I consider these mediations between dance and technology as practices which continue and extend, rather than diminish, the relationship between the body and its worldliness. The arguments for embodiment can be supplemented by those advanced for a new poetics of the virtual body.[3] Utilising the idea of the *technos* as a tool for thought in this essay, I will analyse the creations of some Australian choreographers that make it possible to think about the different bodies which happen in virtual space-time.[4]

Phenomenology in cyberspace

Dance-theorist Suzanne Kozel describes 'virtual reality as a sort of expanded materiality' and sees 'the logic of bodies in technologically mediated environments as an extended or augmented physicality' (30). She does not place either technology or dance, consciousness or bodies, perception and dancing, in any hierarchical relation of privilege. Indeed she presents phenomenology as a means of arguing against a naïve sensory experiencing of the body that would separate embodiment from transcendence. The phenomenologist Merleau-Ponty, she suggests, was as much interested in the perception of aesthetic processes – for instance, the response to a messy tangle of lines or colour in painting – as in the subjectivity of experience. In his study of perception, Kozel locates those ideas which emphasise formlessness, reversibility and disequilibrium, in particular, his notion that the seeing is seen and the toucher touched. When radiation and vibration of the kinesphere (body-self) are reciprocated, perception entails a reversibility based on belonging to a sense of the world different from an other. From this reciprocity of energies, Kozel posits the 'dancing-danced', as a way of saying that the movements of dancing are also danced by external forces that have been set in motion by the dancer. Different kinaesthetic pathways might include the body-consciousness of the viewer, the dancer or another consciousness altogether made visible in dancing.

For Kozel, this model enables the integration of digital image reproduction and manipulation into dance to be seen as another part of the mutability of bodies and spaces in consciousness. There is no equilibrium between technology and the body, only an endless oscillation of vibrations and modalities of dancing or thinking. Thus, technology reframes the poetics of dance, so that it is no longer confined to the materiality of the body and the stage; instead its materialities become multiple, extended and exciting.

> Just because images of dancers can fly, rotate, change size and mutate into anything else does not mean that the physical integrity of a dancer is violated: for what emerges is another logic, one that doesn't have to be non-physical. (Kozel 30)

Technology therefore can be embraced by dancers because it gives them another logic, one that enables them to imagine different bodies. This is a project that can only be undertaken by letting dancers get their hands on technology, letting them see the corpus through a different sense and letting them think corporeally into new spaces of movement.

Whatever this 'virtual poetics' of the mediated body might be, there is still the question of the technology – what is indeed its contribution to thinking? Technology is not the precursor of a virtual body or virtual space but is, as Doane suggests in a provocative essay on 'technology and sexual difference', a concept that, in both its etymology and in practice, involves the use of an instrument for thinking. The *techne* is a process for engendering consciousness, of thought linked to the body through the tool. Whether the tool is 'conceptualised as an extension of the human body, adding to its capabilities and sharpening its efficiency' (3); or whether it is a form of substitution or supplement in the Derridean sense of constituting a lack; or whether it becomes a weapon, a defensiveness against other bodies; it is the operations undertaken with a tool which assist the processes of thinking. What is so rarely acknowledged in dance is that the dancer has always been mediated by technology, her body is so often the instrument or tool of a master discourse, indeed the word 'technique' shares the same etymology. When dancers use technology, however, the dancer becomes the mediator, a consciousness making use of a technology to propose counter-knowledges, those movements of the self that might exist in dialogue with cultural discourses.

While much of Doane's essay is taken up with the gendering of discourses of technology, particularly in the laws of physics, I want to extend her idea that whatever the machine, or the technology, makes possible is analogous to processes that operate in the body, that in turn are associated with thought. What is produced, therefore, in representation by technology is constituted by prevailing discourses of corporeality: so, for instance, when thermodynamics was the dominant science, bodies were also thought of as stable or unstable. Scientific discourses have polarised forces, elements, processes and systems around concepts of sexual difference, so that they tend either towards disintegration (regarded as more masculine) or towards constraint and control (regarded as more feminine). While technology can always lead to physical or material disaster, the assertion of bodies as different in any system 'poses the discursive threat of epistemological or representational crisis' (Doane 8). In terms of dance, this potential for crisis explains some of the fear of disembodiment through technology, but I would also argue that the disturbance of discourse and representation through the body enables dancers to confound certain classical habits of thought. By using and manipulating machines, dancers (feminine in the representational matrix) are no longer moulded by an instructional discourse or philosophy which might reduce them to bodies, but they propel themselves to enter a state of crisis (masculine dynamics), or katabolic instability. They lose control of the body, an archetypal trait of value in dance, as well as autonomy, and they cease to be singular bodies of expression.

This point is illustrated by dancer Trevor Patrick's comments about working with the Australian Broadcasting Commission to produce a dance video: 'the whole structure is geared to the losing of ownership to become the collective ownership and collective responsibility' (Gardner 40). His body, his particular uses of energy in his dancing, were forced to become more social. 'I sort of collaborated against my will ...' and 'I was forced to realise that it could be other' that is, that he could create a more worldly 'product' (45). But in the external and publicly observable body that is the dance video *Nine Cauldrons*,[5] there was still a subjective representation in which he could 'recognise all of my tastes and flavours and things that are I feel a part of me' (40). Out of a crisis of technological representation, came a means of thinking a new question for the dancer. 'I wonder if the others look at it and see in it things that are a part of them?' (45).

Mediators

Critical, then, to this discussion of dance and technology is the notion that technology is an instrument of mediation for a different perception and hence for thought. If thinking cannot happen without a body, as Elizabeth Grosz argues, 'the body provides a point of mediation between what is perceived as purely internal and accessible only to the subject and what is external and publicly observable' (20), the question then becomes what different thoughts of bodies can be mediated with a technology? If body is no pure state of being but a mediated materiality, what is to be seen in the technologised representations of dance? It is these questions of the body, its limits and its relations with others that I will consider in my discussion of the following projects. They are not unique examples – many other dancers are doing similar things – but they represent particular approaches within Australian dance to the use of technology. I offer my discussion not as any definitive statement about an enhanced materiality of dance, so much still exploratory, but more as an analysis of how certain concerns are represented when dancers create body-works in mediated spaces.

In the first part of this discussion I will look at how the technological moves analogically towards vision, a visibility of the body based on similarity, in pursuit of transcendence. In the second part I will consider the ways in which technology shifts perspectivally through space, proceeding through the curves of multiple dimensions, where the body is less certain and more receptive to suffering.

Part One: technology and vision

Choreographer Chrissie Parrott's most recent project has involved the creation of what she calls 'Zardia, a digital dancer ... wandering in a new silent landscape, a digital pixilated space' (28). Utilising the technology of motion capture,[6] a dancer wears a suit with magnetic tape on head, arms, hands and legs as she dances in a room. Cameras record the dancer Claudia Alessi (former dancer in Parrott's company), in three dimensions, both travelling through the space and around the body. The camera sees the dancer as a puppet following the details of limbs but currently only tracking five spinal articulations (there are twenty-four flexible vertebrae in the spine). Once the data is collected, the computer 'smoothes out' particular movements by calculating what might happen in the gaps between the recorded surfaces of each gesture. Parrott can build her 'character' by adding shapes to the figure of revolving ovoids: she can give it muscle bulges, lengthen and shorten limbs or torso, add an epidermal layer made up from scanned photographs (27). In this extended form of dance notation, the body becomes 'the object of a scientific discourse whose aim is to make visible the previously invisible facets of movement' (Doane 10).

In the pilot film *On the Wing*,[7] Zardia's dancing is similar not only to the architectonics of movement investigated by the Bauhaus but also to the figure of 'Kiki' in Fernand Leger's *Ballet Mécanique*: she is a '"machine among machines" ... her facial movements are as mechanical and expressionless as possible. The disembodied legs in the film perform a mechanical dance that differs in no way from that of the film's other objects' (Doane 16). One consequence of machinic mimicry in avant-garde art practice was that the body was regarded 'as a site of inscription rather than as a conveyor of meaning' (16). Parrot's intention with this 'progenitor' of the cyberdancer is, however, to assist in choreography, so that the inscribed figure can be manipulated in whatever ways an operator desires. She will be used by students to teach them about choreography, or by dancers to try out new movements, or by artists wanting to incorporate dance into a digital production. With an electronic dancer capable of real time movement, Parrott hopes to 'lead dance artists towards a new aesthetic' (Parrott 26). An aesthetic that can render the body as a generic style, an object among other objects, and infinitely repeatable in a movement image. The rhetoric is idealist, but is there another logic at work?

It is useful to analyse the construction of the image and ask what is happening to the body? First, the performance takes place in what Parrott calls a 'wired proscenium' (25). The wired proscenium is a virtual space, based on the screen and the technologies of mapping through the camera, but this representational matrix reproduces viewing positions that position the audience outside of the picture. The proscenium is, after all, a nineteenth-century bourgeois conception of the stage. In so far as the dancer is constrained by this viewing space, she remains an objectified image. Secondly, the dancer through 'motion capture' is caught in the seeing apparatus of digital 'tracking systems' thus making the body something to be hunted. According to biologist Paul Shepard, one of our fundamental strategies for knowing another species is through the image we hold of prey; this intelligence, developed through hunting, is linked to our survival (43). The concept of tracking also suggests military or satellite technologies, an invasive or intimidatory structure of knowledge. And yet, by holding the movements of the dancing body in storage, Parrott is able to observe it more closely, to subject it to scrutiny and to modify its potential for movement. Parrott talks about 'the body as the basis for data imagery' (26) and as a technique for survival, a means of taking dance into the next century. What she desires in Zardia and her offspring is the effect that the dancer can produce 'smooth and, in most cases, flawless, organic-looking movement' (26). Ironically, Parrott desires what she has just tried to replace, the appearance of a body that looks natural, even if taken from a body turned into information. The captured body can be classified and the choreographer can assert surface control of the dancer through the composite images. In this kind of work, the choreographer performs an anabolic function, conserving the energy of the dancer's body from its potential loss. This serves an art of reproduction based on a mimetic body, that might release audiences from the mortality of the body.

By way of comparison with Parrott's creation of the captured body, although entirely different because the tracking device is used in the context of a live performance, is Jude Walton's *Seam (silent mix)*.[8] In this work, dancer Ros Warby holds a tiny videocam in one hand behind a screen. As she dances out of sight, the lens traces the arcs and slides of her body at the most intimate level. The microcam renders the body sensuous and unpredictable with the loose flesh of the elbow turning into the knobbly muscles of the neck; finding hairiness a deeply tangled surface texture or the back of the heel crinkling as it rolls on the floor. To critic Eleanor Brickhill 'the image [is] like an ultra-sound of something internal, soft and vulnerable, not quite formal' (11) although some parts of the body remain out of reach of the seeing hand. The normally unseen quivering of a particular limb becomes a continuous line in space, a 'cyclograph', not determined by the conventions of speed or direction, but representing a beautiful, smooth abstraction of the body's surface. With this tool in hand, the power of film or video to create the illusion of continuity out of repetition is reinstated. As with Muybridge's early photographic images, there is an absence in *Seam (silent mix)*; the loss of the labour of the dancer (and the worker as camera operator), so that the dance 'appears to be about the body but in effect causes it to disappear' (Doane 13).

In spite of the dematerialising of the anatomical body in Parrott's work, I am struck by the ways in which the digital dancer rematerialises the human. In the slightly stilted movements of Zardia there are unmistakeable traces of subjective presence. Both the name and form of Zardia carry with them the contingency of Alessi who performs her. Alessi's morphology – her proportion, delicacy and pointedness – infuse the character, as actors do a role, even if Parrott over-writes this specific lived existence when she prepares the script for the adventures of Zardia in cyberspace. A narrative which includes creating a mate for Zardia programmed so that her offspring one day may be free to wander, to be innocent, and hungry to learn. What is beguiling is the utopic and modernist vision at play here, in which technospace is a Paradise before the Fall and the dancer will at last find her true role, that of 'an entertainer and an educator' (Parrott 28). As Zardia cavorts in pink and lime green, a version of Alessi pervades the screen with the malleability of electrons and digitised soundwaves. In this vision, we have slipped from the controlling fantasies of technology rendering the body as machine to a more Romantic vision in which traces of Isadora Duncan are replayed. Haunting the dreams of technology is indeed the body as a kind of limit, an obstacle to happiness because it cannot exist outside the paradigms of vision. In the computer screen, the dancer appears as a different kind of visuality, no longer just coloured lights and floating scarves, but now electronic pathways for freedom in motion.

The vision also involves another subjectivity who labours in creation, the figure of Parrott. The dancer Zardia is a dream of escape for the choreographer, an excited journey away from the endless repetitive strain placed upon dancer's bodies in the company structure towards the machinic reproduction of loss and immortality. Parrott, like Mary Shelley, desires to capture the 'subtleties of movement' and is exhilarated by the 'seemingly limitless creative arena' which technology offers (28). Those committed to the materiality of the social argue that there are productive limitations imposed by dancing bodies working in a collective space, but there are other limits in technological spaces. One of the illusions of technocreation is that this work is undertaken alone – as Patrick observed earlier, there are 'forced collaborations' with camera operators and computer geeks – indeed Zardia would not exist if she wasn't the product of many mediations. The creation of Zardia is, one suspects, the mirror image of Parrott herself, a dancer who wishes to be free and to wander in the technological world creating new children. Naïve, perhaps innocent, she is an information gatherer and yet she also wants to be fertile, to create offspring. Her offspring are to be artworks and not children 'bringing information home to mother' (Parrott 28). This transcendent vision for technology rests on a contradiction that information will be knowledge, and essentially liberating. More truthful to this project is a process of sensible thinking combined with an ongoing passion for the body, whose creation is a digital dancer; and more promising are the potentially new audiences for dance that Zardia might find.

Part Two: technology and space

Company in Space maintains the presence of live dancers in performance, but casts them into a virtual landscape through the actualities of dancing with filmic apparatus, equipment and computer gear. This Melbourne-based company has significantly advanced Australian performance experimentation with interactive technologies, both in redefining the environment of the performer and in their inclusion of the audience as interactive agents in the space of the performance. Utilising multiple cameras, some hand-held and some suspended in the performance space, they generate real-time images of the dancers that are superimposed onto screens and simultaneously manipulated through computer-generated imagery. Embodied gestures are amplified, while both virtual bodies and actual bodies are able to trigger changes to the visual projections of the landscape or cue variations to the synthesised sound-score. Their work is presented in front of live audiences who are located between and across sites in real-time, such as from Melbourne to Sydney or Amsterdam to Melbourne.

This company, directed by Hellen Sky and John McCormick, has a pragmatic aim more concerned with construction than Parrott's projection. They use technology to think about the body as immanent with, and alongside, the apparatus of its transformation, an obstacle resistant to both gravity and disappearance. The dancers are strapped to machines and caught, like the shadows on Plato's cave, in between screen and sources of light. Rather than sensuous and aesthetic, the effect is that of struggle and suggests that the body has no guarantee of dominance over, or resistance to, the constraints imposed by technology. Their most recent work *Escape Velocity* [9] is a useful example of this conundrum of the virtual dancer, because its central motif is the exertion of the human organism wanting to be released from the pull of gravity, the weight of the body.

Escape Velocity opens with dancers Louise Taube and Hellen Sky emerging from below ground level with their two starkly shaved heads rotating as if disembodied. One is reminded of the vulnerability and uniformity of the skull as a container – it presents to audience consciousness an image of detached thought in spite of the thinking that must occur with movement. Is the will to be born thus, head first into the world? Sluggishly, these bodies attempt to rise from the ground to stand, aided and resisted by pulleys and ropes. Testing the weight of newly-found limbs against countervailing forces, they slide along the horizontal, attempt flight and walk backwards up a vertical plane to a perch suspended high above. Each sequence resembles an organism at a biological or evolutionary stage, as bodies discover their conditions of movement by jostling, rotating, bouncing or staggering. The dance is extremely arduous – shifting from tension to collapse – and the noise, a deliberately overloaded static or industrial quality of sound, adds interference to any idealised corporeality of the dancers. The technology is disruptive, preponderating changes in the conditions for matter to live or to move. The human body in this scenario does not disappear, because it is not a machine, but rather is 'subject to fatigue and fatigue-induced error' (Doane 13). It is fatigue which threatens the promise of technology even in cyberspace, where the limitations of the working body have largely been ignored. And if the landscape is hostile, katabolic destruction becomes more likely and the material body will die.

Escape Velocity is as much about landscape as it is about bodies : its environment includes pre-recorded film, floating text in sentence-length strips combine with solarised images of shadows recorded from the floor. If consciousness is disembodied, so are the hyper-text or landscapes rendered indeterminate. Taking it all in as a spectator is no mean feat but the matter of consciousness no longer belongs to an individual body-subject. Bodies, theirs and ours, are already immersed in the trace-making of many and multiple virtual spaces. The visible image of this concept in performance is that of words which rotate around the virtual bodies in response to the spinning of the 'real' dancers. They whirl in the hyper-texts that emanate from their delirium. There is also a sense that signalling can disturb light waves and alter sound; fine red laser beams might reduce visible perception to spots on the body, but the pathways of the body can be magnified in detail on a screen. We are back here not only to the 'dancing-danced' – the dancer leading the danced or the technology leading the dancer – but to the minutely tuned calibration of one thought system encountering another through the dancers' mobility. A model of cybernetics.

A multi-layered space can, therefore, multiply thought processes, requiring one thought to co-exist with another as yet unrealised or unrealisable. An alternative approach to consciousness mapping existed in *Watershed* [10], a performance work created by choreographer Sue Peacock with actor Bill Handley and cameraman Graeme Macleod, where virtual bodies overlaid real bodies in the blurred space of intimate sexual relations. When a couple meet on a bed, or in a bedroom, there is a history, and a hesitancy, about what will happen next. In this work, an overhead camera filmed the two performers from above on a white mattress. These pre-recorded images of sleeping, desiring and erotic gestures between a man and a woman were replayed over the live body doubles in a performance where a sort of seduction takes place: much jumping, some dancing and lots of rolling. Unspoken thoughts were made visible: for instance, what happens when the man is sleeping with his clothes on – yet again – and the woman comes home and wants to make love? The video projections allowed the shadows of thoughts which pass through the mind when bodies are intimate and familiar to be added to the thoughts of the inactive or hyper-active. The female dancer can roll off the bed in her mind, even when and even if the dancer's cellular body is held in the arms of another. The video technology and the couple dancing in this particular collaboration resisted their own clichés, refusing to play into any particular narrative or choreographic resolution of the material; there was always a tension maintained between the content and structure of the desire to project, and the refuge or constraint of the physical. Neither vocabulary – desire imagined or desire activated – was given the final say in the technology of *Watershed*.

When *Escape Velocity* was presented during the International Dance and Technology (IDAT) Conference in February 1999 one dancer and one camera-person were in Arizona, while another dancer and members of the technology team were in Melbourne mixing in visual imagery, sound, computer-generated responses, audience triggers and other interactive exchanges. The dance travelled space, literally as well as metaphorically, physically as well as symbolically. And the dancers have been called 'actual avatars', for not only did they have a cyber-double but a real-double.[11] The duet form is perhaps one way of resituating the logic of dance and technology. In this dance, duets were operative on many different levels, not only by those mediating the work in same-time, same-place locations or between dancers and audiences in two different locations, but in between each of the systems in motion. Ghislaine Boddington watching the work in Arizona: 'the interaction came to us through the projected image – the two dancers heads touching, rolling forehead to forehead with one another. As the camera in Melbourne moved back to capture the whole dancer's body she appeared inside the image of Sky's head – a moving floating memory – a total reflection of herself' (14). The dance of the double makes possible the image of dancers dancing with themselves; something so often suppressed in dance by the idea that the dancer is dancing for the viewer, or for the instructor/choreographer. Virtual dancing is the image of the dancer dancing with an image, which is also the other of herself in movement. When the dancer struggles to make an autonomous move, she also struggles to realise an image. A movement as thought is thus seen as a struggle with a consciousness of another as well as with the material limits of the body. Company in Space, as dancers, are trying to launch thought into the future, even if the body becomes less certain for dance.

Strange questions come to mind for a spectator watching these dances; are these thoughts or movements that have already been uttered; is it possible to get inside someone else's head, actually or only virtually? When a different consciousness invades our thoughts, another body enters into some preserve of the self that is generally protected from invasion. In all these performances, dancing is a system of transposing the self through technology in ways that make the mind less dominant as a unique system and more like a virtual space which different bodies might fill. Thus, the thinking is not about identities but about the exploration of the truths that must exist in 'real bodies' because someone has mediated them. Giving birth to the virtual dance is precisely this process of letting go of the mind's control over technology and enabling bodies to operate with whatever the technologies can do.

Dancing with technology is not only measured (a quantitative enhancement), or a fulfilment (a mechanism of recognition), but a mediation that allows the fragility of the body's materiality to be felt. There are sequences in which the bodies are fluid: the revolution of particles in motion on the screen; the waving of muscles on somebody's back; that produce a redefinition of human-ness. The dance with technology can investigate what a fluid consciousness can do, what it can create, and therefore what thinking must do for bodies to function in and through the world. It is an enabling of thought, or a mediating of virtual space, that can only be done by bodies because consciousness follows the body.

Dancers as mediators

While Kozel with her notion of a 'phenomenological poetics' offers one way of theorising any impasse, or indeed the passage, between dance and technology, I am reluctant to idealise or aestheticise the relationship. Perhaps a more useful way to think about what happens when dancers create with technology is through Gilles Deleuze's description of mediators: '[t]he basic thing is how to get taken up in the movement of a big wave, a column of rising air, to "come between" rather than to be the origin of an effort' (281). The manipulation of technologies and participation in the production process of video, computer and digital technologies have released dancers to some extent from the efforts of creativity in the body. They have got caught up in the movement of the wave, and new technologies have given them a means for continuing their researches on the body in the absence of other structures such as regular companies or funding. Instead of disempowering dance, technology has restored to dancers a capacity to mediate – to network from one sphere of meaning-making to another – that more autocratic and authorial structures at work in dance institutions have often denied them. What is exciting is that this movement has enabled dancing consciousness to become fluid as well as digital, and importantly, more social. Bodily possibilities for representation have emerged that are redefining conventions of perception: 'You have to be liquid or gaseous, precisely because normal perception and opinion are solid, geometric' (Deleuze 292). Or, in dance terminology, because conventional perception and opinion about bodies is anatomical and mechanical, these bodies are seen and felt as electronic and virtual. With the mediation of a postmodern reality, analysis suggests that these 'new' bodies also reiterate images of performance – and the difficulty of liberation from the body – that recur in avant-garde and contemporary arts practice. Perhaps not such a new concept.

But the lesson of these projects is that the choice is not between dance and audiovisual media: it is between creative forces (in both media) and those forces of domestication that would tie bodies down (Deleuze 290). Creative people produce existence, not in the head, but by putting images on a screen or dance steps into a body. Only as mediators do dancers produce bodies which have a way of signifying to others. Dance mediated through technology can also operate as a critique of dance, and its epistemology narrowly defined by modern dance discourses as emergent from, or grounded in, the body. The 'body' is thus only one limit for dance and does not exist as the grounds for a unique subjectivity. Instead, corporeality as technological difference is a project for consciousness that can only be produced by mediators.

References

Boddington, Ghislaine. 'Fluid Space, Fluid Presence'. *Animated* (Spring 1999): 14-15.

Brannigan, Erin, ed. *MAP Movement and Performance Symposium*.(23-26 July 1998). Papers. Canberra: Ausdance, 1999.

Brickhill, Eleanor. 'Hybrid Yield'. *Real Time* 31 (June-July 1999): 11.

Cooper-Albright, Ann. *Choreographing Difference: The Body and Identity in Contemporary Dance*. Hanover: Wesleyan, 1997.

Crary, Jonathon & Sanford Kwinter, ed. *Incorporations*. New York: Zone, 1992.

Currier, Dianne. 'Absent, Mutated, Digitalised, Desexed: Posthuman Bodies in Cyberspace'. *Writings on Dance* 17 (Summer 1997/98): 46-60.

Deleuze, Gilles. 'Mediators'. Crary & Kwinter. 281-293.

Doane, Mary Anne. 'Technology and Sexual Difference'. *differences* 9.2 (1997): 1-24.

Foster, Susan. 'Dancing Bodies'. Crary & Kwinter. 480-495.

Gardner, Sally. 'Making Microdance: Trevor Patrick interview'. *Writings on Dance* 17 (Summer 1997/8): 32-45.

Grosz, Elizabeth. *Volatile Bodies: Toward a Corporeal Feminism*. Sydney: Allen & Unwin, 1994.

Kozel, Susan. 'The Carbon Unit in the Silicon Domain'. *Writings on Dance* 17 (Summer 1997/98): 21-31.

Parrott, Chrissie. 'The Proscenium is Wired'. *MAP Movement and Performance Symposium*: 25-28.

Shepard, Paul. *The Only World We've Got: A Paul Shepard Reader*. San Francisco: Sierra Club Books, 1996.

Notes

1 At MAP Movement and Performance symposium in Melbourne on 25 and 26 July 1998 the audience was provoked into debate by Session Two on new technologies titled 'Ungrounded Bodies/Escaping the Body'. See Brannigan.

2 The title of Dianne Currier's article 'Absent, Mutilated, Digitalised, Desexed: Posthuman bodies in Cyperspace' is evocative of this position, but the article is a thorough and even-handed assessment of some of the forces operating in technological discourse.

3 Embodiment featured prominently during the 1980s in discussions of feminist theory as well as in the arguments with which dance scholars have located the dancing subject, notably in the writings of dance-scholars such as Phillippa Rothfield, Susan Foster, Ann Cooper-Albright and scattered throughout the pages of Australia's academic dance journal *Writings on Dance*.

4 I would like to acknowledge all the choreographers I have discussed here, whose work has been an inspiration to this paper, and thank them for their assistance with details about their creations. I should acknowledge, however, that my approach to each work, after a first viewing, has varied in relation to the access I have had to supplementary resources. Chrissie Parrott's film was viewed only once although I had access to her published conference paper; *Escape Velocity* was viewed live twice and I had access to a video and some printed promotional materials; Sue Peacock's work was viewed once and she kindly provided me with a video and program notes, and Jude Walton's and Trevor Patrick's works were viewed only once, although I made use of publicly printed additional materials.

5 *Nine Cauldrons*, a dance video for Microdance, an initiative of the Australian Film commission and the Australia Council, assisted by the Australian Broadcasting Commission. Directors Paul Hampton and Trevor Patrick; producer Liz Burke; choreography/text/performance, Trevor Patrick; voice, Peter Cummins.

6 Initial research was undertaken at the Western Australian Academy of Performing Arts (WAAPA) at Edith Cowan University, but the first motion capture filming was completed at Medialab (Paris) in 1997/98. Parrott's current work includes a second draft film called *Zardia, the Progenitor* which has been utilised in the choreography of a full-length dance work *Hawk* for WAAPA, premiered 26 November 1999.

7 *On the Wing*, a pilot film by Chrissie Parrott, premiered at the Telstra Adelaide Festival, March 1998, featuring Zardia with assistance from dancer Alessi. 3D animated model using animated Ascensions magnetic motion tracking suit translated with motion sample capture. 3D character created by Ged Wright. Data captured at Medialab studios, Paris (1100 frames animated footage = 48 seconds edited into 4 minute film).

8 *Seam (silent mix)*: multimedia performance premiered at Alliance Francaise, Melbourne, 3-6 October 1998 for the Melbourne 'Mallarmé and the Twentieth Century' Festival. In collaboration with Lisa Barmby, Brighid Lehman, Paul Rogers and Ros Warby.

9 *Escape Velocity* by Company in Space premiered at Opera Australia Studios, August-September 1998. Concept, direction and design, Hellen Sky; computer design and technical realisation, John McCormick; interactive sound design and original score, Garth Paine; choreography and performance, Hellen Sky with Louise Taube.

10 *Watershed,* premiered The Gasworks, Perth, October 1998. Devised and performed by Sue Peacock and Bill Handley in collaboration with Graeme Macleod and Jeremey Nottle (video projection, lighting and sound).

11 The term 'actual avatars' was used to promote *Escape Velocity* at the dLux arts symposium FutureScreen 99 (9 November 1999) at Artspace, Sydney.

Index

Photo 1: *Under Southern Eyes*
Travelling through the Roaring Forties. Photographer Mary Moore.

Photo 2: *Under Southern Eyes*
Drowned bodies. Photographer Mary Moore.

Photo 3: *Under Southern Eyes*
1924: fire at Number 2 Wharf on the cargo ship *City of Singapore*.
Photographer Mary Moore.

Photo 4: *Under Southern Eyes*
1928: the Workers' Waxworks perform the strike on the wharf.
Photographer Mary Moore.

Photo 5: *Under Southern Eyes*
1930s: the Depression. Photographer Mary Moore.

Photo 6: *Under Southern Eyes*
1950s: the ventriloquists discuss social banditry at the Police Academy Floral Show. Photographer Mary Moore.

Photo 7: *Under Southern Eyes*
1980s: Port Adelaide industrial alchemy. Mustard gas and industrial pollution.
Photographer Mary Moore.

Photo 8: *Under Southern Eyes*
1980s: Port Adelaide – a refuge for freaks and social outcasts.
Photographer Mary Moore.

Photo 9
Club Swing's Simone O'Brien holding Kareena Oates at the Victorian Arts Centre, Melbourne, January 1998. Photographer Angela Bailey.

Photo 10
Airated's Isabel da Silva, Deborah Batton and Anna Shelper 1997.
Photographer Lyn Pool.

Photo 11
Sydney Front's *Don Juan*, 11 April 1991: 'Thump Rump' scene. Christopher Ryan, Annette Tesoriero and Nigel Kellaway. Photographer Heidrun Lohr.

Photo 12
Sydney Front's *Don Juan*: 'Java Dance'. Christopher Ryan, Andrea Aloise, John Baylis, seated seduction victim, Nigel Kellaway and Elise Ahamnos. Photographer Heidrun Lohr.

Photo 13
Sydney Front's *Don Juan*: 'Pavan/Fuck Me' scene. Andrea Aloise, Nigel Kellaway, John Baylis, Elise Ahamnos, Annette Tesoriero, Clare Grant. Photographer Heidrun Lohr.

Photo 14
Azaria Universe. Photographer Heidrun Lohr.

Photo 15
Barbara Karpinski. Photographer Heidrun Lohr.

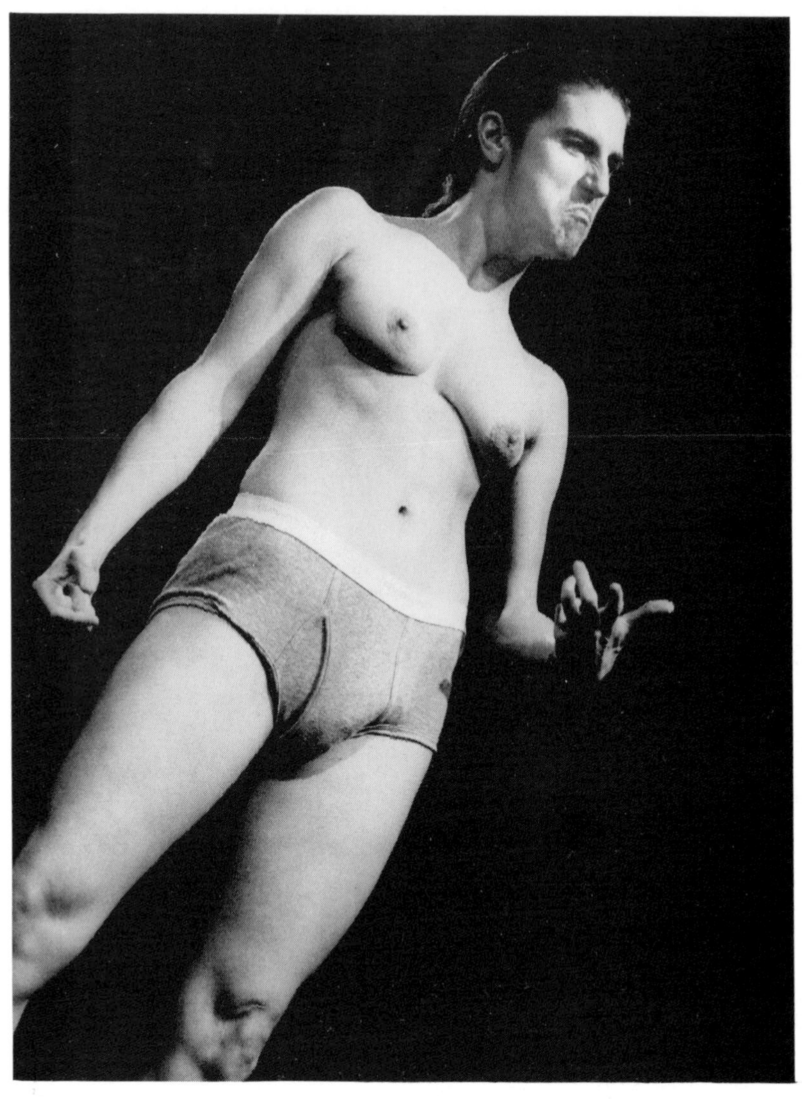

Photo 16
Moira Finucaine as Romeo. Photographer Heidrun Lohr.

Photo 17
'Masculine Force and Intimate Exchanges in the Wrestlers' Gym'. Gleason's Gym, Brooklyn, New York. Larry Brisco (De Garis) offers Chris Moniz some tips. Photographer Sharon Mazer.

Photo 18
Tess De Quincey. Photographer Simon Hunter.

Photo 19
How Could You Even Begin to Understand. Umi Umiumare and Tony Yap. Photographer Sonia Tan.

Photo 20
Fleeting Moments. Yumi Umiumare. Photographer Brad Hick.

Photo 21
Yoni Prior, Michael Kantor, Elisa Gray in *The Dybbuk*. Gilgul Theatre, Everleigh Railyards, Redfern (Sydney), 1991. Photographer Tracey Moffatt.

Photo 22
Milijana Cancar in Lyndal Jones' *Spitfire 123*, Section 3. Lonsdale Power Station, Melbourne, 1996. Photographer Petray Cancar.

Photo 23
David Wicks in Going Through Stages' *Dazzle of Shadows,* Melbourne 1993. Photographer Ian de Gruchy.

Photo 24
Stelarc, 'Sitting/Swaying: Event for Rock Suspension'. Tamura Gallery, Tokyo, 1980. Photographer K. Nozawa.

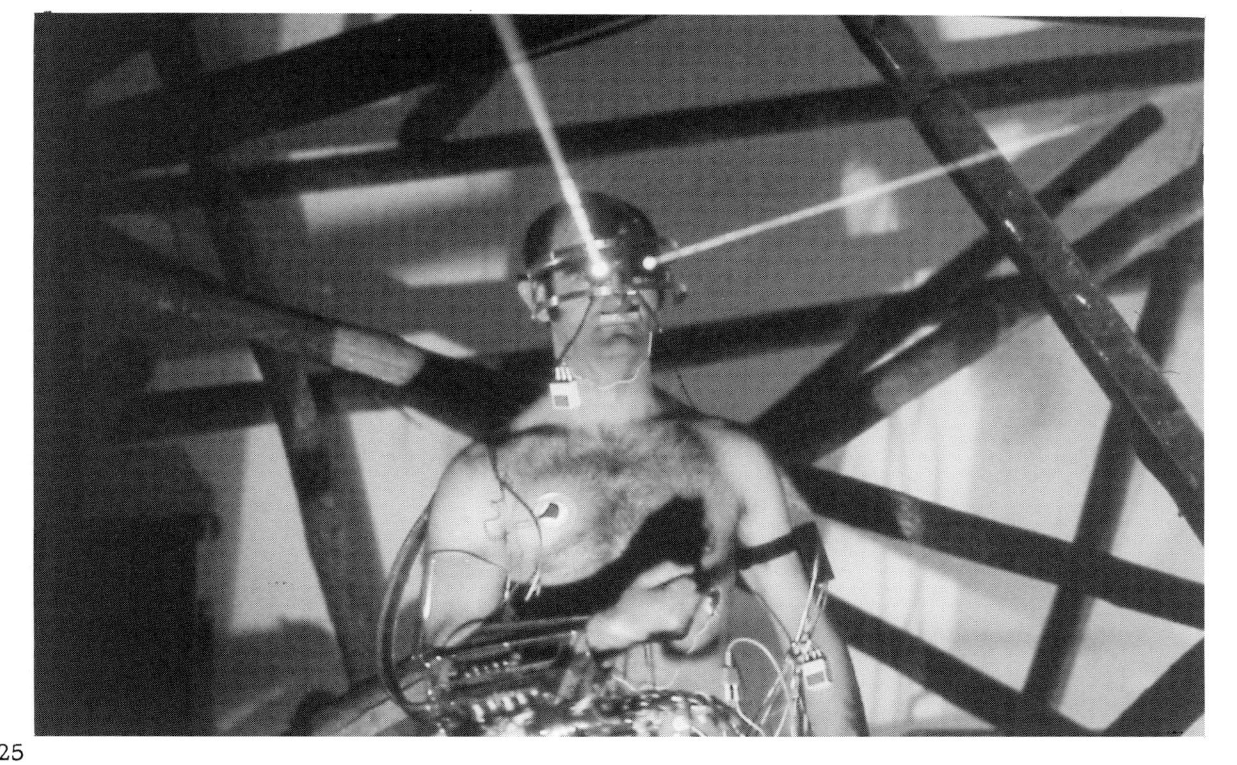

Photo 25
Stelarc, 'Amplified Body, Laser Eyes and Third Hand'. Maki Gallery, Tokyo, 1986. Photographer T. Shinoda.

Photo 26
Possessed by the Meryl Tankard Australian Dance Theatre. Photographer Regis Lansac.

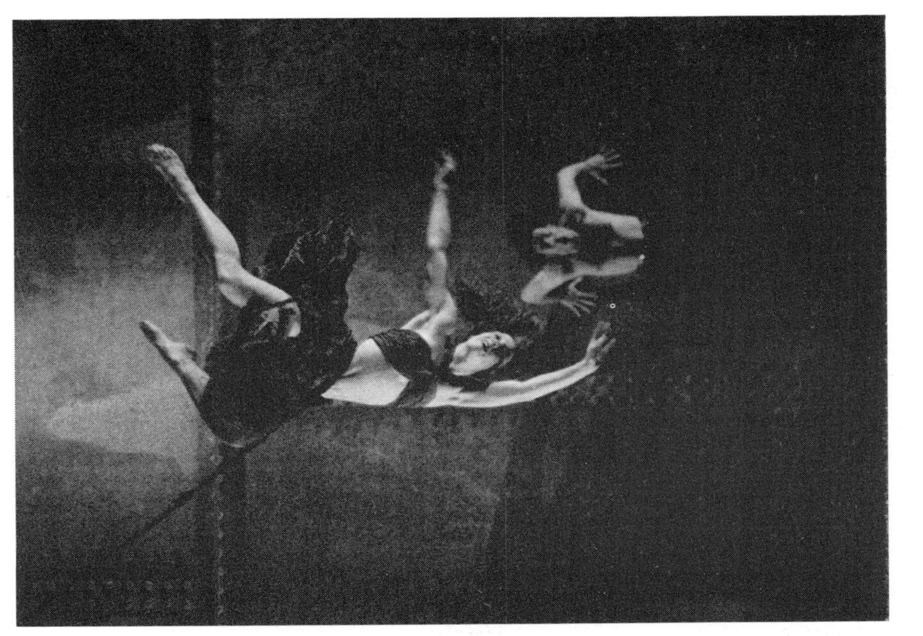

Photo 27
Sara-Jayne Howard in *Furioso* by the Meryl Tankard Australian Dance Theatre. Photographer Regis Lansac.

Photo 28
Louise Fox, Matthew Whittet and John Bell. *King Lear* (1998) by the Bell Shakespeare Company directed by Barrie Kosky.
Photographer Jeff Busby.

Photo 29
Hellen Sky and Louise Taube in Company in Space's *Escape Velocity*. Photographer Jeff Busby.

Photo 30
Hellen Sky and Louise Taube in Company in Space's *Escape Velocity*.
Photographer Jeff Busby.